GW00683351

BEYOND COURAGE

BEYOND COURAGE

Air Sea Rescue by Walrus Squadrons in
the Adriatic, Mediterranean and Tyrrhenian Seas
1942-1945

NORMAN FRANKS

GRUB STREET · LONDON

Published by
Grub Street
The Basement
10 Chivalry Road
London SW11 1HT

Copyright © 2003 Grub Street, London
Text copyright © 2003 Norman Franks

British Library Cataloguing in Publication Data
Franks, Norman L.R. (Norman Leslie Robert), 1940-
   Beyond Courage: air sea rescue by Walrus Squadrons in the Adriatic, Mediterranean
   and Tyrrhenian seas 1942-1945
   1. Great Britain, Royal Air Force. Air/Sea Rescue Service – History
   2. World War, 1939-1945 – Search and rescue operations
   3. World War, 1939-1945 – Personal narratives, British
   I. Title
   940.5′44941

ISBN 1 904010 30 X

All rights reserved. No part of this publication may be reproduced,
stored in a retrieval system, or transmitted in any form or by any
means, electronic, mechanical, photocopying, recording, or otherwise,
without the prior permission of the copyright owner.

Typeset by Pearl Graphics, Hemel Hempstead

Printed and bound in Great Britain by Biddles Ltd, Guildford and King's Lynn
www.biddles.co.uk

CONTENTS

ACKNOWLEDGEMENTS

When several years ago I began researching for a book on all Walrus air sea rescue squadrons, I was in touch with numerous pilots and air gunners who flew in these amphibian aircraft, as well as a number of the men they had rescued. I have acknowledged the help of those involved in operations around the UK in *Another Kind of Courage*, so the following are a list of rescuers and rescuees of the Mediterranean period, a few of the former of whom are the same. Every one of them has my sincere thanks for recollections, photographs, and so on, although in the interim, I know that several of them have passed away.

Walrus aircrew: Arnold Divers DFM, Richard G Eccles, Trevor H Humphrey, Lisle H Newman, Hamish Reid and Alex G Stevens DFC.

The rescued: Lt-Col James A Adams, R Greg Burdick, Maj Richard C Curtis, G/Capt W G G Duncan Smith DSO DFC, Col Leland S Ford, Herbert A Guiness, Lt-Col Raymond F Harmeyer, Lt-Col John C Kelly, Lt-Col Paul G McArthur, William E McGonigle, Lindsey Polwin, Lt-Col Gordon H Rich, Lt-Col Bert S Sanborn and John Schwartz.

Others: Robert F Cutler, Edwin Dalrymple, Col Hugh D Dow, Alison Duffield, John E Fawcett, Robert Karstensen, Joyce Lambert, Sidney Loadenthal, Lyle McCarty, Lt-Col Herbert L Speas Jr., Michael Schoeman, Christopher F Shores, S/Ldr Andy Thomas and G C Tomlinson.

Thanks too go to John Davies and Louise King of Grub Street, and to Colin and Rose Smith of Vector Fine Art.

Thanks to the following for contributing photographs: N F Duke; L Polwin; W A Rance; 12th BG Assn; A Divers; 350th FG Archives via H Dow; Mrs J Lambert; R Eccles; P G McArthur; E Dalrymple; L H Newman; J C Kelly; Andy Thomas; R J Teligzau Sr via Curtis; W G G Duncan Smith; W McGonigle; J A Adams; R F Harmeyer; J A Reid; D Hartwell; V Voss; R C Curtis; J Schwartz; J E Fawcett; B S Sanborn; T H Humphrey; R Guest; H Guiness; L S Ford and G Burdick.

INTRODUCTION

In 1994 PSL published my book *Another Kind of Courage* covering the Supermarine Walrus squadrons, which operated around the United Kingdom during World War Two. It was originally intended to incorporate within it the activities and rescues of the Walrus squadrons in the Mediterranean between 1942-45, but that would have made the book too large. Unhappily, therefore, it was decided to extract the Mediterranean chapters.

However, John Davies of Grub Street Publishing has made the decision to complete the Walrus air sea rescue story by producing this book on the Mediterranean units, which is most gratifying. That is because these stories of exceptional bravery by the rescue aircrew can now be shared with the general public and aviation enthusiasts, as well as the tales of those they saved from watery graves or captivity.

As those who have read *Another Kind of Courage* will already appreciate, it took extraordinary courage to land this comparatively small, single-engined amphibian aeroplane on the sea. The sea was often far from calm, rescues often under the eyes of the enemy, and the pilots were aware that due to weight of extra bodies, or the extremes of weather, not to mention a high running sea, the Walrus might be unable to take off again. Yet the men of the Walrus squadrons rarely hesitated, knowing full well that the quicker the downed airmen were out of the water, the better their chances of survival.

Although we are talking of the Mediterranean rather than the English Channel or the North Sea, the waters off the North African coast, or off either side of the Italian mainland – those extending into the Adriatic or the Tyrrhenian Seas – were no less cold. Anyone enjoying seaside holidays along any of the Italian coasts, or Sardinia and Corsica, will only know the warmth of coastal seas in high summer. Shocked and perhaps wounded airmen who came down miles from shore, often completely out of sight of land, will describe a very different tale of water temperatures. Even if they were in a dinghy, the heat of a summer sun beating down on them, and little or no drinking water, gave them another set of problems, so the sooner they were rescued the better.

What follows, therefore, are the stories of the men who came down on the sea and those very special pilots and observers who unhesitatingly flew out to find them and then pick them up. It took a special kind of courage – and, as the RAF and Royal Navy will tell you, it still does today.

Chapter 1

NORTH AFRICA

By 1942 the air sea rescue organisations operating from the UK for aircraft missing around the British Isles and off the hostile coasts of France, Belgium or Holland were becoming well established. What had begun as mere flights, equipped with a few spotter and rescue aircraft had now grown into squadrons. From the Navy's point of view, their High Speed Launches, also located at strategic places around the British coasts, were either working alone or co-operating with the RAF rescue squadrons.

There was a friendly rivalry between them, the Navy often trying to locate and rescue downed airmen before the Walrus amphibians arrived, while the Walrus men would take delight in being better able to find and rescue men much nearer the enemy coasts, often plucking them from minefields or from under the very noses of coastal guns – sometimes even gunfire.

However, the Walrus crews had soon discovered that with the increasing sizes of aircrew in some bomber aircraft, it didn't take too many survivors to fill and overload the small Walrus flying-boat. More often than not this meant a long-distance 'taxi ride' back to England, but at least the men were out of the cold sea, each moment taking them closer to safety. In these circumstances co-operation with the Navy launches sometimes meant a transfer to the boats, leaving the Walrus free to take off again, or possibly able to become airborne in order to take wounded men to hospital.

There had been little organised air sea rescue till 1941, the early flights being only equipped with Westland Lysanders, Boulton Paul Defiant single-engined turret fighters and Hurricanes, which could only locate downed airmen, and then direct boats to them. It was obviously far more expedient for survival for the aircraft who found men in the sea to have the means to pick them up. Hence the arrival of the Supermarine Walrus amphibian, hitherto an aircraft used for spotting for the Navy and only carried on the larger warships.

There had been little need for air sea rescue in the Middle East in the early months of the war. What action there was around Malta could be contained by Naval launches, while on the nearby continent of Africa, the desert war was mainly fought over the land. However, as things hotted up in the Mediterranean it soon became apparent that a proper air sea rescue organisation was needed as more and more operations were flown over the sea.

What coverage there had been up till this point was undertaken by the Fleet

Air Arm and Navy Walrus aircraft. It is unfortunate that the FAA squadrons did not keep very good records in the early days, and what might have been noted down, has now become lost.

In late 1941, the Fleet Air Arm established a Fulmar Defence Flight on the North African coast, at Fuka Satellite (LG16), situated east of Maaten Bagush, and west of a then little-known place called El Alamein, about 100 miles west of Alexandria. This unit was under the joint command of Alex Ramsey and Bryan Sanderson. In March 1942 this became 889 Squadron FAA.

> The Squadron was formed at Dekheila with Ramsey and myself as joint COs but later he was awarded another half stripe and took over. We were stationed at Fuka to cover convoys proceeding from Alexandria to Malta and we were joined later by a Free French squadron flying Hurricanes.
>
> We remained at Fuka for about nine months and about half way through our sojourn we were given a Walrus for rescue purposes but it was never used and returned to Dekheila shortly before February 1942.
>
> Lieutenant B Sanderson, Fulmar Defence Flight

On 12 February 1942, Sub-Lieutenant Lindsey Polwin flew a Fleet Protection patrol for a convoy sailing between Alexandria and Tobruk. All seemed quiet until Polwin saw some bomb splashes on the sea, which fortunately were some distance from the ships he was protecting. He then picked out the hostile aircraft responsible in the distance and turned to pursue it. It was an Italian Cant Z.1007 tri-motored bomber.

> The engagement turned into a bit of a stern chase. I was not closing too well and the enemy rear gunner was firing back at me and then a tracer bullet hit the cockpit area and set the Fulmar on fire. It suddenly got very warm, very quickly. As was normal when flying in this part of the world, I was only wearing shirt, shorts and boots, which was not much protection against sudden searing heat. I opened the cockpit but the inrush of air only made the flames worse so I shut it again. As I was now being burned about the legs and face – it was time to get out.
>
> Sub-Lieutenant L Polwin, Fulmar Defence Flight

Polwin yelled to his gunner, Leading Airman Norman Davison, to bale out, but whether he did or not Polwin never knew, and he was never seen again. Getting away from the flames was now uppermost in his mind but the next thing he knew was that he was face down in the water, still in his parachute, and the remains of his Fulmar were about 80 yards away. Luckily salt water is very good for burns but everything had happened so quickly, nobody knew where he was or even what had happened. In fact he was some 40 miles off El Adem. Norman Davison, aged 21 and from Northumberland, who was attached to the Defence Flight from HMS *Grebe*, was indeed lost this date.

> When Polwin was shot down, our Fulmars and the Free French boys searched for him for several hours and had given up the search when I

decided to have one last look. Luckily I spotted him and circled him for about an hour and a half before the Walrus finally found us. Although badly burned, Polwin was able to help himself aboard the Walrus and was not placed on the danger list till 48 hours later.

Incidentally, shortly after Polwin was shot down I came down one night off Tobruk and was picked up by HMS *Arrow*, one of the escorts for a convoy on its way to Malta.

Lieutenant B Sanderson, Fulmar Defence Flight

Shortly after Sanderson's gallant effort, and when he was circling Polwin, a Wellington arrived and dropped a dinghy to him, into which he managed to pull himself. Finally came the welcome sight of the RN Walrus, which landed and took him aboard. He was very grateful and felt certain he would not have lasted through the night.

Altogether he had spent six hours in the water. Polwin then began a period of seven months in various hospitals having skin grafts and so on, but he survived, with no small thanks to Sanderson's determined efforts.

*   *   *

ASR Flight ME

There was one RAF rescue unit in existence in the eastern end of the Mediterranean at this time, a unit that would later become 294 Squadron RAF in September 1943. Air sea rescue in the Middle East began in July 1941 to deal with the large number of aircraft in the region, several of which were force-landing in the sea, especially Wellingtons on delivery flights from England via Malta. Up until this time 201 Group RAF had been responsible, using Short Sunderlands and surface vessels. The new organisation consisted of three Wellingtons, which had extra fuel tanks fitted to give them an endurance of 15 hours, a Marine Section of six HSLs – and a carrier pigeon service! It was formed at Kabrit on 13 August 1941 under Flight Lieutenant P W Dawson, a member of the Operational Staff at 201 Group, and was later under Flight Lieutenant G Wright.

In reality it was only a flight, based at LG39, Burg-el-Arab, near Benghazi, in the Western Desert, which it shared with 203 Squadron with its GR (General Reconnaissance) Blenheim IVs. The Flight had three Wellington IC aircraft and in September it moved to Burg-el-Arab, and became operational, thus becoming a Western Desert unit. In November a Walrus was obtained on loan from the Navy and established at Mersa Matruh, augmented by two US amphibians, a Fairchild 91 (single-engined monoplane) serial number HK832, and a Grumman, which had been presented to the RAF by well-wishers in America for air ambulance work in the Middle East. The Grumman was of little use for sea work as it was designed to be used on inland waterways, such as lakes or rivers. It was only to be used in an emergency.

Towards the end of 1941 the ASR detachment was sent to cover forward areas as the army advanced westwards and on 9 January it began operating from El Adem (Tobruk), but as the ground forces began retreating, the Flight was ordered back to Gambut and then Fuka, arriving on 2 February.

In February 1942, Squadron Leader S W R Hughes, a GR pilot, took over command. The Flight began using LG16 (Fuka) regularly, and more FAA Walrus aircraft began to arrive, along with FAA aircrew to man them. Over the next six months, the Flight would receive 67 rescue calls, making 16 successful rescues involving 75 lives saved (in conjunction with HSLs). In June, with further deterioration in the ground war, the Flight moved back to a landing ground near Abu Sueir, one of a whole mass of RAF airfields, some 20 miles south of Alexandria.

One of the first rescues by this Flight occurred on 23 May, the Fairchild picking up the crew of a German Ju88 north-east of Mersa Matruh (either the crew of an 88 of 2(F)/123 shot down on the 21st, or possibly a machine from II/KLG 1), taking off with a total of eight men aboard. The fact that the machine was able to get off with such a large load was not lost on the aircrew.

Then on 2 June, a Walrus and the Fairchild picked up three survivors each from a 221 Squadron Wellington VIII (W5732) lost on 29 May north of Tobruk. The Wimpy crew had been out on a shipping recco from LG05 near Sidi Barrani, port engine failure forcing them to ditch 40 miles north-east of Bardia. The pilot, Flight Sergeant Harry Nixon, did a great job and all his crew safely transferred into their dinghies, although they then had to drift about for three days before rescue. However, the day before this happened, they were spotted by a Blenheim which dropped water canisters and food to them. Nixon's crew were all NCOs, Sergeants Kitchen, Cullen, Irving, Winfield and Spencer. Nixon was awarded the DFM.

Fleet Air Arm
This was followed by a Walrus rescue of the crew of another ASV Wellington VIII that had been reported down 20 miles north of El Amaid on 28 June. 221 Squadron had sent off four Wellingtons on shipping searches. The one piloted by Pilot Officer Alfke had a port engine failure; in fact it lost the entire airscrew and reduction gear in flight. The bomber came down in the sea 30 miles from Burg-el-Arab (310 degrees), but the crew were all able to scramble into the dinghy. They were picked up a few hours later. Alfke's crew were Pilot Officer G F Davey RAAF and Sergeants Rolands, Heard, Ebblewhite and Christopher.

On this occasion it was not the RAF but the Fleet Air Arm who carried out the rescue, the Walrus (W2706) coming from 700 Squadron. The FAA crew were unable to take off so had to taxi to the shore, where the pilot beached the seaplane.

700 Squadron FAA was made up of a number of detachments, one being the unit's Mediterranean Detachment formed in October 1941, and later known as 700 Levant Squadron. In May 1942 it had been absorbed into the MEAF Air Sea Rescue Flight and based at Rayak, near Beirut. Later still it became 701 Squadron FAA. Sadly no records appear to have survived to indicate the crews involved.

Halifax Down
On 6 August 1942, a search was made for a missing Halifax bomber, after a Maryland crew of 203 Squadron reported seeing two dinghies with six men,

north of the Nile Delta. The 203 Squadron crew later reported that they had first seen them after the survivors fired off a green flare and then began waving a red flag. The Maryland's pilot, Squadron Leader Cox, then saw a hospital ship on the horizon and flew to it, signalling for it to make for the dinghies. The ship did so but then, frustratingly, the Maryland crew were unable to relocate the dinghies.

The Walrus, already on its way, was guided to the area, found the men and landed. It took three of the men off and later the same Walrus guided an approaching launch to the other three who were then rescued. The Halifax (W7757) came from 10/227 Squadron, which ditched after being hit by flak the previous evening over Tobruk. 227 were operating Halifax aircraft, part of a detachment from 10 Squadron, pending the arrival of Beaufighters.

*   *   *

283 Squadron

The first RAF ASR squadron at the western end of the Mediterranean, 283, was formed at Algiers in February 1943, with men and aircraft arriving mostly from the UK during the following two months. It became operational in May within the aegis of 323 Wing RAF.

The site at Algiers was a good one. A former seaplane base, it had two large hangars and a slipway into the water. Walrus aircraft were collected from Gibraltar during April and on 6 May it moved to Maison Blanche. One of the new pilots, not long out of training, was 20-year old Sergeant W S Lambert, from Gateshead:

> I had previously met a pilot from an air sea rescue squadron flying Walrus amphibian aircraft over the English Channel and as this seemed interesting work I applied for it and was successful. I was posted to 283 Squadron which eventually formed in Algiers in April 1943. We had previously crewed up with our wireless operator/air gunners before going overseas, and had about a month's practice on sea landings, rescues and take-offs.
>
> From Algiers we made our way eastwards in flights of two or three aircraft to Tunis. On a field beside the Tunis-Bizerta road, my crew and I set up our flight using the fuselage of a crashed German Ju52 transport aircraft as our dispersal HQ. We were warned not to go looking for souvenirs as an American colonel, who had done so, had lost both legs from a booby trap.
>
> Eventually the remainder of the squadron joined up to form a single unit.
>
> Sgt W S Lambert, 283 Squadron

Another young pilot was Leonard Henry Newman, known as Lisle. He recalls:

> Aircrew were trained at detachments of 277 Squadron in England, and the following left by sea in the troopship *Staffordshire*, part of a huge

convoy from Liverpool, arriving in Algiers in April 1943. CO, Flight Lieutenant W Sterne, Sergeants Divers, Lambert, Horne, myself (pilots), Sergeants Prouse, Graham, Bettridge, Botting and Pugh (gunners).

Flying Officer Mears, Pilot Officer Hopkinson, Warrant Officer Peat, Flying Officer Duke, and Sergeants Morabito and Hodges, left with the ground crew a short time before on a convoy, which suffered losses enroute. I believe, but am not certain, their ship was sunk and they were all transferred to another.

At first we were based at Algiers Harbour in an old French aviation hangar for a week or two and then moved to Maison Blanche aerodrome.

Sgt L H Newman, 283 Squadron

The need for air sea rescue in the area was due to air operations now extending off the Algerian and Tunisian coasts following the Allied landing in Algeria – Operation Torch – in November 1942. With the build-up of forces from Gibraltar to the western end of the North African campaign, there were increasing air patrols over shipping into the local ports of Oran, Algiers, Djedjelli, Bone, etc. With the number of German aircraft trying to bomb these ships and the new Allied bases inland, air cover became very necessary and convoy patrols increased. In any event, the end of the battle for North Africa was not far off. Within a few short months, the Axis forces were fighting for their very survival in Tunisia.

The Squadron, commanded by Flight Lieutenant W Sterne, a South African, was quickly in business. Flight Sergeant C Horne and Sergeant S R Prouse spotted a body in the water on 5 May, landed and retrieved the corpse of a German pilot. The next day the Squadron moved to Maison Blanche, also setting up a detachment at Tingley. Three days later Flying Officer R W V Jessett and Sergeant J V Botting rescued three Germans 20 miles east-north-east of Bizerta whilst operating from Tingley. An American P.38 fighter pilot had spotted them and the Walrus (W3074) flew out escorted by P.39 Aircobras from the 91st Fighter Squadron USAAF. Jessett landed at 20.00 hrs and rescued, not airmen, but three German soldiers.

These first successful rescues by 283 Squadron were in fact all Germans, mostly airmen brought down over these Allied ship convoys, just as Tunisia fell. On 19 May, Flying Officer K H Mears, with Warrant Officer N W Peat RCAF and Sergeant R B Hodges RCAF, landed and picked up a German flyer whilst operating from the airfield at Tingley. This sortie was flown at night, in bright moonlight, and Mears set down the Walrus on a calm sea without too much difficulty. The next day, Pilot Officer A Hopkinson and Flight Sergeant A B Morabito RCAF (W2734) in company with Sergeants Colin Horne and Sid Prouse (Z1777) searched long and hard for men reported in the water but failed to find anyone. Horne and Prouse lingered too long and eventually had to land on the water. The next morning Walter Sterne and Norman Peat took off at dawn to locate the downed Walrus, which they did, and they then directed a launch to the spot, carrying a drum of aviation fuel. Emptying the petrol into the tank, Colin Horne later took off and returned to base.

A few days earlier, on the 13th, Newman and Graham had flown to Tingley and were put on the duty roster that afternoon. They did not have to wait long for their services to be asked for:

We were ordered off for a rescue about 2 pm but it was aborted after the engine was started. The rescue was on again at 4 pm, but again we were stopped as we reached the runway. Twice more the call came, and finally we got off at 7 pm. The search area was only 25 miles off Bone but night fell as we got there and we could not see the surface at all from 400 feet.

We returned on a reciprocal course and climbed to 1,500 feet where I asked for a check return course. There was no reply at first, but after about five minutes of calling, I heard a faint: "185 degrees".

The Bone balloon barrage was ahead. Had we had no course, I was going to try and see the foam breaking on the shore, locate the town, and perhaps fly round the back to Tingley or Blida. Failing that I would have put down off-shore in the dark.

However, with a course, we got back to Tingley but I forgot to put the wheels down, luckily, and amazingly, with very little damage, only two plates (nine inches square) needing to be replaced. The Walrus was only out of action till the next afternoon (W3074).

The CO took no notice until I had a row with him because we were late taking off going to the next aerodrome, as Graham and I stopped to have a bit of food. It was mid-day and we had been out on a search during the morning and breakfast had gone a long way down. I'm afraid I cheeked him, being so cross, saying: 'What do you expect on a plate of f...... porridge!' (Using a word I do not normally use.) Sterne said he could have me shot for that, and he then endorsed my logbook for the previous incident, and grounded me. He sent Colin Horne off in my place and I lost rescue chances through that, which Colin certainly gained.

A week later I was reinstated and went to Sebala. After that I was put in charge of detachments at Howaria (Cap Bon), Pantelleria, Stromboli, Salerno, Monticorvino, Ajaccio and Ghisannacia (Corsica).

Flight Sergeant L H Newman, 283 Squadron

Then on 24 May, Pilot Officer Hopkinson and Flight Sergeant Morabito picked up the observer from a Ju88 which had been shot down off Djedjelli by British anti-aircraft fire.

Help and escort at this time came by way of P.39N fighters of the 347th US Fighter Squadron, part of the 350th Fighter Group. Lieutenant Hugh E McColl noted in his logbook on 21 May: "Search for Jerry pilot shot down by flak over Djedjelli on bombing mission." And on the 24th: "Search for Jerry shot down at sea. Found and was brought in by Walrus."

That same evening, Flight Sergeant Lisle Newman flew out with Tony Morabito and Flight Sergeant P H M Graham, searching Cap Serratt for a missing American who had, it was thought, crash-landed on the shore. They finally spotted the P.38 fighter on the beach, the Yank having indeed crash-landed. There was a man seated in the cockpit, so Newman landed and taxied into shallow water – four feet – and the two gunners waded ashore. By the time they had done so, the American pilot had already been found and led to a nearby USAAF camp. As it turned out, the man seen seated in the cockpit was an Arab the US pilot had instructed to stay and guard the machine! Lisle Newman relates:

> While Morabito and Graham went ashore I found the anchor would not hold the Walrus and she finished up in deep water about 70 yards off shore by the time they wanted to be taken off. So I had to get up and hand-crank the engine myself, jumping back down into the cockpit as the engine started.
>
> With everyone back on board, take-off was easy – the sea was calm. On becoming airborne I pressed the petrol gauges to see what we had used and they both showed 'empty'. Discussion followed as to whether the petrol had leaked out, or the dials were wrong. A look at the map showed an aerodrome in the mountains to the south, 20 miles away. Graham and Morabito thought we should locate it.
>
> I took a different view. To hunt for an aerodrome in unknown mountains with cloud on the tops, and the possibility of engine failure, I thought was an extremely dodgy prospect. As our normal return would be along the coast, I kept just over the sea so that if the engine did fail I could glide-land onto the water, and in the event of a break-up we could reach the shore by dinghy. If all went well we could anchor off shore and wait for help.
>
> The radio was quite useless – out of range – but of course, all went well, and we landed at dusk without mishap. Back home we found that the petrol gauges had indeed been faulty.
>
> Flight Sergeant L H Newman, 283 Squadron

283 Squadron Lose Two Men

Many of the customers of the Mediterranean ASR squadrons would, of course, be Americans, due to the large USAAF presence, and Norman Peat and Sergeant Frank Bettridge (in Walrus W2734), searched for and found the pilot of a P.38 Lightning, 53 miles east of Bone on 27 May. However, when Peat tried to take off he lost a float and they themselves had to call for help. It was now getting dark and an aircraft and an HSL were beaten by the darkness and Peat and Betteridge were reported missing. The following morning search aircraft were out early but they found no sign of the Walrus, nor did they find anything the following day. Their deaths at sea had to be presumed. Did something untoward happen? They should have been well placed to save themselves, having dinghies and equipment. Perhaps we shall never know. The luckless American Lightning pilot was Lieutenant F W Sanders of the 48th Fighter Squadron, 14th FG, who had initially been reported missing on the 26th.

> Peat and Bettridge were drowned off Cape Rosa trying to rescue an American pilot who was also lost. There was, I believe, a radio message to say their Walrus was sinking and there was something wrong with the dinghy. The CO blamed the dinghy safety ground staff member, but there was no proof of anything.

I was sent with Graham to search but we knew it would be useless from the start. After that we carried two extra dinghies – pilot types, but of course, no parachutes. This was because it was considered that as we flew most of the time at below 400 feet, they would not deploy in time anyway. Often we flew as close to ten feet as possible to keep in the sea return to avoid hostile radar.

Warrant Officer Peat was probably at that time the most experienced pilot; unshakeable and reliable, and a great loss at that stage. Frank Bettridge, from Salford, was very young, extrovert, terribly keen to make something of his life after the war. He wanted to be a civil engineer but had had to leave school at 14. He asked me if I could teach him about fractions in our spare time. I said I would – having fortunately had the benefit of a tremendous educational chance – but he was gone too quickly.

We also lost Flying Officer Duke who became ill after swimming and was sent back to Canada not long after losing Peat and Bettridge. There were no replacements.

Flight Sergeant L H Newman, 283 Squadron

The Squadron now moved to La Sebala No.1, situated just north of Tunis. Then, on the 30th, Hopkinson and Morabito (X9471) rescued Lieutenant C M Lindstrom, another P.38 pilot of the 48th US Fighter Squadron, 14th Fighter Group, who was to score at least three victories against the Luftwaffe over North Africa. Earlier in the day Sergeants C Horne and Prouse flew out and rescued four American crewmen from a B.25 Mitchell, ten miles off the island of Pantelleria. The bomber, from the 340th Bomb Group, had been shot down in flames off the island, while being escorted by Spitfires of the US 31st Fighter Group.

This island, situated almost mid-way between Cap Bon, Tunisia, and Sicily, was still occupied by the Italians and would be until 11 June 1943. There were several bombing raids on the island and on Sicily too, which increased 283 Squadron's activities. On 31 May for instance, Hopkinson and Morabito in one Walrus shared in the rescue of seven US airmen from a B.17 Flying Fortress, in two dinghies, with Flight Sergeant L H Newman and Sergeant Pugh.

My first rescue with Pugh – always known as 'Puff'[1], who was Welsh, very young and very boyish, nice fellow – was off Cap Sidi Ali. We found the men with no search needed. Seven in one dinghy, one of them, a gunner, with his nose hanging on by a thread of skin. Their skipper had taken off his jacket and placed it around him and was cuddling him in an effort to keep him warm. Dried blood covered the gunner's face. The picture of that skipper and gunner always remains with me.

We took off four and said we would return for the rest. I then found that due to a long swell I could not get off. We ran out 11 miles and as soon as I got close to pulling her off, she porpoised, knocking off the speed.

The Fortress skipper said he would return to the dinghy in order that I could try to get off with just three. He was certainly thinking that his

---

[1] Pugh was also referred to as 'Puggy'.

gunner was in urgent need of hospital treatment. As we returned him to the dinghy, Pilot Officer Hopkinson – known inevitably as Hoppy – arrived in another Walrus. He got off with four after I finally made it with three. He may have had a better plane – there was a great difference in aircraft – or he may have just been a better pilot.

Long swells were almost the worst from which to take off. The Walrus wanted to porpoise, jumping out of the water 20-30 feet, or more if one does not close the throttle. The Pilot's Notes say do not on any account fight a porpoise, as it will break the machine up. In the end, everyone on the squadron will have, at one time or another, fought a porpoise and got off successfully.

I fought one once after a practice landing at sea off Corsica, with a Canadian air gunner aboard for a joy ride. His bomber squadron shared our airfield. When we got back to the Mess their CO asked me what I had done to 'Hank'. "He came in just now, his eyes standing out like chapel hat pegs and couldn't speak, but finally blurted out that he had never had such a ride in his life!"

Flight Sergeant L H Newman, 283 Squadron

On the morning of 3 June, Sergeants Bill Lambert and 'Puff' Pugh were scrambled from Korba, (on the Tunisian east coast) after sighting two men on Zembra Island firing distress signals. For reasons not recorded (probably the water was too shallow) the crew were ordered back to base after contacting HQ, but took off again at 15.25 in order to guide a minesweeper to the men. After arriving in the area, the ship sent a dinghy ashore to pick up three stranded and wounded Americans.

The Tunisian campaign and the war in North Africa had now been won but the Allied efforts were now reaching northwards, the island of Pantelleria still being in enemy hands. Out in the Mediterranean too, the island fortress of Malta still survived and soon this would become the stepping-stone to the next offensive moves in the Middle East – the invasion of Sicily.

The Allied air forces of both the British Desert Air Force and the American 12th Air Force would very soon be undertaking support missions and tactical bombing sorties to both Sicily and mainland Italy. This would naturally involve much over-water flying just as the RAF and US 8th Air Force in England had to over-fly the Channel and North Sea. Suddenly, Air Sea Rescue would take on an increased workload in the Middle East theatre of operations.

* * *

284 Squadron

The softening up of Sicily began in June and continued until the invasion of the island – Operation Husky – on 9/10 July 1943. As a direct result of the upcoming invasion and the certain knowledge that both American and British flyers would soon be battling over the sea between North Africa and Sicily/Italy, another Walrus squadron was preparing for action. This was 284 Squadron.

This unit was formed on 7 May at Gravesend, England, specifically for overseas duty. The first commander was Flight Lieutenant R F Hayes, who was confirmed as CO on the 20th. Reginald Hayes had previously been with 277 ASR Squadron. 284, with six Walrus aircraft, started their move to the Middle East on 27 May, first going to Liverpool, where the aircraft carrier HMS *Battler* awaited them. The party got aboard on 3 June, sailing from Larne, Belfast, where a convoy had been prepared to sail for Algiers, leaving at 14.30 on the 5th. They would eventually arrive at Hal Far airfield, Malta on the very first day of the landings on Sicily.

One of the pilots of the new squadron was Sergeant James Andrew Reid, known to everyone as 'Hamish – the mad Scotsman'.

> I was transferred in January 1943 from 530 Squadron on its disbandment, where I had been flying Hurricanes in this Turbinlite night-fighter squadron. I then joined 277 ASR Squadron at quite an interesting period of its development. It was at that time that they were bringing in the modified Spitfire IIs equipped with a small Lindholme dinghy which could be dropped from the flare chute. So the Spitfires were assuming a dual role of search and escort for the Walrus aircraft on the pick-ups. I joined the Flight at Martlesham.
>
> After a suitable period of conversion, a couple of trips in a Defiant and a few training trips in a Walrus, then four or five searches in Spits, I went off on leave and came back to the Squadron, to find myself on a Middle East posting. This was May 1943, and was the formation of 284 Squadron. Reg Hayes was the CO, Eccles the adjutant, and Warrant Officer Ken Hall the senior NCO pilot, and the most experienced Walrus pilot in the whole Squadron.
>
> I suppose I had the second highest number of Walrus hours – about ten, plus four hours dual, so we weren't a tremendously experienced squadron. 'Sticky' Glew was a most experienced air gunner and we also had another experienced man, Norman Pickles. We were a pretty mixed bunch.
>
> We were following in the footsteps of 283 Squadron who had formed a couple of months earlier and who had gone out to North Africa. 284, we understood later, was essentially needed to cover the invasion of Sicily.
>
> We went out to Gibraltar in a slow convoy – OS 49/KMS 161 – aboard the escort carrier HMS *Battler*. We were rather annoyed we were not put on the ship's rum ration, neither did our officers do the necessary, and slip out some spirits from the wardroom for us! So we NCOs were soon a pretty bolshie bunch, especially when we were asked, when we were 300 miles away from Gib, if any of us who were ex-Spitfire pilots would be prepared to fly off 13 Spits, which were being sent out. We didn't go much on that idea, which was just as well, as out of the 13, seven went over the side. We felt rather sorry for the Navy 'Middys' and Sub-Lieutenants, who'd been brought out from Gib to take these from the deck.
>
> We arrived at Gib, spent a few days there, then we were transferred by DC3 aircraft to North Africa. We spent some time in Algiers then three days in the back of a lorry travelling to Bizerta, and finally out to Malta in a Sunderland – probably the most comfortable part of the trip we had

had since leaving the UK.

The time spent on Malta, prior to the actual invasion of Sicily, was spent in getting in some practice sea landings, training up the crews and finding out who fitted in best with each other. As far as I recall, it was D-Day plus three that we went into the first airstrip on Sicily, which was at Cassible. Simple thing – dirt strips carved out of a vineyard, probably 6-700 feet long. The main trouble was, we were extremely short of aircraft. We had no ground crews – they had not yet caught up with us – and our aircraft and MT had been sunk on a ship on the way out, so the question of a shortage of aircraft was something which was not fully resolved for some months and was to plague us. In fact, in the beginning at Cassible, we virtually had to inspect and maintain our own aircraft and had to fly back to Malta for any major inspections.

The first fuel we managed to obtain was after Catania harbour had been secured, where we scrounged a three-ton truck and managed to get 1,000 gallons of 87-octane in two-gallon cans. Filling a Walrus from two-gallon cans was not a very rewarding task in the heat of a Middle East summer! But we persevered and all in all it was an experience.

Sergeant J A Reid, 284 Squadron

Meanwhile, at La Sebala, 283 were still busy as June progressed. On the 5th, Sergeants Lambert and Pugh picked up four men from an American B.25 Mitchell just 15 miles south-east of Pantelleria, three of them being wounded. Heavy seas prevented the Walrus from taking off again but later a minesweeper came to their aid, off-loaded the Americans, and took the Walrus in tow. The crew came from the 379th Bomb Squadron, 310th Bomb Group and were 1st Lieutenant S C Schlitzkus (pilot), 2nd Lieutenant R G Werner (co-pilot), Staff Sergeant Teeple (radio), and Staff Sergeant Edwards (gunner).

On 5 June I was detailed to effect a rescue which turned out to be just off the island of Pantelleria. It took some time to spot them, but fortunately I saw star shells and altered course to a dinghy, which I could now see. I dropped a smoke float to establish the direction of the wind, there not being any aids such as T-markers or windsocks at sea, and upon landing, taxied up to the dinghy. This enabled my WOP/AG to open the front hatch, hook the dinghy with a boat hook, and then fasten a rope from the aircraft, allowing the dinghy to drift back to the rear hatch and admit the occupants.

When it came time to take off I found I could not do so, what with the state of the sea and the extra weight of the four Americans, survivors from a B.25 bomber. I decided to head for the Cap Bon peninsular which was about 60 miles away, as I thought this would provide some shelter from the seas. Just before making landfall I came across a minesweeper anchored for the night, and they took the Americans, and we also spent the night on it.

Sgt W S Lambert, 283 Squadron

Bill Lambert later expanded on the later stages of this operation:

> Puggy and the pilot of the Mitchell took up continuous pumping of water from the Walrus. Then I spotted the minesweeper *Espiegle* (J.216) and I stopped the engine at 20.50 hours. A rowing boat was lowered by the minesweeper and a tow line passed across and fixed to a bar by the undercarriage lever. The rowing boat came to the back hatch on port side and the Yanks and ourselves were taken off.
>
> The kite was rather damaged during this operation. The Yanks were taken to the sick bay and I had a bath and a change of clothes. I then went out at around 22.30 to secure the Walrus again as the towline had broken. Towline was now fixed to a High Speed Launch (ML 1230) which had arrived and it took the kite to Sousse the following day.
>
> In the morning we were taken off the minesweeper and into Sousse by HSL 139. The Walrus came into harbour about 17.30 on the 6th. There was a lot of water in her but it was all pumped out.

Lambert and Pugh had been unable to send a message back to base, so at first light on the 6th, 283's CO Walter Sterne was out searching, and found the Walrus, an HSL and the minesweeper. William Lambert received an Immediate Distinguished Flying Medal for his actions.

Flying Officer Mears and Flight Sergeant Botting rescued Lieutenant Paul G McArthur of the 79th Fighter Group on the 10th, ten miles to the north-west of Pantelleria. He was the top-scoring fighter pilot of the 79th, and in the battle which ended with him being in the water he had shot down two German Me109s and two Italian Mc202 fighters. After he'd baled out of his aircraft (X-83) his dinghy was only half inflated but he hung on and was finally rescued at dusk. Because of the heavy seas, they were unable to take off, and McArthur helped with the bilge pump, and then the engine stopped. Later a corvette came to their aid and towed them into Kelibia Bay. Paul McArthur recalls:

> As near as I can remember, we were based on Cap Bon, Tunisia – 87th Squadron, 79th Group. Our mission was to roll some 500 lb HE bombs into hangars (dug in) on Pantelleria island. Don't know whether the bombs found their target or not. I was shot down during the engagement and spent the night in a rubber dinghy. Lieutenant Anderson was able to get back and give directions and the Walrus came out.
>
> Once they'd picked me up the Walrus attempted to take off but the sea was too rough. During the attempted take-offs we sprung some leaks and we all had to pump water all night. Next day a Canadian corvette moved in and put a tow on our Walrus and towed us to Kelibia Bay.
>
> Someone waded out with a glass of scotch which didn't go down too well on an empty stomach with lots of salt water I recall! I spent the night and left for my squadron next day.
>   Lt Paul G McArthur, 87th FS, 79th FG

After the war Paul McArthur remained in the US Air Force, serving as a test pilot at Wright Field, and also in the Strategic Air Command (SAC), as a B.29 pilot in Korea. He retired in 1970 and went to law school.

* * *

More Trade off Pantelleria

An American Spitfire pilot of the 308th Squadron, 31st Fighter Group was rescued off Pantelleria on the 11th. Shortly after midday, 18 Spitfires had provided convoy cover during which 36 German fighters – Me109s and FW190s – came into the area, and were seen about to attack. While bomb-carrying Me109s of the Jabo staffel scored one hit and one near miss on the ships, five 109s were claimed shot down but one Spitfire pilot baled out. This was Lieutenant Gordon H Rich, whom 283 rescued. Many years later, Rich was to retire from the USAF as a Lieutenant-Colonel. Flying during the action was Lieutenant Edwin Dalrymple (a future FBI agent) of the same Squadron:

> In mid-June 1943, after the surrender of German forces in North Africa in May the 31st Fighter Group, 308th Squadron was based with its Spitfires at Korba North field on the Cap Bon peninsula. At this time we were flying missions over and around the island of Pantelleria, escorting bombers and seeking Axis fighters. On the 11th, the 308th engaged a number of enemy fighters and during the battle, Gordon Rich was forced to bale out several miles due east of the island.
>
> Immediately after our return to base, the 308th returned to the area where he had baled out, this time escorting a British Walrus. Lieutenant Matt W Mosby rode in the Walrus with the British pilot. We flew well south of Pantelleria to avoid detection by the enemy based there. We then helped lead a Walrus around the southern tip of the island and east of there, where, after a brief search, Lieutenant Rich was seen floating in his Mae West. The Walrus landed on the water, Mosby assisted in getting Rich aboard, and then the pilot skilfully took off and returned safely to Korba.
>
> It was learned later that Rich had failed to attach his dinghy to his parachute harness and thus had spent several hours in the sea with only his Mae West to support him. After the successful completion of this mission, several 308th personnel tried to reward the rescue pilot with a few gifts and 'alcoholic consumables' but the RAF pilot rejected them all, saying he was merely doing his job. The official 308th logbook commented: 'Such modesty and devotion to duty is not rare among the British we've met'.

The successful rescue crew were Colin Horne and Corporal Jaggers of 283, the operation timed from 16.00 to 18.50 hours. Gordon Rich tells his own story best:

> I remember the events clearly. Ed Dalrymple and I were both members of the 308th FG. I was shot down while flying a mission covering the invasion of Pantelleria. We were bounced by some Me109s and in the

ensuing fire fight I was hit in the engine, which began to smoke. I successfully baled out from about 8,000 feet, at approximately 12.30 pm. After hitting the water I was unable to retrieve my dinghy and spent the next five hours in my Mae West swimming towards the island.

In the meantime, the RAF Air Sea Rescue Squadron had been alerted and a Walrus was dispatched to search for me. An enemy attacked his fighter however, so he returned and asked for a fighter escort. A twelve-ship escort and search group of the 308th went back out with the Walrus.

About 5 pm two Spitfires buzzed me and the pilots waved. I then saw the rest, and the Walrus, off in the distance. The Walrus flew over and landed, then taxied up to me. Lt Matt Mosby, a 308th pilot, was standing up in the bow of the hull and he pulled me aboard. I was unhurt except for a small cut on the calf of my right leg which had snagged on the latch on the canopy as I baled out. I stripped off all my wet clothes and the crew gave me a blanket to wrap myself up in.

The pilot turned to take off but was unable to do so due to the choppy sea. He then taxied into the harbour of Pantelleria where the water was calmer and we got off all right. Fortunately, the island had been captured about 3pm!

When we arrived back at our base at Korba they took pictures of us. I am sure I entered the names of the pilot and crewman in my pilot's logbook but I later lost it during one of the moves in Italy.

I was very fortunate to survive. After swimming for five hours I had made little progress towards the island and I was getting cold and very tired. When I saw the Spits and the Walrus it was an answer to my prayers. I can't say enough in praise of the RAF Air Sea Rescue service. They did an outstanding job under very difficult and dangerous conditions.

Lt Gordon H Rich, 308th FS, 31st FG

For The Record
During operations to and around Pantelleria, 283 Squadron rescued a total of 18 aircrew between 1-12 June 1943. Since it had begun rescue work, it had collected 37 downed airmen in six weeks whilst being under Tunis Fighter Sector. (At the time 283 moved to Palermo, Sicily, in August, the total had risen to 67.)

* * *

On 13 June, Mears and Botting rescued a German pilot 15 miles from Pantelleria. There had been an air battle the previous day and the 4th US Squadron had shot down two FW190s, a Me109 and damaged two other 190s. They had found one of the downed German fighter pilots – Leutnant Franz Perz, from II/SLG2. He has variously been claimed by flak and by a fighter from the 350th US Fighter Group, but in any event, ended up a prisoner of war – but alive.

However, the Walrus had come under fire from the island and was hit, Mears being forced to land back on the water. He was faced with a difficult decision but finally had to taxi to the island. They eventually made the harbour and motored in.

They knew they were running a great risk as it was not certain if the island had yet been totally occupied by Allied troops or was still in part-possession of the enemy. The gunfire had convinced them that some hostile troops were still around. One imagines the German pilot had similar thoughts but of a slightly different nature. Luck was with them, however, and they found themselves greeted by a small Allied garrison that had only been in possession of the island for a short time. The gunfire that had hit them must have been about the final act of defiance from the defenders.

Mears was unable to radio their whereabouts to the Squadron as the new garrison had no signalling equipment, and the previous owners had destroyed theirs. It was not until a HSL arrived bringing in supplies that they managed to persuade the skipper to tow them back. They were then able to clear up the mystery of their disappearance.

Meantime, Walter Sterne was given the rank of squadron leader on the 24th, underscoring the success and the status of the Squadron. This was following a sortie three days earlier to rescue an American fighter pilot from the 14th Fighter Group. Captain R E Dekker, of the 37th Squadron, had been reported missing and Sterne himself flew out to search but found nothing. Landing to discuss further the loss and the man's possible whereabouts, he then flew off again at 10.50, this time escorted by some of the American Lightnings. They headed for a spot near the Sicilian coast and successfully located the man in a dinghy and made a rescue within sight of the island's south-west coastal area. Captain Dekker had been in the water for 27 hours and was found three miles off the island of Marettimo, west of Sicily.

Also that morning, the squadron had another successful rescue under their belts, this time nine miles off Cape Mostefa. The previous night a Wellington of 142 Squadron had been part of a raiding force bombing the railway marshalling yards at Naples. On the way home however, for some unaccountable reason, they began to run short of fuel.

Sergeant H L Pleydell finally had no choice but to ditch off the North African coast, after his wireless operator, Sergeant J Slater, sent out a Mayday call. Pleydell suffered some minor injuries but he and his all-Australian crew were quickly in their dinghy. At first light, three of 142's aircraft, led by its CO, Wing Commander A R Gibbes DFC, were out searching for their missing companions, found the dinghy and then called up the ASR boys. Sergeant Colin Horne and Flight Sergeant Botting were soon landing nearby and took the five men aboard. The others were Sergeants H W Gee (navigator), J Lynch (rear gunner), and A E Evans (bomb aimer).

Mears and Botting rescued survivors from a B.26 Marauder from the 437th Bomb Squadron, 319th Bomb Group on 30 June, who had gone down returning from a raid on Trapani. The bomber's pilot, Lieutenant A L Graves did not survive, but his crew did: Lieutenants Davis and Matthews, Sergeants Matunio, Disciscio and Chard. Mears had to taxi the two miles back to the nearest safe beach.

By June, the Squadron had made more than two dozen rescues, picking up around a score of Allied airmen and seven Germans, plus helping to guide rescue services to several others. This included two Germans rescued on 6 June, 12 miles east of Kelibia by Horne and Prouse, in a very rough sea. Early on this day, Sterne and Sergeant Botting rescued four US airmen but the Walrus received some damage so all four had to be transferred to a HSL, while the aircraft was towed home by a naval motor boat.

Air Commodore K B Cross DSO DFC, Air Officer Commanding 242 Group wanted to make an aerial reconnaissance of Lampedusa Island at this time, and chose a Walrus flown by Squadron Leader Sterne in which to do it on 14 June, which has much to say for the Walrus and for Sterne.

* * *

Back in England yet another ASR squadron was being formed, 293 coming into being on 28 June 1943, with 20 crews from the OTU at Bircham Newton, Norfolk. They began training on twin-engined Warwick aircraft specifically for ASR work in the Mediterranean. The CO was Squadron Leader R H McIntosh AFC, who had been with 280 Squadron until March, and whose DFC was about to be Gazetted. This new unit found itself going to North Africa, first to Blida, then to Bone.

Although essentially a Warwick squadron whose aircraft would be used for long range search and rescue flights, in April 1944 they would begin to have some Walrus aircraft too and a few experienced Walrus men would be transferred to the Walrus flight.

* * *

We return now to the ASR Flight at the eastern end of the Mediterranean (still not yet known as 294 Walrus Squadron), which by early 1943 was operating from Misurata on the Libyan coast. The Flight had moved from Abu Sueir to Burg-el-Arab in November 1942, as the El Alamein battle had once more moved the front line westwards. Detachments were also located at Gambut, Benghazi and Sidi Barani. With such a stretch of coastline to cover, a Blenheim flight was formed in January 1943 and another Walrus flight in February.

Assists
While the stories of Walrus rescues is the main thrust of this book, there were many rescues by surface vessels which were aided by Walrus aircraft, guiding boats of various descriptions to downed airmen. One, which must have been made by the ME Flight and occurred on 2 January 1943, was quite dramatic.

On this day a mission by the US 12th Bomb Group to attack Heraklion airfield, Crete, from their Gambut air-base got fouled-up at the start. A sandstorm blew up just before take-off time during which 36 B.25s were milling around blindly in the dust, and only 12 managed to get airborne (six 81st and six 82nd Squadrons). Aircraft #39 piloted by Lieutenant John H Holmes, from Des Moines, Iowa, ran into more trouble half way to the target. Navigator Monroe P Schwartz, from Philadelphia, saw that the right engine was trailing smoke and after some discussion it was decided to press on. This they did, bombed with the others, then turned for home. About a third of the way back the right engine began to pound and splutter, forcing them to feather it. Fuel was a problem with all the delay at take-off and suddenly the left engine stopped.

Holmes ditched successfully and everyone got out, including a sergeant newsreel photographer who had chosen this raid to go along for the ride! The top gunner and the radioman had banged their heads but eventually all seven men were in a five-man dinghy. For the next 25 hours the men waited, knowing they were hopeful of rescue as other B.25 crews had seen them ditch. There was some anxious moments as a valve stuck and air started to leak from one section of the dinghy but it got sorted out.

Early next morning a Wellington hove into view, then began circling in order for a fix to be made. Not long afterwards, Mitchells from their own squadron began to arrive to help keep the dinghy in view. The same, or another Wellington, came back and dropped smoke floats and some supplies, but five more hours passed, during which time the sea got up and it began to rain. Then a Walrus arrived overhead but by this time the sea was too rough for a landing. Then a Hudson arrived, and someone in the rear turret was seen to be taking film shots of them. Finally the Walrus fired off some flares and then a boat appeared – a RAF HSL.

Once aboard the boat, the airmen found that things were still not going well. The storm broke and the HSL skipper decided to drift rather than risk trying to battle it, and so the HSL's crew and the rescued airmen had to endure three days of battering, with only limited food stocks. Later it was thought that the storm was the worst anyone in the area could recall. On day four it abated and the sun came out, and at last the HSL could head for shore with the last of its fuel. It had been low on fuel and food as it had previously been on another rescue trip and been diverted to help.

* * *

The Middle East Walrus Flights made a few successful rescues during the final build-up to victory in Tunisia. On 19 April, 603 Squadron provided three Beaufighters for air cover to the convoy *Merit*, which began soon after first light. 603 Squadron was at this time a Navy Co-operation unit under 201 Group and were based at Misurata West.

On patrol, Flight Sergeant J Goodfellow and Sergeant L G Maynard in Beau V8372 'J' began to have engine trouble so turned for home but before they reached the coast they were forced to ditch. Aircraft 'H' with Flight Sergeant R H Giles and Sergeant L Coulstock escorted the limping Beaufighter but they were unable to inform base by either W/T or R/T of its position so flew back to Misurata to report verbally. Ten minutes later they were in the air again, escorting a Walrus flown by Lieutenant Borland. He was taken to the spot in the Gulf of Sudra where he landed and picked up the two men.

On the following day, the 20th, the first RAF Walrus arrived at Goubrine and immediately became operational.

The Flight also had a detachment at Sidi-Bou-Cobrine, and on 25 April –

Easter Sunday – they had two rescues and some excitement. 92 Squadron, led
by Flight Lieutenant Neville Duke DSO DFC, took off at 10.35 for a sweep off
the Tunisian coast and although no enemy aircraft were found, intense flak from
the Ras-el-Fortass area clobbered the Spitfire IX flown by Flying Officer R H
Probert RCAF (EN458), which forced him to bale out ten miles east of Korba.
When the squadron was forced to leave, he was seen sitting safely in his dinghy.

Neville Duke wrote in his diary:

> Escort to some Kittys on another Cap Bon expedition but saw nothing.
> P/O Probert was hit by flak as we crossed the Cape and turned back and
> had to bale out off the coast at Korba. After lunch we escorted a Walrus
> out to pick him up and found him OK about six miles off the Hun coast.

Meantime, 145 Squadron of the Desert Air Force were flying cover to 239
Kittyhawk Wing of three squadrons on an anti-shipping patrol. As they swept the
Gulf of Tunis they too met intense AA fire which hit the Spitfire flown by Flight
Lieutenant I H R Shand – a Rhodesian – (ER982) shortly after mid-day. Soon
afterwards, he too was in his dinghy.

The first Walrus, 'A', piloted by Sub-Lieutenant Oldknow, was airborne in
response to the Mayday call at 13.15, and escorted by six Spitfires from 1 SAAF
Squadron. He located Probert in his dinghy 12 miles from Korba, landed and
soon had him aboard. Probert had been happily paddling around for just over
two hours and his only complaint was that he had lost one shoe of a pair he had
only purchased the previous day! Rex Probert won the DFC later in the year.
Neville Duke and 92 Squadron were also part of the escort cover.

The Shand rescue was also successful – just. Sergeant H G C King had taken
Walrus 'C' out, escorted by 12 Spitfires of 417 Squadron but at first they could
not spot the dinghy. King then flew a pattern search and found Ian Shand on the
fifth leg, six miles off Hammamet. However, as the Spitfires circled the area, all
the activity had attracted some attention and suddenly two Me109s dived onto
two of the Spitfires, shooting down Flying Officer A E Pourboix. The other
rescue was still in operation as enemy fighters, six more Me109s, turned up, but
the South Africans kept them at bay. They were also engaged by the Spitfires of
1 SAAF Squadron and one Messerschmitt was damaged. As it turned out, Ian
Shand too was about to receive the DFC.

Later, 244 Wing noted its deep admiration and gratitude to the two Walrus
pilots who had carried out their tasks so successfully despite the dangers and the
presence of enemy fighters. It was one of the rewards the Walrus crews had,
knowing they had saved men from certain death or capture by their efforts.

Just two days later it was the pilots of 1 SAAF Squadron who were to feel
grateful. They had seen how a rescue had been made on Easter Sunday, now one
of their pilots gained first-hand experience.

Lieutenant C A Halliday took off with his squadron at 4.50 pm, which was
led by Captain W M 'Bushy' Langerman. Their Spitfire Vs were to fly a sweep
in company with two Kittyhawk squadrons round Cap Bon and down to Tunis,
chiefly on an anti-shipping strike, but the Kittyhawks did not make the
rendezvous. A couple of ships were seen through some cloud but then Colin

Halliday's aircraft developed engine trouble. The temperature began to rise but as the engine sounded fine he thought it must be a faulty gauge.

He stayed with the formation till they neared Tunis but then glycol began to stream from the engine and he was forced to bale out south of Hammamet, after calling Langerman. He tried to glide south-east, accompanied by Captain J R Lanham, but then 'bandits' were reported to be in the vicinity so it was time to take to his parachute.

By the time he had departed, his cockpit had been full of smoke, fumes, and flames were now coming from the engine. Halliday inflated his Mae West on the way down and when he was about to hit the sea, took a deep breath. He came back to the surface only to find himself entangled in the parachute lines. Luckily the parachute floated sufficiently to give him time to fully inflate his Mae West, release the dinghy, climb in and pull the 'chute in with him, keeping the 'D'-ring as a souvenir.

He put on the yellow cap which was in the dinghy, meant to be worn to help people spot a man, but was disappointed to discover there was no rum in the emergency kit, and that he had lost his escape aid box. He then recalled seeing it shoot up past him as he baled out. Halliday was a little miffed as he had always been curious as to what it might contain and now the opportunity to find out had eluded him.

Thinking the dinghy was drifting inshore he began to paddle out, wanting to avoid capture. High overhead he could see four Spitfires orbiting and after a while saw a Walrus escorted by more Spitfires, which, as they neared, broke away to search for him. They soon spotted the yellow dinghy and cap and then the Walrus was landing close by. He was pulled on board but in doing so he lost the grip on the 'D'-ring, the parachute and one gauntlet. Moments later they were airborne.

It was now almost dark and he was given a coat to put on but very quickly they were landing at Goubrine Landing Ground. He had been rescued by Sergeant King, who had had an escort of ten Spitfires from 145 Squadron. They had found him off Reyville, his position being made easy to find due to a large patch of oil nearby. As the Spitfires had circled above the Walrus they had been subjected to gunfire from the shore but nobody had been hit.

As 1 SAAF moved to Sicily in mid-July, Colin Halliday bagged a Me109G near Syracuse on the 13th, although because his seat moved forward he did not see what happened to it and once he'd sorted the seat out, there was no sign of the German although there was something burning on the ground far below. Unhappily, on the 19th, Halliday was shot down and killed following an attack by Hauptmann Franz Beyer of IV/JG3. Both wings of his Spitfire broke away before crashing. He did not get out. Beyer achieved 81 victories before his own death on 11 February 1944 over Holland.

Sergeant King was again busy on 16 May, searching with his crew for a downed Kittyhawk pilot 11 miles from Hergla. They found nothing until they saw a large patch of oil, and then a man in a Mae West. King landed and picked up Leutnant Bruno Losen, who turned out to be the German pilot of a Me410 (F6+YK) of 2/(F)122, shot down over Medjej. His crewman, Unteroffizier Willi Keller had not survived.

By the end of May 1943, as the Tunisian battle ended, the Flight was thinking it should have more Walrus aircraft, and that the Blenheims should be replaced by more Wellingtons. The crews also believed the most forward detachment should be in Tripoli. In June six more Wellington crews arrived and were sent to Shallufa for ASR training.

However, the Flight lost its Fairchild on 17 May and was lucky not to lose two pilots. At 07.18 Pilot Officer D Harcourt and Flight Lieutenant Wright were airborne, doing circuits and 'splashes' (bumps!). Almost an hour later 247 Wing informed the Flight that they had received a call from the Fairchild that it was in trouble two miles off the coast. The Navy were sending out a launch and a Wellington was also flying out.

Apparently in one take-off the Fairchild had hit an underwater obstruction and been forced to ditch. For some reason, Harcourt was not wearing a Mae West, so once the Fairchild had sunk, he had little option but to strike out for the shore, leaving Wright clinging to an empty tool chest.

The Wellington arrived to find only wreckage but did see one man in the water and guided the launch to him. This was Flight Lieutenant Wright, who once aboard, told the crew to head for shore in the hope of locating the swimming Harcourt. This they did and half way to the beach, found Harcourt and pulled him safely on board.

The Flight almost lost another Walrus on 25 July. Flight Lieutenant Bleby in the Derna detachment's P5669, was making practice landings in Derna Harbour, but damaged a float as aircraft hit a sudden swell, but he got it down again safely, with only Cat.II damage.

A Difficult Decision

Lisle Newman remembers a difficult decision Colin Horne had to make on one occasion, off Cap Bon, operating from Korba North, Tunisia.

> Three army soldiers went out from the shore in a wooden boat for pleasure, perhaps even fishing, and must have lost their oars. The sea became very rough, and the wind gale force. They were spotted drifting.
>
> F/O Mears and Sgt Hodges went to look, and returned without splashing down, saying the sea was impossible and that a HSL should be called. It had to come from Tunis and round the Cape, southwards, to Korba North position. Whether one ever started out I do not know.
>
> What were the orders for Colin and Sid when they set out later I do not know either, but they splashed down to find the sea with 12-foot waves and wind gusting at over 60 mph. This threatened to capsize the Walrus on each turn required.
>
> Two of the men managed to scramble aboard the Walrus, I believe by swimming the last yard or two from the boat. The third man was so petrified he would not leave. Twice Colin put the wing over the boat but he would not leave it or attempt to grab the wing struts.
>
> In the end Colin considered they would all drown from the Walrus capsizing if he did not abandon the attempts. They took off with the two they had got, the high wind-speed no doubt helping them once she had

jumped out of the water. In any event the main frame of the Walrus was twisted and it never flew again.

How dreadful to leave someone. How courageous to go in the first place. No time to think; instant decisions to make. As I had fallen foul of the CO [the porridge incident related earlier] it had put Colin and Sid in my place at Korba. What would I have done? I guess I would have followed orders but if it had been left up to me . . . .? The thought still makes me shudder; I am not a Colin Horne.

* * *

Rocky Hodges, our Canadian air gunner, was killed in a strafing raid while in a tent at Korba North. Sid Prouse was hit in the leg and was in hospital at Maison Blanche for some time but returned after his wound mended. Colin Horne, Ken Mears, and John Howells, our medical orderly, were in the same tent but were unhurt.[2]

Horne and Flight Lieutenant Sterne had fallen out early on, and literally hated each other. It had started before I met either of them – at Shoreham I think. It was personal but I don't know what.

Colin was ex-merchant navy, public schoolboy, extrovert and flamboyant. When he was ranting on one could tell him to shut up and he would pause, then laugh, saying – "I am going on a bit aren't I."

On the sea in a Walrus he was absolutely fearless. After demob he lived in Kenya and South Africa.

Flight Sergeant L H Newman, 283 Squadron

---

[2] Flight Sergeant Robert Bertram Hodges RCAF was killed in action on 7 June 1943 and buried in Medjez-el-Dab war cemetery.

Chapter 2

SICILY

Operation Husky

The invasion of Sicily took place on 9/10th July 1943 and as the battle front moved forward, so too did the Walrus squadrons. With the amount of aircraft operating from Malta, North Africa and even Pantelleria (from 15 July) they would have plenty of customers in the coming weeks. Mediterranean Air Command anticipated this which resulted in the formation of 284 Squadron. Thirteen Walrus aircraft were obtained from Admiralty stocks at Gibraltar. Initially it was thought that the 13 would all go to 284, whereas six were slated for 283 Squadron. The Deputy Director of Air Sea Rescue eventually sorted the confusion out following a visit to MAC, making it clear that six of the 13 were to form 284, with the others going to 283 to help with the invasion.

As July began, 47 Squadron's torpedo-carrying Beaufighters had good reason to thank 283 Squadron, who were still in Tunis, for they had crews rescued on successive days, 2nd and 3rd July.

An armed-reconnaissance on the first day, led by Flight Lieutenant J R Hastings, saw Flight Sergeant J E Carroll and Sergeant T Frewen ditch and get into their dinghy. The leading Beau circled the spot, sending the third crew back to base to raise the alarm. Shortly afterwards three German Me109s turned up, forcing the circling Beau to jettison its torpedo and head south low and fast, and the 109s to break off three minutes later. With the alarm duly raised, a Walrus crew was scrambled, crewed by the CO, Walter Sterne, Dick Eccles and Sergeant Pugh.

> We scrambled to search for a pilot and navigator of a torpedo Beaufighter on a course of 40 degrees for approximately 88 miles. We found them eventually and landed on a very rough sea. With the load and the swell we didn't manage to get airborne and with the loss of power in the motor we started taxying for home. A HSL met us and the two 'pick-ups' were taken on board.
>
> We had another shot at take-off which was again unsuccessful so we taxied on through the night. We rested for an hour or two and then couldn't re-start the engine. We were picked up by a MTB [motor torpedo boat] from a convoy about 26 hours later and the Walrus was towed back with us.

Four days later I flew to Malta to join 284 Squadron which was my
original posting.

Flying Officer R G Eccles, 284 Squadron

While the technique of picking up a downed airmen was described in my first
ASR book *Another Kind of Courage*, it is worth repeating here, and in the words
of Dick Eccles, when I asked him why the Walrus crew sometimes had two crew
members and occasionally three:

> Interesting you asking about operating with two pilots. I'm sure there
> was no definite rule about it, but I was in favour of it as in many cases it
> was necessary to have another [third] crewman. The Walrus had .303
> machine guns stowed fore and aft, which in my time were never used,
> and had removable covering. If the person to be rescued was not in a
> dinghy, the second pilot operated the covering of the forward hatch and
> threw a rope to the survivor who held it. The forward movement of the
> aircraft brought him around to the side where the gunner, with cover off
> the rear fuselage hatch, caught him and helped him on board. Extremely
> difficult without the third man.
>
> Similarly in the case of German survivors, it would have been pretty
> dicey with one crewman looking after, say, two of them. In one case we
> had the report that there was only one man in a dinghy and as we wanted
> to avoid extra weight due to distance and petrol, we only used one pilot
> and a gunner.

Lisle Newman also has some observations about operations from the North
African coast during the first part of his tour:

> It is my personal opinion that the control of rescues was not far short of
> appalling. On one of my sorties the ground people were 40-50 miles out
> in their calculations and dithered over the positions.
>
> My other gripe was the radio. We carried Morse radio but had no station
> to connect with, so we had a huge and heavy radio on board, which was
> in the way most of the time, giving us an unnecessary load when it came
> to take-off. Our radio was for fighters flying at great heights and was
> utterly useless when flying close to the sea at more than 20 miles out.

Flight Sergeant L H Newman, 283 Squadron

* * *

On 3 July, 47 Squadron mounted a shipping strike, led by Wing Commander A
M Taylor. The three Beaufighters found five armed trawlers at 10.38 am and
began to work them over with cannon fire. However, Flying Officer C A
Ogilvie's Beau was hit by flak in the port engine and staggered away in a
southerly direction. Ogilvie maintained height at 2,000 feet for a while but then,
with both engines smoking and one undercarriage wheel hanging down, he was

forced to ditch. He and his navigator, Sergeant A G Williams, got into their
dinghy as Wing Commander Taylor, who had followed them, circled and got off
a Mayday call.

Sergeants Lambert, Divers and Cromie of 283 Squadron, took off in a Walrus
at 15.35, landing at Bone to refuel, then taking off again at 17.35. After a search
they found and picked up the two men, but they had to taxi back for seven hours,
and then the amphibian ran out of petrol. The next afternoon, HSL 176 arrived
and took off the survivors, plus Lambert and Cromie, who'd become unwell, and
then, with Divers, a New Zealander, staying at the controls, the Walrus was
towed into Bone harbour. Arnold Divers recalls:

> This was an unusual rescue. We flew from Maison Blanche and refuelled
> at Bone. Late in the evening, almost at the end of our search pattern,
> approximately 38.26N/08.20E we located a dinghy containing F/O
> Ogilvie and Sgt Williams of 47 Squadron having ditched after clearing
> the coast south of Sardinia. Although making a successful landing in
> failing light and rough seas, attempts to take off were impossible. The
> VHF set then blew up as a result of dangerous bouncing on and
> sometimes under the high seas. Sooner than sit like shags on a rock
> awaiting daylight we thought it prudent to taxi away from the Sardinian
> coast and head back to North Africa. After taxying for over nine hours the
> engine through lack of fuel faded out. We were, after many long hours of
> waiting, eventually located by HSL 176 and HSL 182 and towed into
> Bone, finally returning to base after the Walrus was refuelled, and the
> plugs cleaned and serviced, on 6 July. Fortunately during the whole time
> I was the only one not sea sick. On reflection, I feel the years spent deep-
> sea yachting off the Otago coast prior to WW2 were helpful in many
> ways during my Air Sea Rescue service.
>
> Sergeant A Divers, 283 Squadron

Bill Lambert had made some notes too, which read:

> Two attempts at take-off. No bloody good – wire broke off starboard float
> and the IFF blew up. Taxied approximately 160 degrees and engine gave
> out at 02.10 hours. Saw a Hudson aircraft at 08.00 – two cartridges fired
> – and aircraft seen again at 10.00 hours and again at 11.55. HSL 176
> arrived at 12.20 and we were taken aboard and given a meal. HSL 182
> came up and took Wally [Walrus] in tow, Divers staying on board.
> Arrived at Bone 17.00 hours, and the Wally came in at 19.00.

Unhappily, Ogilvie, who became OC B Flight in September 1943, was
reported missing on 6 November, last being seen over Yanni Bay with a
Messerschmitt 109 on his tail.

A Walrus Loss

The very next day, the 4th, the Squadron made a successful rescue but lost
a Walrus. An American pilot, Lieutenant Marks, had come down 10 miles

north-east of Cap Bon and Flight Sergeant Lisle Newman, along with Sergeant Jock Graham, found him, landed and picked him up. However, the rough sea swamped the Walrus and it sank. The three men clambered into dinghies and were later rescued by a HSL from Pantelleria.

> Lieutenant Marks was only 25 miles off Cap Bon when we located him. Jock and I flew low over him and I tried to drop a smoke bomb for wind direction, but it would not come off the rack. I could see the clamps move but there was no release.
>
> In consequence I only had the waves to give me wind direction, and luckily they were large enough to break, allowing foam to tail back on the wind. I set the gyro compass on them and we attempted a landing which ended in taking off the port float which caused the Walrus to sink.
>
> I must have had drift on for the float to break. This is not easy to see on moving water, although very easy to see on land. Also, I now know, as a sailor with experience with yachts, that the wind can change in an instant by five to ten degrees. That may have happened then. I went for a flat landing, whereas I should have used a rough sea attitude.
>
> Our training in the beginning was not good enough. Three shared two-hour training stints on three afternoons in my opinion is not enough to start to land on any sea. This meant, of course, that most of us learnt as we went along.
>
> Squadron Leader Sterne's refusal to let pilots practice was a big disadvantage to pilots like myself. Mustn't risk the aircraft or use the petrol. It was a short-sighted policy in my opinion. Things such as weather, navigation, flying at night, they were all nothing compared with getting off of a rough sea and a long swell. That is the crucial aspect of air sea rescue Walrus flying. Even the thought of German interference is also of little regard.
>
> Flight Sergeant L H Newman, 283 Squadron

This rough weather at sea continued until the 5th, at which date Sergeant Colin Horne and Sergeant Graham rescued Captain Carpenter of the US 316th Fighter Squadron, 324th Fighter Group (P.40 Warhawks), 25 miles out from El Haouaria. Being unable to take off they had to taxi into the harbour at Pantelleria.

* * *

The 5th US Fighter Squadron, 52nd Fighter Group, shot down two Messerschmitt 109s on 12 July. The next day Sergeants Lambert and Pugh, escorted by Spitfires, rescued Unteroffizier Franz Schmidt, one of the 109 pilots, north of the Tunisian coast – position 37.45N, 09.49E. On the 18th, Sergeant Arnold Divers of 283 picked up Lieutenant Townsend of the 310th Squadron of the 86th Bomb Group, who had been drifting in a dinghy for 20 hours. He was 43 miles to the south-east of Pantelleria. This outfit had been flying from North Africa in transit to Sicily where they would begin operations on the 22nd.

Within days of the successful invasion of Sicily, 283 Squadron and the recently formed 284 Squadron were preparing to send detachments across to the island. On the 15th 283 in fact sent two aircraft to Pantelleria, and on the 31st, Walrus aircraft finally landed on Sicily.

A few days earlier, on 27 July, 284 Squadron had scored its first success, picking up a P.40 Kittyhawk pilot – Lieutenant Donald E Harwood of the 65th Fighter Squadron, 57th Fighter Group, ten miles south-west of the toe of Italy. The Walrus crew consisted of Sergeants D J Lunn, G F Brown and Warrant Officer N Pickles (X9506). In this same mission, the 57th Fighter Group had Major Glade B Bilby of the 64th Squadron bale out through engine trouble. A search was made for him too but he was not found until the next day – the 28th. A Walrus of 284 Squadron searched for him the next day but a HSL picked him up and brought him back. Bilby would end the war with four air combat victories.

284 Squadron was now operating aircraft from Malta, Sicily and Algiers. The Malta detachment was based at Hal Far, which was commanded by Squadron Leader J H Ashton DFC. OC Comms and ASR units were also based there.

Thirteen Hours in a Dinghy

Then on the 31st, in the midst of 284 moving bases, Reg Hayes and Sergeant C S Taylor took off (in W3012) with an American officer on board who knew the exact location of a fellow pilot – Lieutenant J C Kelly of the 86th Squadron (The Commanches), 79th Fighter Group, 9th Air Force. Kelly had been shot down the previous evening during a fighter-bomber mission, but had not been picked up before darkness fell. Flying to the spot there was no sign of him so Hayes began to widen the area of search and eventually they found the dinghy and pilot ten miles further to the east. He was east of Andrea, in the Straits of Messina, having been paddling desperately away from the nearby hostile shore once realising that the tide was taking him in. Jack Kelly recalls:

> I was leading a Flight of P.40s carrying 500 lb bombs for a targeted harbour on the north-east coast of Sicily. After I released my bomb and pulling up from a rather steep dive, I noticed white smoke coming out of the engine and realized I'd been hit and was losing coolant. I tried to gain as much altitude as I could with my excess speed and then headed towards the sea some distance away towards the east. My engine ran for about five minutes before it over-heated and finally seized.
>
> I glided with a dead engine as long as possible and was about half to one mile out to sea and at about 1,000 feet when I baled out. I had undone my radio connection and seat belt while gliding and just rolled over to an upside-down position and fell out. All the while I was being escorted by my squadron mates until, due to fuel limitations, they had to return to base. As it was late afternoon there wasn't enough time to launch an air rescue before nightfall.
>
> The next morning at first light I could see this flight of P.40s looking for me at about where I came down. As they were too far away to see me in my dinghy, it occurred to me to toss out my orange dye marker which made a huge slick on the water and made my position visible. Major Fred

Borsodi, the squadron leader, was the first to spot the slick and called in my position to air sea rescue.

I was rescued by the crew of 284 Squadron RAF, and the US pilot on board was Lieutenant Gordon Gibson.

Former Technical Sergeant Sidney Loadenthal was a member of Kelly's Squadron, and says:

I was a Tech. Sergeant and Flight Chief in the 86th Squadron, 79th Fighter Group from October 1942 until 25 June 1945. I kept a diary from the time I left the US until I came home in 1945. Lieutenant Kelly was a pilot and flying ship No.64 when he went down, the ship being in my Flight. In my diary I wrote: '# 64 Lt Kelly was hit with shrapnel and had to bale out; he was in a dinghy for 13 hours before he was picked up.'

This was not Kelly's first adventure of baling out, as he also relates:

Previously, around January or February 1943, when fresh out from the States, for combat experience I and several others were loaned out to the 57th Fighter Group. I was with the 66th Squadron. My first time out, flying tight wing (a dumb tactic) on Captain Zipser, we got into a dog-fight with a well known Me109 outfit[1] and I got blown out of the sky without warning. Never saw him. Engine on fire, no controls, I went over the side at 340 mph. I woke up floating in the shroud lines. I guess the shock of the 'chute opening at that speed knocked me out. Anyway, I managed to untangle myself, saw my plane burning in the distance, and landed. This was about 100 miles west of Benghazi. As we'd been taught, I gathered up my parachute and ran as far from where I'd landed as I could. Then flattened myself and lay still somewhat hidden from view by scrub bushes. After a while I saw what appeared to be a German command car about a half mile away. Not seeing any sign of life they eventually left. I didn't move for several hours. An Arab passed within 20 yards of me but didn't notice me. Towards late afternoon I picked up my 'chute and started to walk on a line that would take me towards our lines and the water.

Around dusk, I stopped when I noticed four to six soldiers with their rifles aimed at me. Not knowing what to do, I sat down and as they drew close, pulled a corner of my 'chute and sort of waved it. Then I heard, "It's a Yank." Talk about luck! They were part of the forward elements of the 8th Army. So I ended up as a guest of the Argyll and Sutherland Highlanders. No more than 500 yards to the west was a forward element of Rommel's Desert Corps.

The next day I hitchhiked my way back to my unit. Since I'd been listed as missing in action, I had to track down my belongings, which had been shared by various buddies. They'd figured I didn't need them anymore.

---

[1] The German unit was II Gruppe of JG77, the date, 13 January 1943.

John (Jack) Kelly survived the war to become a Lieutenant Colonel in the US Air Force.

* * *

With the heavy fighting over and around Sicily, the Walrus crews were kept busy. On 1 August, Flight Sergeant E J Holmes with Sergeants G F Brown and C S Taylor (X9506) were sent out to search six miles north-east of Catania. In the air they were re-vectored five to eight miles east of Cap St Andrea. There they located Lieutenant Henry A Barker from the 65th Fighter Squadron, 57th Fighter Group. Landing, they pulled the pilot aboard but were unable to take off again so taxied south. This was just after 20.00 but within half an hour they had reached quieter water and were able to get off, landing back at Cassible at 21.15.

Two days later this same 284 Squadron crew were out again at 08.05 to search one mile south of Riposto. Together with a fighter escort, they scoured the surface of the sea but only spotted oil and wreckage off shore. With no sign of a pilot they returned to base but as they were off Augusta, a radio call sent them back to a spot three miles north-east of Catania, and one mile off shore. Here they located Sergeant J Howell-Price of 3 Squadron RAAF, in the water – not in a dinghy. Despite fire from enemy shore batteries, the Walrus landed, picked up the Australian, and took off down-wind – in a hurry!

Howell-Price had been strafing ground targets along the roads around Mount Etna, led by Flying Officer R L Matthews. They had shot up three trucks and a gun position, but coming under heavy AA fire, Howell-Price's P.40 (FL291) had been hit in the cooling system. He had flown out to sea, saying he was going to bale out, but in the event he ditched 1½ miles off Catania harbour. After the first abortive search by the Walrus, 3 Squadron sent out a search of their own, the latter's CO, Squadron Leader Reg Stevens, finding Howell-Price in his Mae West. Thus the call for the Walrus to return.

Once on the water and pulling the downed pilot aboard, the Walrus came under gunfire, which gave everyone a certain impetus to get off quickly. Meantime, Stevens picked up the position of the guns from their flashes and attacked. It was an 88 mm gun battery, and although he silenced it, his own aircraft was badly hit and he later had to crash-land, fortunately on the right side of the Allied lines on Sicily, 3½ miles from Augusta.

A Busy Day
On the 4th it was Denny Lunn, Norman Pickles and Flight Sergeant J Bradley's turn in X9506. Six Spitfires of 72 Squadron had flown escort to Bostons on an attack upon Adriano. On the return flight enemy aircraft were reported but having turned, the Spitfires found the 'bogeys' to be friendly aircraft. Having seen the Bostons out of danger the Spitfires then went down to attack ground targets in the Catania area. A blockhouse was strafed and left on fire near Miscali but light flak hit the Spitfire flown by Flying Officer G N Keith DFC RCAF (JK637), while he was at 100 feet. Keith climbed to 2,000 feet and at three miles east of Mount Etna decided to leave the aircraft.

Sliding back the hood he undid his straps and went over the side, only to smash his left leg on the tailplane as he did so. He came down into the sea where the Walrus found him and picked him up, but it was obvious that the Canadian was in a bad way. Getting him back was hindered by rough sea, which made it necessary for the Walrus to be taxied to calmer water near Augusta where they were then able to get airborne. Keith was taken to No.25 Mobile Field Hospital but he died later that evening and was buried at Cassibile next day. George Keith had been an outstanding pilot, having seen action during the Dieppe Raid in August 1942, then with 72 Squadron over Tunisia and later over Sicily. He had claimed eight combat victories, five since the invasion had started. He was 22 years old.

The day was far from over for Denny Lunn, for within minutes of landing back with the injured Keith, he was off again with Sergeants Brown and Flt Sgt G Paxton in the back, and sent to a spot 400 yards east of Catania, where they landed and rescued Sergeant A W Walker of 250 Squadron. Once back in the air and heading for base, they were vectored five miles further north, and just a mile off-shore they located and rescued Pilot Officer H J M Barnes of 112 Squadron. With the extra weight Lunn could not get off so began to taxi. It was then found that somehow a hole had been punched in the port wing float, which had filled with water. Three men were sent out onto the starboard wing but rough seas continued to send water into the aircraft, forcing Lunn to turn for the coast. He beached the Walrus south of Catania (X9593) and a High Speed Launch later brought the men back. A few days later the Walrus was repaired and flown back to the Squadron.

Sergeant Walker was an Australian, and engine trouble had forced him to ditch his P.40 Kittyhawk (FR302) into the sea off Catania, but he was only in the water an hour before rescue. He had been No.2 to his CO, Squadron Leader G B Johns, dive-bombing targets near the town of Fiami Freddo. Walker continued to fly with 250 Squadron until 19 October, a date on which he was forced to belly-land after being hit by ground fire over Italy. Although his aircraft was seen to disintegrate, news later filtered in that he had survived and was in hospital, eventually returning to the Squadron in early November.

The other rescued man was Martin Barnes who had been part of a sortie of 12 Kittyhawks out to attack ground targets. The Wing Leader, Wing Commander John Darwen DFC and Bar, organised the mission flying north over Etna and then, upon his command, every aircraft turned sharply to the right to sweep down on any columns of vehicles spotted, hoping to be out to sea before any defensive fire could be instigated. It didn't quite work out that way, and ground fire hit several P.40s, shooting down one and damaging Barnes' aircraft so severely he had to bale out over the sea. Another machine staggered home with its rudder shot away.

This same 4 August saw 284 move its Algiers detachment to Sicily, while the next day, a detachment of two 283 Squadron Walruses moved to Palermo.

* * *

The team of Holmes, Brown and Taylor were successful again on the morning of 8 August in R6588. That morning they were sent out to a position 12 miles south-east of Catania, meeting up with a Spitfire escort on the way. Passing the

12-mile 'position' without seeing anything, they carried on for three more miles, but then saw an oil patch. One of the escort fighters dived low over a dinghy, whereby Holmes descended, landed, and picked up Lieutenant Henry Sherboudy of the 65th Squadron, 57th Fighter Group, hit by ground fire whilst attacking motor transport in the Randozzo area. The man was unconscious and once aboard, with a sea swell of five feet, take-off became impossible, so once more the Walrus had to be taxied. Three miles off Catania, they met a minesweeper and HSL 2593. With the help of the minesweeper's crew, the injured pilot was transferred to the launch. Holmes was now able to get airborne and landed back at 11.30.

It was back to rescuing a German on the 13th – which was a lucky date for him – during an afternoon sortie by Reg Hayes, Brown and Sergeant A Heseltine (X9593). Taking off from Cassible, Hayes headed to a given location five miles north-west of Messina. Flying to the west of Mount Etna to avoid the bomb line, heavy flak was experienced off the coast at Milazzo. Back out over the water, they eventually spotted a man, Unteroffizier Arnold, who turned out to be a navigator of a Dornier 217 bomber. If the German thought his troubles were over he had to think again as the engine of the Walrus cut on the way back and Hayes had to make a forced landing in a vineyard north of the airfield, but nobody was injured.

With Friends Like These . . .
Warrant Officer K G Hall, with Flight Sergeant J Berry, scored a double on the 17th. Flying to a position five miles north-east of Cape Spartivento, they were escorted by five Spitfires of 43 Squadron, operating from Lentini East airfield, which 284 were about to have as their base. They failed to find the original airman, but around 50 minutes after the search began, two Mustangs appeared from the north and had the bad grace to shoot down one of the Spitfires! Flight Lieutenant N W Lee baled out 400 yards from the shore at Bianco, and he was fortunate enough to have a rescue aircraft right on the spot.

As if to add farce to the already unbelievable situation, the offending Mustang was then hit by enemy gunfire from the coast and its pilot quickly joined his recent 'victim' into the water, 100 yards from the hostile beach by Cap Bruzziano. Ken Hall happily picked him up too and brought both men back. There must have been a very interesting conversation between the two damp fighter pilots in the back of the Walrus.

The Mustang pilot was Pilot Officer J L Griffiths from 1437 Flight, his machine being HK947 'A'. Oddly enough, 43 Squadron's records show Lee to have landed back at base in his Spitfire at 16.55 hrs. However, Spitfire BR290 was lost this date, so either the recording clerk got it wrong, or 43 did not like to admit having one of their aircraft shot down by a 'friendly' Mustang.

*   *   *

Missing??
While these sorties by 284 Squadron were in progress, 283 Squadron had not been idle. On 5 August, the same day as a detachment moved to

Palermo, Flight Sergeant L H Newman and Sergeant Graham had created a bit of a mystery by failing to return to base from a sortie.

Although some accounts note that they picked up three German airmen from a Ju88 shot down on the night of the 3/4 August, a NACAF report records that two Spitfire pilots from the 2nd US Fighter Squadron, 52nd FG, located a boat in which, apparently, sat three German soldiers trying to escape. The Walrus crew ran into difficulty and failed to get back.

They were finally towed into Palermo harbour on the 10th, with a long story. Back with the Squadron, Newman and Graham explained that with five bodies on board they could not get off, so headed for Sicily but soon realised they were going to run out of fuel before reaching it. The sea was very rough and Newman decided to alter course and make for Salerno Island, which they reached that night.

However, in doing this they ran a very big risk, as they were not sure whether the island had yet been occupied by Allied troops or was still in enemy hands. Luck was with them, and, like Mears and Botting's adventure back on 13 June, they were greeted by a small Allied garrison that had been in possession of the island for only a very short time. It was not possible for the stranded men to communicate their whereabouts to the Squadron as the garrison had no signalling or radio equipment, and as exactly happened earlier, it was not until a HSL arrived bringing supplies that they were able to hitch a lift and be towed back to Sicily. It was only then that the mystery of their disappearance could be cleared up. Lisle Newman recounts the whole story:

> At 6 pm on 4 August, the American 52nd Fighter Group was ordered to leave from Pantelleria Island and fly to Palermo, Sicily. The Americans packed all night and at approximately 8 am, 30 Dakotas arrived to take their stores, while the three squadrons of Spitfires took off.
>
> Our detachment of Jock Graham, myself and four ground staff were on the aerodrome and the latter four were ordered to leave with the Americans, while Jock and I awaited orders with our one Walrus [Z1784]. All had departed by 11 am, the Walrus looking very lonely on a completely empty aerodrome.
>
> Orders came very soon. Proceed to Palermo, refuel, obtain fix for a rescue and get off again immediately. "And take revolvers with you!"
>
> We duly arrived at Palermo, refuelled, got the fix – Sardinia, 80 miles. We located three men in about $1\frac{1}{4}$ hours. Jock thought they were fishermen; do we have to splash down? I said they couldn't be; we're going down. Landing we discovered they were German soldiers, out of food, out of water, and trying to escape from Sicily. We ordered them to get aboard and they came quite willingly, our conversation being in broken French and sign language.
>
> The waves, although only a foot or so high, kept throwing the German boat back on us and I was having difficulty in clearing it. Graham climbed on to the wing where it was fouling and pushed it away but still the sea brought it back and at length I thought I could just miss it. I throttled up but it came back and smashed the starboard aileron.
>
> There could be no take-off now, so it was back by sea, but with not

enough fuel to make it to Palermo, and there was only about an hour or so of daylight left. Radio was useless – out of range.

I steered a reciprocal course till about 10 pm, and could see only foam, with wind and waves rising. I was now afraid the port float – the one that always trailed in the water – would not stand the pounding caused by the Walrus rolling in the heavy sea. We therefore heaved to (stopped the engine) and tried to make her face the waves by use of a drogue, but it didn't work. Three times every minute she rolled, and the port float crashed down on the water from about four feet.

I found that by putting the wheel over fully one way when the float went in and reversing it when it came out meant the air over the ailerons on that side took off half the bang. Three changes a minute and I became a mechanical man – I could do it with my eyes shut. My arms began to ache a bit at first but after a while they got used to it. I knew I must not risk stopping. After three hours the wind and the waves dropped. Very relieved I stopped too, while the rest on board just slept throughout.

About an hour later aircraft could be heard from the direction of Palermo. Jock woke up; whose were they, Allied or German? He thought they sounded British, and asked if he should send up a distress flare. I thought it was too risky, we didn't want a bomb dropped on us.

We had hardly finished discussing it when a large flare dropped to the south-east of us, followed by another, then another – about 15 falling in all. The sea was like daylight as far as one could see, but we just lay in the shadow by a few hundred yards. Then some American ships opened up in Palermo Harbour and bombs were dropped. The noise was terrific but we lay safely, drifting in the darkness, which had returned.

Jock stayed awake while I went to sleep behind the wheel. Daylight came at 5 am, and the sea was virtually calm, but we were surrounded by a dense fog right down to sea level, with visibility restricted to around 20 yards. It was obvious we couldn't start taxying now in case we hit something in the water which we couldn't spot.

I knew I had not enough petrol to get to Palermo, even if we had not drifted too much off course during the night. I told Jock I was pretty thirsty, not having drunk anything for 24 hours, but he said we had nothing left on board. Jock and the Germans went for a swim while I dozed and half slept.

The fog finally lifted about 11 am. To our amazement there was an island standing up in the morning sunlight, 8-10 miles away. Jock and I looked at our map. The only islands were west of Sicily and I could not imagine that we had drifted that far. And did Germans occupy it? Because we had only taken off from Palermo yesterday after a hurried arrival, we had no map showing the island of Ustica, which was what we were seeing, and which sat over 30 miles north of Palermo.

The day went by with no sound of aircraft or any sightings. It was hot, sunny and clear, really enjoyable if one could have been in the position to enjoy it. We heard later that the 52nd Fighter Group had put up their whole Wing to search for us, plus our own squadron, but to no avail.

As the day progressed, Jock and I discussed our options. I finally decided on a plan. I could not afford to risk another night at sea, and we could not manage another 24 hours without water. So we would wait till one hour before darkness fell and then go for the island. We should arrive just before dark and it would give us the whole day to be found by someone.

At about 4 o'clock I found four cans of water in the stern of the Walrus and divided it into five and drank it – half a pint each. At 6 pm I told Jock to get up into the wing and start the engine, it having to be cranked to get the flywheel going. It started at once.

Darkness was falling as we approached; large rocks formed the shore line. I saw a tiny inlet between some of them. I told Jock to open the hatch and sit right out on the bow holding the towline. I would cut the engine and let us drift in, and once he could jump onto the rocks, he should do so, then fend off the bow to prevent damage. He did it perfectly and we lashed her up between two rocks.

No sooner had we done this than down over the rocks came dozens of people, mostly children. One man came to me and informed me that he had been put in charge by the Americans. Asking if any Americans were still on the island he told me no, but that a nearby hospital will put us up. The son of the hospital doctor was introduced and I was told he would take us to the building. The lad was about 18 and with some broken French and a little English, he became our friend and interpreter while we were on the island.

With a jabbering crowd following, he conducted us to the hospital, a matter of a mile or so distant. Once there, they gave us an egg each, some water and bread. Then they gave us a room with five beds. We met the doctor, who could not speak French or English, then a man came in, clicked his heels and introduced himself as the local mayor.

We then went to bed. I told Jock to tie his revolver to his wrist by the lanyard and have it with him under the blankets, with the first chamber of six empty for extra safety. I slept fitfully, bitten terribly by mosquitoes, my chest looking like a case of measles the next morning, but it was super to sleep. The others never stirred.

Next morning the doctor's son came and told me the fishermen had towed the Walrus into the harbour with their rather unreliable old boat. We all went to the harbour after we got up, and while Jock kept an eye on the Germans, someone took me out to where the Walrus was anchored. There was absolutely no damage, and I was very relieved that the fishermen had retrieved her from the rocks.

I pumped out the bilges for about an hour – which is normal when a flying boat is on water a long time. I toyed with the idea of seeing if the fishing boat might be able to tow us to Palermo, but it seemed doubtful so we abandoned the thought.

On the morning of the 9th a high speed launch arrived with an Air Commodore on board. They had come to arrange a radio station for direction finding on the island. They had also been told by an over-flying Wellington en-route for Maison Blanche, that a Walrus had been seen lying at anchor in the harbour. They had thought it odd so had reported it. The Air Commodore said he would arrange for a pinnace to come and take us in tow, meantime he relieved us of our three Germans.

The pinnace arrived as promised and the young captain asked if we were in a hurry, because if we weren't they would like to enjoy a day on the island. We said we were happy at that, moved on to the boat and they gave us some welcome good food. The inhabitants were all over us and that afternoon we made up a team from the pinnace and played them at soccer in a dried-up reservoir, watched by an admiring crowd, especially of young women. We won for the honour of England but it was in tremendous spirit.

Late afternoon saw us riding donkeys and we were invited to the mayor's country house for supper and to be introduced to his family. The boat's crew were invited too, the doctor's son again acting as interpreter. We sang English songs to them and they sang Italian songs to us.

Next day we were towed back to Palermo, mechanics and aircrew coming to the harbour to welcome us home. They had first thought that we had been captured by a German submarine. The squadron adjutant had asked the CO if, after two days of absence, he should inform headquarters for onward transmission to Air Ministry of our non-return. Fortunately for both of our parents, the CO said they should hang on for a day or two as he couldn't believe we had gone.

The following day we worked on the Walrus with the ground crew and by evening the engine made a spluttering start. Jock and I ran it between the US navy ships for half an hour to try and stop the spluttering and warm it up. We finally took off and having agreed with Control not to fly a circuit, came in straight down the runway at the airfield.

My thanks are due to the good people of Ustica for their generosity and kindness to five strangers. This will never be forgotten by me; I only wish I could have told them.

Flight Sergeant L H Newman, 283 Squadron

*   *   *

Walter Sterne, in company with Sergeant Pugh, was out at 11.15 hours on the 7th to continue a search mission begun the previous day for an American fighter pilot. They found him – Lieutenant Montgomery of the 4th Fighter Squadron, 52nd FG – and landed back with him at 13.10. He had been in the sea 35 miles north-east of Palermo.

The Heavily Armed German
Arnold Divers and Tony Morabito fished out a German – Leutnant Joachim Zantropp – on 10 August. He was a pilot from the third Gruppe of KG100, whose Do217 had been shot down by a Beaufighter. As Divers remembers:

> [The German] had been shot down after doing a night intruder raid on our Palermo airfield a couple of nights prior to his rescue. I remember Flight

Sergeant Morabito calling out to me from the front hatch after we had landed and taxied to the pilot in the dinghy, saying: "Christ, he's a bloody Hun." After getting him aboard I asked Tony to search him. Tony relieved him of a wrist compass, a flick knife, a Mauser pistol and a Luger. The German was most arrogant and insisted on knowing his pick-up position and where we were taking him. I suggested to Tony to tell him nothing and to keep all maps of the area away from him.

According to later information received from the American de-briefing officer, the German pilot, after being stripped, was found to have a .22 Italian Beretta pistol strapped to the inside of his upper leg!

Sergeant A Divers, 283 Squadron

Squadron Leader A C G Wenman was leading 154 Squadron on the 12th as escort to Kittyhawks on an anti-shipping patrol over the Gulf of Gioia just north of the toe of Italy. This was an area where escaping Axis troops had been crossing to the mainland. On the return flight, Wenman's engine packed up and he was forced to bale out of his Spitfire IX (EN520), ten miles south-east of Vulcano Island. Two of his men circled him whilst the third returned to base to arrange help. The call went out to 283 Squadron who sent Arnold Divers and Tony Morabito off to the scene, picking him up and returning him home. Wenman, who had led his squadron since March, completed his tour of duty ten days later.

A week later Divers and Morabito picked up Lieutenant C E Simpson, shot down two days earlier (the 17th) while escorting US B.26 bombers to Caserta. They had been sent out to find three men in a dinghy but spotted Simpson, from the 71st Fighter Squadron, 1st Fighter Group, and a dead body, north-east of Ustica, which was 52 miles north-east of base. Simpson had been flying a P.38 Lightning.

A Land Rescue

Not long after returning from this sortie, Divers and Morabito were off once again (in Z1777), as Arnold Divers recorded:

One of the rescues which I like to think was perhaps perfection was listed on the 19th of August 1943. On this occasion it proved to me the wonderful versatility of the Walrus. We were ordered to a position on the beach west of Termini, west of Palermo. Our instructions were to pick up a wounded man. A landing was made on a calm sea for a change. Wheels lowered and under full power we ran up over the shingle beach to the smoke fire indicating our pick-up spot, which was still under enemy small arms fire.

We loaded the injured chap in great haste into the rear hatch, roared over the beach back to the water, raising the wheels, followed by a perfect water take-off back to base at Palermo.

This to me was what air sea rescue was all about, getting in quickly, making the pick-up, getting out and airborne at great speed (90 knots being a fast cruising speed when airborne) then flying home.

> In the entry in my logbook mention is made of an airman being rescued but I do believe he was a US soldier with serious gun shot wounds to his jaw. An incidental memory is that I was given his wallet, which was just the fattest I'd seen, full of US dollars and local currency. I gave the wallet to the doctor standing by with an ambulance on landing.
>
> Sergeant A Divers, 283 Squadron

Four men from a B.26 Marauder of the 444th Squadron, 320th Bomb Group were rescued by Hopkinson and Botting on the 22nd, off the island of Ustica, to the north of Sicily, two others not being found. The 320th had made a successful raid upon the Salerno marshalling yards, together with aircraft from the 319th Bomb Group, escorted by A.36s, which was a dive-bomber version of the P.51 Mustang. Approaching the target, 34 Marauders of the 320th went in ahead and below the 319th but were intercepted by large numbers of Me109s, while others flying above dropped delay-fuse bombs on the 319th Group. Several Marauders were hit, one seen going down to sea level, its top-turret gunner still blazing away at the 109s.

The 320th also fought the 109s, which developed into a running air battle, while the A.36s desperately tried to ward off the German fighters. The formation leader, Major J Scott Peddie directed the fight and the air discipline over the radio as the target came up and the bombing hit rail, rolling stock and yard buildings. Peddie was wounded by an exploding 20 mm cannon shell, but remained in the astrodome of his B.26, directing the formation and the defensive fire, for which he received his country's DFC. After the bombing the Group dropped down to sea level and headed for home. Six Marauders from both Groups failed to make it back.

Then on the 25th Horne and Pugh searched for another downed P.38 pilot but found nothing. However, a VHF call from an unknown aircraft led the Walrus crew west where they found and picked up a German Ju88 pilot – Leutnant Rudolf Bohn, 45 miles north-east of Termini. He is believed to be the sole survivor of the 88 shot down by a 219 Squadron Beaufighter VI on the night of 25th – 01.30-05.00 hours.

The 219 Squadron crew had been Wing Commander A D McN Boyd and Flight Lieutenant A J Glegg (V8882), who reported their success at 13,000 feet in the Sebala area. Archie Boyd was 219's commanding officer and this was his eighth victory. He and Glegg went on to score ten in all for which Boyd received the DSO and DFC, and Joe Glegg the DFC and Bar.

Towards the end of August 283 Squadron had a detachment at Palermo, and early in September the main Squadron assembled there, leaving just a small detachment at La Sebala. By this time the Squadron's total rescues since 12 April were 67 live and three dead. Squadron Leader Walter Sterne was awarded the Distinguished Service Order on the 28th, while Sergeant William Surtees Lambert received his Distinguished Flying Medal. Sterne's DSO was the only one awarded to air sea rescue aircrew during the war, which in itself seems amazing considering the outstanding valour shown by many of them.

Nevertheless, it seems that the men in Sterne's squadron did not like the man very much, and he rarely flew or put himself down on the flight roster after

Tunisia fell. And as one pilot put it: ". . . he was extremely lucky not to meet with an 'accident'. He was the absolute opposite to Reg Hayes, CO of 284 Squadron, who led by example." Newcomers to the Squadron after this period were convinced he never put himself down on the flying roster at all, and some thought he hadn't even made a successful rescue himself. (He had actually rescued at least eight men from the sea.) Sterne did tend to spend time at Headquarters, and as another pilot recalled, seemed to take half the unit's whisky ration with him to butter-up the top brass. What good this achieved is uncertain.

However, Sterne's squadron did a lot to raise the morale of flyers in the fighting squadrons and no doubt his DSO reflected the courage and heroism which had been bestowed on the squadron as a whole. In 242 Group's records (Bizerta HQ) the total number of people rescued as at 16 July totalled 66 in the Tunis area since 26 May 1943, and three days later this had risen to 74 – by Walruses and HSLs.

* * *

Well We Tried!

Along the North African coast to the east, the ASR Flight that would later become 294 Squadron were still doing their best, even though much of the war had moved away from their area of operations. During August they made a few rescues operating from Gambut and LG07, although the first attempt on the 6th was far from ideal.

A Hurricane pilot had been reported in a dinghy a short way out from the coast, roughly north of Sollum. Two Wellingtons from Gambut and a Walrus from Landing Ground 07 (situated along the Mersah Matruh to Sidi Barrani road) failed to locate the man but then a Walrus crew from Gambut found him and landed on a rising sea. However, they were not able to reach the dinghy, nor was the pilot then able to take off again. Another Wellington spotted the Walrus in difficulty and directed a HSL towards it, but this became unserviceable and unable to take the Walrus in tow. In a worsening sea, the crew was taken off and the Walrus (X9582) later sank during the night off Bardia. The HSL was fixed and all returned safely. Meantime, the Hurricane pilot had fortunately drifted ashore and made his way back to his base unaided!

The next day, the 7th, at 16.45 pm, a Walrus crew watched from their airstrip as a Kittyhawk crash-landed on the sea half a mile north of Mellaha, outside Tripoli, and were airborne from there within ten minutes. They located the pilot immediately but without a Mae West. Despite a rough sea which was going to prevent take-off, the pilot landed the Walrus and picked up the P.40 pilot who was exhausted but uninjured. The Walrus was then taxied into Tripoli harbour where a launch took him to the quay.

Desert Rescue

An unusual rescue took place on 18 August 1943, not from the sea but from the desert. The previous day 212 Flying Control passed on the position of a downed American Warhawk pilot, from a colleague of the stricken pilot, giving position

31.25/21.07 – in the Libyan Desert! The Walrus crew from the Rescue Flight, Lieutenant A Whitworth, with Sergeant R W J Forbes and LAC Taylor (X9584) went off but were unable to locate him before nightfall. Early the next morning they were off again, found the missing pilot, landed and brought him back to base none the worse for his night out.

Another different rescue came about on the 29th. Flying Officer L Wilson, Flying Officer B F Ramsden and Sergeant L Palmer operating from El Arish, were sent off soon after dawn to find a crashed Spitfire and pilot nearly on the island of St Jean, at position 31.12/33.20, which was not far from Port Said. Reaching the spot they found it marshy and for landing off shore the sea appeared too shallow. A HSL was seen off shore but it was having trouble negotiating a passage through the shallows. Therefore, Wilson dropped his wheels and put down on a nearby flatish sand-strip where the pilot came to them. Getting him aboard, Wilson went to take off but the Walrus (X9479) sank in a patch of soft sand then put its nose into the ground. Although the speed was only around 20 knots, the crunch damaged the fuselage. Finally, the crew and the Spitfire pilot paddled themselves to the HSL using the aircraft's dinghy and left the Walrus under guard by one of the HSL crewman. It was later salvaged by 58 R&SU (Repair and Salvage Unit) but did not return to the Squadron.

*   *   *

Back with 284 Squadron, Dick Eccles had arrived on Sicily and in early September 1943 rescued two German airmen, then went on to make one of the more famous rescues of the Sicilian campaign.

> When I flew to Malta with 284 Squadron we had no successful rescues during the three weeks on the island, although I was scrambled when a SAAF Baltimore went down, but the crew luckily pranged next to a fishing boat which picked them up instead.
>
> One of the missions caused amusement as a Walrus was sent to rendezvous with three aircraft to do 'escort duty' for them. We thought it was a leg-pull but we flew to Sicily accompanying three Piper Cubs [two-seat high-wing cabin monoplanes] and we were there in case they had to ditch.
>
> On 4 August the advance flight of 284 went over to Cassibile on Sicily and we were fairly busy with no real success and then we moved up to Lentini East, and on the 2nd September, I was scrambled with Ken Hall and Flight Sergeant Bradley [X9498], to a spot 30 miles from Panchino.
>
> The search was made easy by the presence of a Sunderland that we had been told was waiting for us. They sent us a message that if we were going to pick [the downed airmen up] we must have guns at the ready! This we did and on board came Unteroffiziers Walter Young and Josef Bierer. Young was old for a pilot and we brought him up front, Bierer on the other hand was surly and aggressive. They were unarmed but my gunner kept Bierer covered all the way back.
>
> Flying Officer R G Eccles, 284 Squadron

Duncan Smith Takes a Swim

It was a spur of the moment decision which led Wing Commander W G G Duncan Smith DSO DFC and Bar, leader of 244 Wing, Desert Air Force to fly a sortie in the late morning of 2 September. The invasion of Italy was coming up and he decided to take a look at one of the last two remaining airfields the Germans were using near Catanzaro.

With his wingman, he took off in his Spitfire VIII, with his personal 'D-S' on the fuselage sides, and headed away from Sicily towards Catanzaro. In the event the airfield seemed totally deserted, so as planned, Duncan Smith headed across the 'instep of the toe of Italy' to Crotone to check on a second airfield but this too was clear of aircraft.

As they headed out to sea, the fuel warning light came on, telling the WingCo to switch from the auxiliary tank to his main fuel tank:

> I reached down and pulled the lever which I found extremely stiff, so gave it a hard pull and the wire of the Bowden cable to the cock on the main tank snapped. Reaching frantically beneath the instrument panel I tried unsuccessfully to find the wire so was unable to activate the main cock. Within seconds my engine began to splutter, then stopped.
>
> Having already pointed my nose south, out to sea, I began to glide away from the enemy coast, hoping to stretch it as far as I could before having to bale out. I was lucky that nearby, P H 'Hunk' Humphreys, the CO of 92 Squadron, was on patrol, for he heard my 'Mayday' call, then called Ops and the ASR boys.
>
> The thought did cross my mind whether to crash land and hope to stay out of sight until our invasion forces reached me in a day or so, but decided against that, trusting that the ASR chaps would have me out and home in an hour or so. Then my No.2 confirmed that Ops had a fix on us, so when I got down to 2,000 feet I baled out, although I somehow drifted against the side of the Spitfire and gave my leg a crack against the tailplane.
>
> Hitting the water, I released the parachute and grabbed the line for the dinghy but to my horror found that somehow it had parted company and sunk out of sight. I was more than a little worried at the prospect of a long sojourn in the sea, for having taken off at the last minute, I only had on shirt and shorts, plus of course, my Mae West, which was now my 'only visible means of support.' I had even lost my mosquito boots on the way down.
>
> To be on the safe side I began to swim towards the shore, recognising Cape Vaticano, about two miles off. I swam for an hour with the hot sun blazing down, burning my skin, which became most uncomfortable. Also my leg hurt and I found a deep gash round the knee which was bleeding badly. Resting on my back for a while I observed that a current seemed to be taking me away from the coast and further out to sea.
>
> I began to swim inshore again and looking at my watch, discovered that I had already been in the water for an hour and a half. Another hour passed slowly. So much for a quick rescue!

Meantime, aircraft were out looking for the Wing Leader. 1 Squadron, South African Air Force sent out four Spitfires at 1.40 pm led by Captain Jan van Nus, taking over the search from another squadron; two Spitfire Vs flew at 500 feet, covered by two Spitfire VIIIs at 1,000 feet. They scoured along the shore of the Gulf of Eufemia but only found an empty dinghy. What in fact looked like a dinghy turned out to be a ship's life-belt. Then 145 Squadron took off to search, and they located Duncan Smith – in his Mae West – a quarter of a mile north-east of Tropea, which was six miles north of Vaticano.

During this search, Lieutenant Cecil Golding of 1 SAAF had to break off due to engine trouble. With his engine cutting, he climbed and as he then descended through some cloud near Taormina, he spotted two Focke Wulf 190s almost on the water, flying north-east. Despite his struggling engine he immediately turned after them but his engine did not allow him to close in. The two 190s were cruising along blissfully unaware of Golding's Spitfire, but soon became aware as the South African, in desperation, opened up at long range on the left hand one. They quickly beat it north!

At 2.20, six Spitfires of 145 took off to escort a Walrus of 284 Squadron but the Walrus developed engine trouble and another had to be made ready. Meanwhile the Spitfires continued flying over the WingCo, remaining in orbit until relieved by 417 Squadron RCAF. With 145 Squadron was their American CO, Lance Wade DFC, and Flight Lieutenant I H R Shand DFC, from Rhodesia, who had been rescued by the ASR Flight back in April. Duncan Smith continues:

> When I heard the sound of aircraft engines I looked to see some Spitfires, but they were some way off. But then one detached itself and came towards me. Frantically I tried to fire off one of my distress flares, but they were all too sodden and useless. The Spitfire went over me, circled a couple of miles off and then came back. I began splashing the water with my arms and legs, then it was over me but turning, then dived down towards me. I saw the pilot waving and knew I'd been found. It was a great relief!
>
> Minutes later more Spitfires were circling, their engines deafening, but what a sweet sound. For another 20 minutes I waited, then the Walrus came into sight, landed and was coming towards me. A rope was thrown – I was safe. Or was I?

The Walrus had taken off at 3.30 pm with Sergeant R Brown at the controls, and Dick Eccles, with Flight Sergeant Jack Berry down the back. Escorting it were four Spitfires from 1 SAAF Squadron led by Lieutenant A O M Vialls, while six more led by Captain Johnny Secombe headed straight for the rescue area, overtaking the Walrus en-route, with Vialls and company in tow.

Eventually the Walrus arrived and landed but almost immediately three Me109s dived out of the sun and commenced to strafe it. At the same moment, three more German fighters, two at least being FW190s, attacked the six Spitfires circling over the Walrus at 500 feet; the four Mark VIIIs with Mike Vialls were higher up, at around 2,000 feet.

As the German fighters struck, Lieutenant R L Cherrington's Spitfire burst into flames and went straight into the sea. Mike Vialls saw this and chased after 'Cherry's' victor for 15 miles over the Gulf of Eufemia, but although he fired all his ammunition at it, the 190 finally escaped. It appears these fighters came from 1 Gruppe of JG/52 (who may have been escorting FW190s of 2/SGK 10), Unteroffizier Alfred Scharl claiming a Spitfire for his fifth victory; his war total later reached nine. To quote from Vivian Voss's history of 1 SAAF Squadron:

At 16.05 hrs, Mike Vialls led four Spitfire Mk VIIIs, from Milazzo to Tropea, to escort the Walrus, which was to pick up the Wing Commander. Twenty minutes later six Spitfire Mk Vs took off to fly direct to the WingCo and to orbit him till the Walrus arrived. These latter passed the slow Walrus, with its escort, ten miles south of Cape Vaticano. When the Walrus arrived off Tropea it alighted on the water, and picked up the Wing Commander. The escorting Mk Vs were circling at 500 feet, the Mk VIIIs at 2,000 feet. Immediately after he had been pulled aboard, three Me109s swooped down out of the sun, fired at the lower aircraft, and strafed the Walrus. Mike Vialls saw the 109s flash past, and shouted to the lower Spits to duck. Dick Cherrington's aircraft was hit between the cockpit and the nose, and it burst into flames and crashed into the sea. After this one lightning attack, the Me109 which had shot Cherry down made off east. Mike dived after it and chased it all over the Gulf of San Eufemia, firing short bursts at it whenever he could, until he expended all his ammunition. The 109 took violent evasive action and escaped.

Immediately after the first attack by [the] Me109s, more enemy aircraft came down on the Spitfires. Pilots identified, in all, three Me109Gs, two Mc202s, two FW190s and a Re2001. Hector Taylor, who was flying No.2 to Mike Vialls, opened his score during this dice. Hector saw splashes in the water as a 109 strafed the Walrus. This 109 now pulled up behind him and Mike. The latter was diving after another E/A, and Hector turned to face the 109 which was on his and his leader's tail. Another Spitfire now attacked the 109, which, after a steep turn, dived towards the coast, with Hector on its tail. As he closed in, the 109 pulled up in front of him. Hector gave a quick burst, and then a second. The 109's hood flew off, and also some debris. The aircraft turned on to its back and dived straight into the ground, where it exploded in flames.

The Walrus was holed in several places by the strafing, but no serious damage was done. When the enemy fighters had broken away, the Spitfires reformed above the Walrus and escorted it back to base.

The Squadron was sad at losing Cherry. He was a fine fellow, and a good pilot. He would have been 21 years of age the next day.

I/JG52 lost Gefreiter Wolfgang Schlüter in this action, north-west of Tropea.

Down on the sea Duncan Smith had indeed been hauled into the Walrus, and hearing several loud explosions he felt a stinging blow across the back of his neck which spun him around. Then he passed out. Richard Eccles who was in the Walrus, continues the story:

We took off to search for Wing Commander Duncan Smith in an area north of Vaticano. We found him swimming away from the beach as the tide was taking him in, as he was only about a mile off. His Mae West was keeping him afloat but he was pretty tired having been in the water for about five hours. We were just getting him aboard when our escort radioed, "Look out, they're coming down sun!"

We were pretty well shot up being sitting ducks, as it were, but we managed to get airborne and beat it for Milazzo. If we had stayed on the water 30 seconds longer we would have sunk. We took off at 40 miles an hour, the Walrus threatening to stall several times but it got us back.

Flying Officer R G Eccles, 284 Squadron

The Walrus had its controls smashed, petrol was pouring on the hot exhausts, the upper wing was damaged and water had been coming in through a number of holes beneath the water line. The Wing Commander finally came round, by which time Berry had already wrapped him in a blanket. Duncan Smith continued:

> When I came to, I found myself covered in a blanket. A man was grinning at me and trying to force brandy between my chattering teeth. He said: "You feeling better? Sorry about the mess in here." He pointed to debris lying about, and about six inches of water swilling along the floor. "It won't be long before we land at Milazzo. I wouldn't be surprised if the skipper has to crash-land. The old Walrus is in a shocking state." He then told me about the rescue operation.

Berry had in fact covered two holes near the rear of the Walrus with his hands to prevent more water coming in before they got airborne. They landed at base at 17.00 hours.

> We got back to Milazzo safely, the pilot making a brilliant landing. I was whisked away to an American field hospital where my leg and neck wounds were treated, and although they wanted to keep me in bed, I persuaded the doctor to let me return to Lentini. Hunk Humphreys landed after escorting the Walrus back and he told me of the air battle. The news that one pilot had been lost took the edge off my euphoria, but all I wanted now was to get back and thank everyone for what they had done, and especially Ian Shand, who by chance, had found me in the first place. With a bottle of brandy I went in search of him – the first drink had to be with him.

Wing Commander W G G Duncan Smith, OC 244 Wing

Like many wartime stories, this dramatic rescue received coverage in a number of newspapers, not least of which was the *Johannesburg Star* (similarly repeated in the *Cape Argus*), under the headings of 'SAVED PILOT UNDER FIRE' and 'FEAT OF TWO SPRINGBOKS: RESCUE PLANE RIDDLED'.

The story of how two South African pilots helped to save the life of a Royal Air Force wing commander was told today by the pilots, says Sapa's war correspondent at Messina.

One pilot was in command of a Walrus rescue aircraft which picked up the wing commander off the Italian coast. The other, who belongs to a South African Spitfire squadron, destroyed a Messerschmitt 109, which attacked the rescue aircraft as it was about to take off.

The Walrus pilot is Flying Officer Richard George Eccles, aged 27, of Johannesburg, a well-known athlete. He was studying dentistry at Edinburgh University, where he won three Scottish national championships when he joined the RAF in 1940.

He flew Spitfires until he went to North Africa about four months ago to do sea rescue work. He has several rescues to his credit, including German pilots.

RESCUE PLANE RIDDLED

He was standing by when he received a report that Wing Commander W G G Duncan Smith had baled out and was floating in his life-jacket. Escorted by four South African Spitfires, Eccles located Wing Commander Duncan Smith, who had been in the water more than five hours.

The gunner in Eccles' plane had just pulled the wing commander through the hatch in the rear of the fuselage and Eccles was preparing to take off, when a Me109 riddled the aircraft with machine-gun and cannon fire. "I was absolutely helpless while the German riddled my aircraft until it looked like a sieve," said Eccles. "The controls were smashed, petrol was pouring from the tanks on to the hot exhaust and water was pouring in through the holes made under the water line."

If he had stayed on the water 30 seconds longer, his aircraft would have sunk, so he decided to take off. As he did so he had the satisfaction of seeing the Messerschmitt being shot down by a Spitfire. He managed to get the Walrus into the air at 40 miles an hour. It was a hair-raising flight during which the aircraft threatened to stall several times. He brought it down safely at Milazzo.

Many years later, in 1981, after the publication of Duncan Smith's book *Spitfire Into Battle* the whole story was brought out again in Johannesburg in a book review:

Spitfire into Battle, by Group Captain W G G Duncan Smith DSO and Bar, DFC and two Bars, by John Murray; reviewed by Charles Barry.

It's a small world. A book by a distinguished RAF fighter pilot is dropped on your desk for review. Looking through the "Dramatis Personnae" next to the foreword, you see your wartime pal Hannes Faure's name.

Immediately your mind rolls back 36 years. Could the author be the same group captain you met on leave in Italy, the man whose name you had forgotten but who told you he had named his dog Hannes after the popular SAAF fighter pilot wing leader you both knew so well and admired, an anecdote you had dined out so often on in the intervening years?

Yes. It is the same chap. From his home in Scotland last week, he confirmed [it was] a bulldog, found lost in Taranto, obviously off a British warship as ". . . nothing could have been less Italian-looking. I named him Hannes because he had the same pugnacity." It's a small, small world.

Chatting about the air war with ex-RAF fighter pilot Dick Eccles in Johannesburg a couple of days later you tell the story of Hannes the dog and say you are reviewing a fascinating wartime autobiography by the man who owned him.

"Did you ever meet a Groupie named Duncan Smith?" you ask. "Yes, indeed," says Dick. "I pulled him out of the drink off the west coast of Italy just before the invasion." It's a small, small world.

Tribute to both Lieut-Colonel Faure and Flying Officer Eccles are paid handsomely in these memoirs, though Dick Eccles is not mentioned by name. Of Faure writes Duncan Smith: "He was one of the calmest men I ever knew. Nothing upset Hannes, and the tougher the situation the better he liked it: an ideal type in a tight corner."

Of his rescue he tells how he spent six hours in the sea supported only by his Mae West after baling out of his Spitfire which had fuel problems. A Walrus amphibian piloted by Dick Eccles – who had previously flown operations in Spitfires from Britain – landed on the sea nearby, and as "Smithy" was being pulled out of the water, a number of enemy fighters appeared and strafed the sitting Walrus. ("It's strange the things you do instinctively," mused Dick Eccles this week. "I remember putting my arms over my head to ward off the bullets!")

"The Walrus was badly holed below the water line and a cannon shell had pierced the wing tank, but luckily, though petrol spewed all over the place, the old bus did not catch fire." writes Group Captain Duncan Smith. "The blow I felt (as he was pulled aboard) was a bullet going through the collar of my Mae West, grazing my neck before smacking into the Walrus. We got down at Milazzo (Sicily) safely after a brilliant landing by the pilot."

Group Captain Duncan Smith died in December 1996, and as this book is written, his son Iain Duncan Smith is a Member of Parliament and leader of the British Conservative Party.

John Robert Berry, a New Zealander, was awarded an Immediate Distinguished Flying Medal for this and his work on earlier rescues. Sergeant Brown, whose initial in 284's records is shown as 'R' appears to be, in fact, G F Brown (RCAF), who later went to 293 Squadron ASR as a Flight Sergeant, and with this unit became a Warrant Officer and received the DFC in 1944.

Other awards which came to members of 284 Squadron during September 1943 were DFCs for Flight Lieutenant Reg Hayes and Warrant Officer Ken Hall, while Sergeant D J Lunn received the DFM.

On the day Duncan Smith was rescued, 284 Squadron moved to Lentini East, while still keeping a Flight at Milazzo, which is just west of Messina, under Warrant Officer K G Hall.

* * *

To end this chapter Arnold Divers records some interesting aspects of his time on 283 Squadron in North Africa, Sicily and later Italy.

During my time on the Squadron I saw very little of Squadron Leader W Sterne and other officers. It appeared to me I was the one sent out to establish advanced flight bases such as airstrips east of Algiers, Cap Bon, Pantelleria, Salerno, Naples, etc. This made me bitter that as a Sergeant, Flight Sergeant and later as a Warrant Officer, I was performing the duties of a flight commander on an NCO's pay, without the authority of an officer and without resources such as food and accommodation, and no priority to transmit messages and arrange transport. At some forward bases the 52nd US Fighter Group were most helpful supplying many of the basic needs I was unable to obtain through normal RAF channels.

The American pilots, on many occasions, allowed us to eat in their officer's mess. In order to avoid embarrassment we removed our badges of rank and wore only our flying insignia. To obtain a few comforts and necessities for our advanced detached units, I masqueraded as an officer wearing only my pilot's brevet [wings]. Perhaps Sterne did assist me to finally become commissioned but unfortunately all too late to be of any assistance to the organisation of 283 Squadron and its detachments.

Sterne once proudly introduced me to Sir Keith Park, me being the only New Zealander on 283 Squadron. Sir Keith not only attended the same High School as I had done, but had also lived only two blocks away in the same street in Dunedin when his father was a professor at the University of Otago. During the visit he allowed me to have an hour flying in his stripped down Hurricane IIC, as I had made a comment during our chat that I found the Walrus awfully slow.

Some of the more pleasant distractions during my service with 283 included shooting at washed-up mines on the east coast of Corsica from Bastia South, the enjoyable swimming, picking kerosene tins of grapes and fishing on the island of Pantelleria. The underground hangars built by the Italians on that island were a remarkable piece of engineering.

Chapter 3

THE WAR MOVES TO ITALY

With the island of Sicily taken by the Allies in August 1943, the assault upon mainland Italy was planned for September. On the 3rd, the day after Wing Commander Duncan Smith had been rescued, British and Canadian troops crossed the Straits of Messina to land on the toe of Italy and began, with their American ally, the long haul up 'the boot'.

An armistice had been signed with the Italian government, but German and Fascist troops had still to be defeated. This was not going to be easy and so began the Italian Campaign which would last till the war's finale.

By this date, 283 Squadron had a detachment at Palermo, but would soon be based here, while a detachment was at La Sebala. 284 Squadron had its A Flight at Lentini West, with its B Flight at Milazzo East. 294 Squadron was still in North Africa, while in Tunisia, a new squadron had recently arrived – 293. This latter unit had originally been formed in England during June 1943, from the OTU at Bircham Newton, Norfolk, under the command of Squadron Leader R H McIntosh DFC AFC, who had previously been with 280 ASR Squadron, flying Hudsons and Ansons. It wouldn't be operational until November, but would see considerable active service during the Italian Campaign.

On the night of 18 September a German Heinkel 111 had been shot down and the next day 283 Squadron were out searching. Flying Officer Mears and Sergeant Smith had originally been out soon after first light to look for any signs of a missing Beaufighter 80 miles north from 283's base at La Sebala, escorted by fighters from 73 Squadron. They found and picked up two German airmen, one having a thigh wound. Later during the morning, Flight Sergeant Lambert and Sergeant Keeble, still looking for the Beau crew, spotted and rescued two more Germans, in position 37.40N/10.20E, off the Tunis coast.

Bill Lambert noted in his logbook that his two Germans were the pilot, Unteroffizier Sowade, aged 21, and the observer, Feldwebel Hofmann, aged 20. He also recorded that a HSL picked up the missing Beaufighter crew.

* * *

Hamish Reid was still with 284 Squadron, and he gives us a view of the Squadron at this time:

284 did some pretty sterling work because we were picking people up north of the Messina Straits. Denis Lunn picked someone up, if memory serves me right, inside Catania Harbour before it had been taken, so life certainly had its moments.

In September the Squadron as it still was, moved to Lentini and continued ops. What was happening, was as the lines moved northwards, we were following up on the most immediate aerodromes. We then had a detachment which Ken Hall took, with myself included, up to Milazzo, right on the north coast of Sicily. By this time, of course, Sicily had been taken and we were now in a position to cover the Salerno landings.

A pattern was beginning to emerge; that the Squadron would split into detachments/flights of two or three aircraft and this was to continue throughout the period I was with it. So Ken Hall, 'Sticky' Glew, Paxton, Norman Pickles, and myself plus some others – 13 in all – including one of each groundcrew trade, went forward. We had a wonderful time there because, close by, there was an MT dump of all sorts of Italian vehicles and again, we were in our usual carved-out vineyard. Our quarters were three rooms in a battered farmhouse, but when the Spitfire squadrons, which had been using Milazzo, moved out to the Italian mainland, we found ourselves with 450,000 gallons of aviation fuel in a dump at the other end of the strip, which was right on the water's edge. One came into land over the seashore there. The locals were coming in and pinching the petrol at night, so there were little gun battles up and down the strip, for there was also an abandoned ammo dump there, with discarded machine-guns and so on. But we got rather tired of this, so we went into the small town of Milazzo, about 5-6 miles away. We came to a deal in order to stop this looting, and said that if the Mayor sent a signed chit, we'd give them some of the petrol in exchange for wine or other suitable barter. After all, we were on dawn to dusk readiness so hadn't the time nor the men to play about with night patrols around the dumps. So we finished up with an electric generator for our lighting, and a motley collection of transport.

An Italian Sergeant-Major and his Corporal – deserters I suppose – from the Italian Air Force, had attached themselves to us and were wonderful mechanics, so we got a motor pool going, restoring all these vehicles. Plenty of wine, eggs, even the odd sheep (we found we had an armourer among our ground crew who had been a butcher in civilian life) and as long as the aircraft were maintained and there were enough bods to do the necessary trips, it was like a summer camp!

Also, because the chaps we picked up from the sea often needed to stay overnight, we could draw extra rations for them. We could, of course, fly them out or arrange for them to be picked up by their squadrons, but in the meantime there were plenty of extra cigarettes, etc, so everyone was quite happy. This lasted until the end of October at which time the detachment ended.

Flight Sergeant J A Reid, 284 Squadron

Hamish Reid was involved in the rescue of two American Spitfire pilots on 21 September, one being a Group Commander. The 31st US Fighter Group had been in action on this day, which resulted in Colonel John R Hawkins and Flight Officer Clifford W Nelson of the 309th Squadron, going into the sea. Both were between 10 to 15 miles off Stromboli, an island to the north of Sicily. Ken Hall DFC and Sergeant Heseltine picked up the Colonel (in W2757), during the morning, while Hamish Reid and Sticky Glew got Nelson, in the same Walrus, in the afternoon.

> I remember Ken Hall bringing in the American Colonel and when he was back at Milazzo on dry land, recall him being more concerned with drying out the money in his wallet on a board in the sun, than having a brush with death.
>
> J A Reid, 284 Squadron

Mail Run Mishap

On 24 September, Flight Sergeant G F Brown and Flight Sergeant J W Bradley of 284 (in W3012) were scrambled to locate and rescue the crew of a twin-engined Albemarle of 296 Squadron, which had gone into the sea south of Agrigento, Sicily, whilst on a flight from Tunisia, with its crew and two soldier passengers. Flying Officer Gordon L Wilson, the pilot, later made out the following report:

> On the evening of 23 September it came to my notice that my [usual] aircraft was unserviceable and consequently I should have to fly P1382, an aircraft normally flown by P/O Vandenburgh. Two days previously he had experienced a fire in the starboard engine whilst starting up. The aircraft had been inspected at Bizerta and was found fit for flying and the machine was flown back to base without incident. On return to the squadron the occurrence was reported. On making enquiries at the flights I was assured that the engine in question had been thoroughly examined and no faults traced. At 08.00 the following morning I took off for Italy with a load of 3,400 lbs and full fuel tanks in the bomb-bay. Maxwell, Ward and Lidgett were in the crew positions, Regimental Sergeant-Major Ryan in second pilot's seat, and Sergeant-Major Devine in the rear of the fuselage.
>
> The aircraft took off and climbed normally to 2,000 feet. At 09.20 we were between Pantelleria and Sicily when a sudden change in note in the starboard engine occurred. Instruments, including engine temperature and pressure were normal; boost was '0' and revs. 2150. The revs. dropped slightly but built up again almost immediately. The engine note now became harsher and vibration commenced. I asked F/O Maxwell for a course to steer to the nearest aerodrome; he answered almost immediately and I set course for Sicily. I instructed the WOP to transmit SOS which was answered at once by Malta [Control], who gave me a course of 130°. I ignored this as Sicily was already visible and obviously the nearest place.

In the meantime the air gunner attempted to inform SM Devine in the tail of our situation but was unable to do so since Devine was asleep and could not be reached because of the freight.

The Vokes filter on the starboard engine had become loose and was vibrating between 2-3″ from the front of the engine cowling. Flight Sergeant Lidgett returned to his turret and informed me of his inability to warn Devine. I throttled the starboard engine right back, opened part port throttle fully and putting the airscrew in fully fine pitch, attempted to fly at about 110 IAS. The aircraft was losing height between 400-500 feet per minute and was difficult to control. I operated the aileron and rudder trimmers fully against the good engine, but even so, due to the low speed it was necessary to take the aileron control fully over. The aircraft was now at approximately 700 feet.

I considered feathering the starboard engine but the aircraft was losing height so rapidly that it became obvious that within the next minute or two we should hit the sea. I informed RSM Ryan to inflate his lifebelt. I then gave the order over the intercom to prepare for ditching. Maxwell stationed Ryan in the crawl way beneath the escape hatch and locked up the second pilot's seat. The WOP continued to transmit, preparatory to clamping down the key.

At about 100 feet the Vokes filter became detached from the starboard engine and fell away. The engine itself was vibrating to such an extent that I expected it to break up. I instructed WOP to open the escape hatch and the crew prepared for impact. At about 30 feet I cut back both throttles and made the most level approach I could, ditching tail first without flap at about 95-100 IAS. The tail of the aircraft broke away about eight feet from the end of the fuselage. SM Devine was thrown clear. The aircraft sank about eight-ten feet in the water and I became aware of a fire in the cockpit and water pouring in through the nose and hatch. I found the escape hatch blocked by a body which I pushed upwards, finding myself rising to the surface. The aircraft floated to the surface and I saw the dinghy had automatically inflated. The aircraft was on fire along the whole fuselage and the starboard engine was also on fire. All the crew and passengers were afloat except for the gunner, who was still in his turret, which was facing aft. I climbed up onto the port wing, feeling very dazed and found the aircraft practically breaking up and sinking. The turret was surrounded by flame and Flight Sergeant Lidgett was shouting loudly. As the aircraft sank, the guns commenced firing and F/S Lidgett's cries ceased. In a minute the aircraft had sunk completely.

The dinghy was towed away from the aircraft by Flight Sergeant Ward and passengers and crew assisted each other aboard. The dinghy was floating upside down and despite our efforts could not be righted. This task was made more difficult because the dinghy was not equipped with ropes. Within five minutes we were located by an American C.47 attracted by the column of smoke and the aircraft dropped what looked like a Lindholme dinghy but after Maxwell and Ward had swum out and retrieved it, we recognised it as an emergency radio set.

At 12.00 we were located by an ASR Wellington which marked our position with smoke floats and a short time afterwards a Walrus landed and picked us up. The pilot attempted to take some of the mail bags aboard, which were still floating but this was impossible and he promised when he returned to base he'd arrange for a boat to salvage whatever remained afloat. The Walrus took off and landed us at Gela West.

On D-Day in Europe – 6 June 1944 – Wilson and his crew were back in England and flew a night sortie, towing a glider into the assault area, near Caen. After releasing the glider their Albemarle was riddled by ground fire, which set both engines on fire and shot away the controls. Wilson ordered his men out despite only being a couple of hundred feet up. He made certain everyone was out before he left the cockpit and his parachute opened just as he crashed down onto the roof of a house, and he was wounded in the right leg. The village in which he found himself was deserted but in the middle of a battle with mortars and machine guns going off all around him. He remained on the roof until some British soldiers arrived and he was eventually sent back to the beach area. Here he met up with Maxwell and Ward, plus his bomb aimer. His replacement air gunner was reported missing. Gordon Lee Wilson was awarded the DFC.

The Squadrons Move Again

283 Squadron began a new detachment at Monte Corvino, Palermo, on 26 September – Flight Sergeants Divers, Newman, Graham and Morabito with two aircraft. A second detachment went to Sidi Ahmed (Bizerta), again with two crews and two aircraft.

In late September 1944, 284 Squadron moved to Scanzano, on the northern coast of the Gulf of Taranto, then in early October, moved again to Gioia del Colle, inland, about 25 miles north of Taranto itself. Within a short space of time, the Squadron was moved yet again, this time to Brindisi, situated on the east coast of the heel of Italy. Hamish Reid continues:

> The finish of our detachment at Milazzo was quite an interesting story. Ken Hall flew the remaining Walrus over [to the mainland] and Sticky Glew and myself set off with the ground crew and our motley collection of Italian vehicles – plus our two Italian types – travelling by road to Messina, we got across the Straits and eventually arrived in Taranto where 284 had their Headquarters. We expected to be welcomed with open arms, bringing much required transport to the Squadron but, instead, found we were not at all popular because we'd taken three weeks to do the trip and had been posted as missing!
>
> Possibly that was because we'd taken aboard an extra 700 gallons of petrol for the trip so we hadn't stayed at any official staging posts, just picked ourselves little villages and swapped petrol for bread, wine, etc. Sticky and I reckoned we and the ground lads deserved a bit of a break but Reg Hayes didn't take a very good view of it – but that's life.
>
> Flight Sergeant J A Reid, 284 Squadron

From Gioia, on 10 October, Flight Sergeant Ted Holmes and Jack Berry flew to Foggia for a briefing, then took off in Walrus W2757 and flew to Treniti Island, in order to try and find some Germans and possibly a Spitfire pilot of 244 Wing. 92 Squadron had celebrated its fourth anniversary of reforming by shooting down a Dornier 17z bomber off Termoli on this day, although one of 92's pilots had gone down from its return fire.

Holmes and Berry made a search and found an oil patch which led them to a dinghy. They landed and found it was not their Spitfire man, nor a German, but a Croat airman. He was badly injured with severe leg wounds so Holmes decided to get him back and into hospital without delay. Having done this, he flew back to the area, escorted by 92 Squadron, and having made yet another ribbon search, found a second Croat, picked him up and continuing the search, discovered yet a third Croat airman. These three had in fact been part of the Dornier's crew, but unhappily, there was no sign of the missing Spitfire pilot.

It was learnt that the crew had flown from Moscar in Yugoslavia, and they were flying on a shipping recco and did not know that Termoli was in Allied hands. In fact they only knew Foggia, much further south, was in Allied hands by listening to the British radio! When they were asked about what their German ally thought of the war, one of the Croats replied that they were too disciplined to think.

The Dornier had been about 18 miles north-east of Termoli. 92's patrol was led by Flight Lieutenant J H Nicholls DFC. Warrant Officer L B McKay RCAF had attacked in turn but his No.2 saw McKay's Spitfire hit by return fire and go down. He saw McKay bale out but did not see the parachute open. Laughlan McKay was not found in the subsequent search and has no known grave.

Walrus Lost to Me109s

Messerschmitt 109s of III Gruppe of JG27 based in Greece shot down a Walrus on 30 September; it was not a machine from the rescue squadrons, but is mentioned here in case anyone thinks that it was.

Flight Lieutenant F E G Rashleigh DFC was an officer with HQ Royal Air Force Middle East and was piloting the Walrus to Kos in order to improve communications. With him was his navigator, Sergeant Clifford Platt, whose unit is shown as being a Personnel Transit Centre. They had the great misfortune of being spotted by marauding 109s over the sea between the islands of Lesbos and Kalimnos and stood little chance. They were claimed by the Gruppenkommandeur, Major Ernst Düllberg, who would end the war with 50 victories, 33 scored whilst with JG27. Francis Rashleigh had won his DFC in 1941 serving with 202 Squadron. He rescued three downed airmen in the desert, who were surrounded by Arabs, and who appeared to be upset by the rescue, for he took off amidst much rifle fire.

Sole Survivors

Dick Eccles made the next rescue, on 20 October. The previous day, 14 Squadron had sent out one of its Marauders (FK127 'K') on a reconnaissance between Durazzo and Lizza Island. It failed to return so a search was mounted at first light on the 20th, carried out by Hudsons from 608 Squadron, as well as 14 Squadron's own Marauders. Flight Sergeant H W Bates of 14 Squadron located one man in the sea clinging to a petrol tank, and dropped a dinghy to him. They saw the man get in and then they called for a Walrus. Dick Eccles and Jack Berry scrambled in X9506 at 12.45 pm, heading out 86 miles from Triola on a course of 025 degrees, being then led to the spot by another Marauder. Locating the dinghy one mile from the island of Cazza, off the Albanian coast, being circled by a Hudson, Dick Eccles prepared to land.

> We scrambled to an area near the island of Vis in the Adriatic. It was rumoured that there was a Luftwaffe aerodrome on the island and so strict radio silence was essential. It could be difficult sometimes to get a man into the Walrus with just one air gunner [crewman], rather than two, but on this occasion, we wanted to avoid extra weight due to the distance/petrol relationship. We were also escorted by Spitfires.
>
> As it was, we were lucky, and found Sergeant Ritchie, the only survivor of the Marauder, very quickly. His legs were in pretty poor shape from exposure and immersion, but the rescue proved uneventful. We were photographed landing back at base, and when we were getting Ritchie out of the Walrus.
>
> Flying Officer R G Eccles, 284 Squadron

Sergeant H Ritchie had been the second pilot of the B.26 Marauder. His pilot had been Flying Officer Adam M Cameron, but he and the other four men in the crew – Flying Officer G Ingram, Flight Sergeants W G Williams and Colin V Proud, with Sergeant C Leslie, had all been lost. Ritchie said they had suffered aileron failure and were forced to come down in the sea. Ritchie was thrown clear on impact and he thought all the others died in the crash.

A Night on the Ocean Wave

Back in the Adriatic Sea, 283 Squadron rescued five crewmen from an American B.25 Mitchell from the 82nd Squadron, 12th Bomb Group, 9th Air Force on 3 November, from a very rough sea. Flight Sergeant A Divers RNZAF and Sergeant E F Keeble effected the rescue but it was once again the old story of not being able to get off again. In this case, the angry sea gave the Walrus such a battering that it had to be abandoned, and all seven men were taken aboard the hospital ship *Seminole*, and taken to Naples following a ten-hour ordeal on the water. Arnold Divers retained this report of the mission from 355 Wing records:

3 November 1943

15.45   One Walrus 283 Squadron scrambled to search for dinghies holding five men, reported in position 3901N, 1418E. Pilot, F/Sgt Divers RNZAF, Wop/AG Sgt Keeble.

16.05   Aircraft airborne from Palermo.

17.10   In target area. Commenced ribbon search.

17.35   Sighted single red Very light 6/7 miles NW. Wind 080 degrees, 15 mph. Light rapidly failing, sea moderate swell. Some whitecaps.

17.45   Alighted on sea and, by the light of the a/c's searchlight, saw two dinghies lashed together, containing five aircrew from a ditched B.25 of 82nd Bomber Sqdn, 12th Bomber Group. Names as follows:

1st Pilot	1st Lt Devlin
2nd Pilot	2nd Lt McGonigle
Bombardier	1st Lt Steinberg
Air Gunner	T/Sgt Stephens
WOP/AG	S/Sgt Keyes

    The B.25 had been hit by flak over the target area, silencing one engine. The a/c subsequently got out of control and the crew baled out in the area 3901N, 1418E, which is approximately where they were located and picked up by the Walrus.

17.55   The Walrus attempted a sea take-off with intention to return to base and make a night landing. The aircraft porpoised violently and the attempt was abandoned due to the heavy swell, darkness and excessive weight.

18.10   Threw out drogues and decided to spend the night on water with intention to take off early next morning. Bilge pump in use and thereafter manned every hour.

19.00   Sea and wind increased, causing the a/c to role very heavily. Engine started to keep her into wind and to reduce buffeting.

21.00   Noticed slight list to port and that the port mainplane failed to rise out of the water due to leaking of the port float.

23.30   List to port became very pronounced, the mainplane bending under the weight of the seas and causing it to wrench at the wing post. The Air Gunner (Sgt Keeble) climbed on to the starboard wing to counteract the list. In this he was only partially successful.

4 November

00.30   The pilot (F/Sgt Divers) relieved the AG on the wing for one hour, whereafter alternate spells of shorter duration (owing to the cold) were spent by both members of the crew on the starboard wing.

02.30   Sighted light on horizon to NW. Seas now breaking right over the aircraft.

03.00   Fired two star green-red Very light.

03.10   Signalled for help by Aldis lamp.

03.20   Ship trained searchlight on Walrus who replied with a two star red Very light.

03.30   Motor launch drew alongside and took off the five survivors of the B.25. The Walrus crew explained their intention to remain with their a/c in the hope of keeping it afloat until morning when they hoped they would be sighted and be able to have the aircraft taken in tow.

03.45   The a/c was now practically heeling over and the chief mate of the M/L ordered the crew to abandon the a/c. The IFF was blown up but no explosion was heard owing to the noise of the sea. Ropes were

thrown to the a/c because the heavy seas made it no longer possible
for the M/L to heave alongside. The Walrus crew were then half
dragged and half swam to the launch and were put on board the
hospital ship *SEMINOLE*, bound for Naples. The Ship's Master
gave the crew a written statement that he had taken the seven men
on board, [and that] in his estimation, the a/c would not survive the
night owing to increasingly heavy seas.

The survivors of the B.25 were handed over to the USAAC
Embarkation Officer at Naples, whilst the crew of the Walrus, after
spending the following night on the ship, two nights at 3 RAF Base Area
and one night at Catania, were eventually returned to Palermo at 16.00
hrs on 8 November.

Injuries to Survivors

One survivor sustained injuries to his ribs but all the others escaped with
minor cuts and bruises.

The Walrus crew were little the worse for the adventure although it is
pointed out that the pilot, F/Sgt Divers, was actually convalescing
after an attack of malaria and undertook the sortie as no other pilots
were available at Palermo at that time.

Lieutenant William E (Bill) McGonigle, the surviving second pilot of the B.25,
wrote to his uncle about the rescue, in a letter dated 9 November 1943, a copy
of which Bill sent to me:

Dear Uncle Doc,

How is everything going back home? I guess you thought I had forgotten
all about you folks – but believe me I haven't, and have just been pretty
busy.

I had a pretty interesting experience, which I know you would
appreciate but I don't want Mother to know because she might worry too
much. You were over here the last time, so you know it is only part of the
game. I would also be careful whom I showed it to as it might have some
material in it the enemy could use.

We took off the other day on a bombing mission, and I was flying co-
pilot with Paul Devlin. We all fly co-pilot over here on our first mission
and it is a good idea. Anyhow, he hit plenty of Jerry ack-ack before we
got to the target and he's a pretty good shot. We were hit a few times but
held formation and dropped our eggs. We came off the target and headed
back home. We knew we had been hit, but everything seemed OK. We
had gotten about half way back home, when the right engine began
throwing oil. Our gunner, Sgt Lourrie Stephens, called over the
interphone and told us about it. Paul tried to feather the right engine but
evidently the feathering system was shot out and we were left with a
windmilling prop and not any oil which meant the engine would burn out
soon. Paul gave the order to stand-by to bale out, and I crawled around

behind him to try and hold the wheel while he got out. Our trim tabs for the tail rudder were broken or something and Paul was holding full left control and the ship was still rolling to the right. By that time, Jimmy Steinberg, the bombardier, had the emergency hatch kicked open and the plane went into a spin. Paul yelled "bale out," and away we went. I bounced around a bit and finally went out through the hatch head first, waited to get clear of the aircraft and pulled the rip-cord. I didn't have any sensation of falling, when the chute opened it gave a slight jerk and I was just standing in the air.

I saw the plane hit and miraculously the dinghy life raft released itself. I saw it and tried to drift my chute towards it. Almost before I could realise it I hit the water and kicked out of my chute. On the way down I had lined the raft up with a cloud so I took out in that direction. The sea was pretty high so I could just catch occasional glimpses of the raft. Finally I got there and climbed aboard. I heard a yell and couldn't see anyone so I yelled to "wave your arms". Finally I saw Paul and was plenty glad to know he had gotten out as he was the last to leave the plane. The oars of the raft were broken up by the impact so I took off my clothes and swam, pulling the raft behind. I grew tired of this soon and climbed back in and found a piece of oar about 2' long, so I paddled and Paul swam and we got together.

He had taken pretty much a beating inside the plane before he got out and was just about at the end of the rope. We felt a little better to have company and about that time we heard another yell. This time it was our gunner and we got him aboard. Next we found the bombardier and at last the radioman. Most of them were in the water so long they were half paralysed, and because we only had one paddle, I did most of the rowing.

As I was pulling up to the radioman, an Irishman by the name of Keyes, I said, "This bus is too crowded, wait for the next one." He said, "To hell with you Mac, I have my token." We all had a good laugh and felt better, now that the gang was all there.

When we went down, Lt Franklin dropped out of formation and got our location by some good headwork and had to get back home as he was running out of gas. We went in about 10.30, picked Keyes up at about 13.00 and about 14.30 a plane flown from our squadron came out. We shot a flare at him and he located us and circled us and dropped another raft. We picked it up, lashed it to ours and were more comfortable. It was about dark and we were sweating out having to spend the night out there on a rough sea, when we sighted an English amphibian. We shot a flare and he came in and landed on that rough ocean. He taxied up and the sea was so rough I didn't have a chance to get my clothes – it was all we could do to get aboard.

He tried to take off, but the sea was too high, he couldn't get flying speed, so he decided to wait until dawn for the sea to quiet down. Instead of calming it became rougher and by 1 am in the morning the amphibian was listing badly and about ready to sink. At that time we saw some lights in the distance and Sgt Divers, the pilot from New Zealand, started up the motors and taxied towards them. When we got closer we sent up a flare and a SOS. It turned out to be a US hospital ship heading for .... to take on some patients.

They immediately sent out a life boat and picked us all up, including the Limeys. As soon as we were on board we had hot coffee, toast and some cold cuts and also a very tasty cigarette. They gave us each a pair of pyjamas and put us to bed with a couple of sleeping pills. In the morning a nurse came in and served us a breakfast of hot cakes, ham and eggs, orange juice, buttered toast and coffee. An orderly came in and took our measurements and fitted us with some new clothes – so we were all fixed up. We stayed on the boat for 36 hours, had good food, saw a movie, danced with the nurses – all in all we had a wonderful time.

When we hit port we left the ship and were flown back to our outfit. It was a great experience and after it ended so well we didn't have too many regrets.

It was Paul's last mission (after 50 missions you can return to the States) and also Steinberg's. I'll hate to see them leave but they had an adventurous ending.

Paul is going to try and call mom up when he gets back, but I told him not to say anything so don't you do it either. Aunt Marge might even spill the beans so be careful and I'll be seeing you folks soon.

Your young godson,
Billy

P.S. The boat sent out after us had to turn back because of the weather, so we owe plenty to those two English boys.

Billy McGonigle received a commendation for this adventurous day and night, which read:

1. On 3rd November 1943, Lt McGonigle was co-pilot in a B.25 airplane, engaged in a combat mission over Ceprano, Italy. While over the target area, Lt McGonigle's airplane was repeatedly hit by enemy anti-aircraft fire, and was seriously damaged as a result of this action. While on the homeward journey to his base in Sicily, Lt McGonigle's airplane developed serious engine trouble over the Mediterranean Sea, necessitating immediate 'Bail-out' by all crew members. The crew successfully left the airplane and parachuted into the open sea, and after their landing in the icy waters, were left helpless without the aid of a life raft; their only means of support being the standard life jacket. Lt McGonigle and several other crew members noticed a life raft on the water while on their way down by parachute. After reaching the water, all crew members were soon exhausted and did not have the strength enough to swim for the raft, but Lt McGonigle, through sheer determination and will, managed to overcome his shock and temporary exhaustion, and swam for the raft. He then rowed the lifeboat in the immediate vicinity

of the crash, and picked up all fellow crew members after 2½ hours, just before darkness was setting in. All the men in Lt McGonigle's crew have stated that they did not have strength enough to swim for the raft, and all agree that they owe their lives to Lt McGonigle.

2. In recognition of Lt McGonigle's excellent achievement, and his strong determination to save the lives of his fellow soldiers, which he successfully accomplished against great odds, it gives me pleasure to commend him.

John W Shinners,
Major, Air Corps,
Deputy Group Commander.

The story was issued at the same time as a PR press release by the 82nd Squadron, based at Gerbini, in central Sicily, not far from Catania, and parts of it are reproduced here:

Flying at 12,000 feet, the 12-plane formation levelled off and dipped lower, as ordered, for the final approach to the target. It was about then, with the target in sight but still some distance, that puffs of smoke and dull thuds in the sky signalled that the enemy was alert and attacking with flak, and AA guns sent tracer bullets ever closer.

Midway through the bombing run anti-aircraft fire tore into Devlin's aircraft and the plane shuddered. "We knew we were hit. We could hear it and we could feel it. But we didn't know how bad it was. Our plane seemed to be under control and we still had bombs to drop so we went in on the target", McGonigle recalls.

As soon as the mission was accomplished the squadron hustled out of anti-aircraft range and headed for home but [when] Devlin's plane was only a few miles from the target with lands-end well in sight it became apparent that the Devlin plane could not hold its altitude and it dipped low over the water.

Once over the sea the damaged starboard engine became totally useless and was smoking, which presented another threat. One of the crewmen, a Lieutenant Steinberg, breathed easier as the damaged airplane cleared land and headed out to sea. The Lieutenant, a bombardier, is Jewish and didn't relish the thought of being captured by the Nazis.

Once over the water, the pilots set out to feather the smoking starboard engine but the feathering device didn't work and the propeller windmilled, adding to the danger and threatening more trouble. It wasn't long before everyone aboard knew they would have to abandon the aircraft and Captain Devlin gave the order to inspect parachutes and get ready to jump. A jump rotation was directed and it was decided that Devlin would handle the controls while everyone evacuated except McGonigle. Then Devlin would jump while McGonigle held the controls. Once Devlin was clear, McGonigle would hold onto the controls only long enough to get into position to jump.

"As soon as I turned loose of the wheel the plane went into a spin and threw me out through the bottom escape hatch. The plane's tail just missed my head as I twisted clear of the wreckage and watched it plunge toward the water", McGonigle reported later. "Then I made a point of counting the 'chutes which had opened ahead of mine and found the other four (besides his) floating safely downward. I saw the plane hit the water and was surprised to see a tiny life raft pop out."

Since McGonigle was the last man out he landed in choppy water closer to the raft and the rapidly sinking airplane than anyone else. It was clear the plane was sinking and pulling with it the life raft which was secured to the wreckage with a single rope. All the crew had life jackets but it was obvious that the only life raft in the vicinity would sink with the plane if someone didn't cut it loose. McGonigle decided it was his responsibility to get to that raft before it disappeared into the sea. It was about this time that he noticed also that other planes from the squadron had observed the whole bale-out operation and were circling to offer whatever help they could, and hopefully noting the position of the men in the water.

An official report of the incident said crew members who landed in the cold, choppy waters barely had strength to unbuckle their parachutes and tread water in their life jackets. "Lt. McGonigle", the report said, "through sheer determination and will, managed to overcome his shock and temporary exhaustion and swim for the raft."

He reached the life saving equipment in time to cut the raft loose from the sinking aircraft wreckage and climbed in. Paddles which are standard equipment on such rafts were missing and McGonigle decided he would strip off his uniform and swim with the raft in tow towards the other crewmen, now scattered over a broad expanse of the Mediterranean Sea. It was approximately 2$\frac{1}{2}$ hours before the five crewmen were all in the life raft. The afternoon sun was still shining and planes overhead were making notes of the location of the downed airmen. After that the observation plane took off, supposedly to seek help, dropping another life raft. McGonigle swam to it and tied it to the original life raft as back-up equipment. They then waited. McGonigle, who had discarded his clothing to swim to the first life raft, commandeered the raft's only blanket.

About dusk a British single-engine plane – a Walrus – spotted the rafts, landed on the water nearby and taxied to the five men who had begun to get more anxious as darkness drew near. The five airmen left their raft and climbed into the rescue craft with near disastrous results. The tiny plane, now seriously overloaded with approximately 800 pounds representing the combined weight of the five crewmen, also faced the difficulty of taking off in a sea which had grown rougher as darkness approached. The pilot, an Australian [sic] sergeant, tried repeatedly to take off on the choppy sea and then both Devlin and McGonigle tried their more experienced hands at getting the craft airborne. For the next 10 to 12 hours the plane drifted while firing occasional flares to attract the attention of anything that might be in the vicinity.

Shortly before midnight they lost a wing float to the elements and it seemed uncertain whether the craft would remain afloat. It was just before dawn, about 4.30 am, when flares attracted the attention of a hospital ship, which came cautiously closer until the distressed men aboard the British plane recognised the red cross on the ship's side and magnified their efforts to attract attention.

Once it was established that the hospital ship and the rescue aircraft were both allied forces it was relatively easy to pull the two craft together and get the downed airmen aboard. "There were two hitches", McGonigle told his friends. "First, the Australian pilot refused to leave his ship to be rescued until we pulled rank and ordered him onto the hospital ship. Second, I had lost my clothes in the process of our exploits in the Med, and just before we made contact with the ship I lost my blanket. I boarded that ship stark naked."

In 1995 Bill McGonigle told me:

As co-pilot I climbed out of my seat, stood behind Paul Devlin, and took control of the wheel to try and hold the ship level until Paul got out of his seat and prepared to jump through the lower hatch. Meantime the rest of the crew baled out. We ejected almost simultaneously as soon as he was in position. I believe I was first out and Paul immediately behind me. [Not according to the official report.]

We all received Purple Hearts, and later I received the Air Medal with Oak Leaf Cluster and the Distinguished Flying Cross. Later I was recommended for the Silver Star but our outfit was transferred to a different theatre (India) and evidently it was lost in the shuffle because I never received it.

This was the first of my 66 combat missions and I became first pilot soon after the incident. There were 45 of us in the replacement crews that arrived in the Mediterranean Theatre on November 1, 1943. Of those 45, only 22 were left after 22 missions.

Man on the Beach

Later in the month, 17 November, 284 Squadron were heavily involved in a most dramatic rescue. Five days earlier an American B.25 Mitchell of the 321st Bomb Group had been lost returning from a raid and the crew had baled out over the sea off Gryhee, but two men came down on land, and one, Sergeant Hilton, found himself on the Albanian coast, where he hid from capture. Meanwhile, the rest of the crew were picked up by an Italian Cant 506B seaplane being used by the Allies, with a now, pro-allied Italian crew.

With five men rescued and two missing, believed prisoners, that seemed to be the end of that until the 16th. On that day, Squadron Leader W T Page, the CO of 126 Squadron, baled out of his Spitfire. His parachute failed to deploy and later his body was seen floating in the sea, so an attempt to recover it was made on the morning of the 17th.

At first light, a Walrus with an escort of two Spitfires from 249 Squadron flew out towards the Adriatic coast to search for Page's body but instead they spotted a man waving from the nearby beach, close to the mouth of the Semini River. 284 Squadron aircrew had been warned that there might be a survivor or two from the missing B.25 near to the coastal area. Indeed, on the 13th, one had been spotted on the coast of Albania, and although 284 had agreed to a rescue attempt, this was later cancelled. Now, after five days, it seemed likely the man or men had by now been taken prisoner. In the Walrus, Flight Lieutenant Reg Hayes and the seemingly indestructible Sticky Glew of 284 Squadron, circled the man and then decided to land off shore.

One very grateful Sergeant Hilton was quickly on board after his six-day ordeal, but his relief was to be short-lived as the Walrus then became stuck on a sandbank. Meanwhile, 1435 Squadron had sent out four Spitfires to relieve 249 Squadron and when they arrived at the mouth of the Semini, they saw the stranded seaplane below. They began to orbit above it with two of 249's Spitfires, but the latter two were soon forced to break off and return to their base as fuel ran low. However, two more 249 machines arrived, piloted by Flight Sergeants J D Sheeran and K L Dale, a Canadian. As these two pilots went down for a closer look, 1435 called to say that they had company – some Me109s had turned up and were spotted up in the sun. These were flown by pilots of JG27 from their base at Kalimaki, northern Greece, and they attacked both the Spitfires and the stranded Walrus.

In the mêlée which followed, Flight Sergeant Dennis Sheeran (EF638 'K') gave a *Tally-ho!* call that he was engaging, but that was the last they heard of him. Dale attacked a 109 but it flew off and then he attacked another which staggered away with smoke pouring from its fuselage. He was unable to see if it crashed as more Messerschmitts began to arrive.

Another 109 attacked the Walrus and as the three men on the ground took cover in some nearby marshes, Flight Sergeant E A Rushmer of 1435 Squadron went for it and scored some hits.

In between these attacks, Reg Hayes and Sticky Glew emerged from their hiding place and with Hilton's help, tried to free the Walrus but then the 109s started coming down again. Four times they crept from their cover position, and each time they were spotted and strafed. Sticky and Hilton were both slightly wounded during these attempts, which in any event were proving totally fruitless.

One Me109 came in at deck level and 1435 Squadron engaged it, then chased the German inland to within ten miles of Berat where it spun in and the pilot baled out. By now the message that the Walrus crew were in trouble had been sent back, and Denny Lunn and Heseltine (W3012), already out on another search, were told to locate the CO and his Walrus, but, having found them, they had no choice but to return to base first in order to refuel. They took off again at 14.10 pm and relocated them, then to avoid another problem with sandbanks, decided to land on a nearby inland lake at Kneta-E-Kavestese, which was really an inland bay. The three men on the ground quickly got to the Walrus, clambered aboard and Lunn took off and returned everyone back to base.

It is not certain if JG27 lost one aircraft or two during this action, but Leutnant Hans Hetzler of the 12th Staffel was wounded. Sticky Glew couldn't have been seriously hurt for he was back in action on 14 December with Denny Lunn and Norm Pickles, but a Cant 506B beat them to a rescue of a Spitfire pilot. However, two days later, Lunn, Pickles and Paxton (W3012) did get their man.

A flight of four bomb-carrying Spitfire Vs from 249 Squadron escorted by six more as top cover, had this day made the Squadron's first fighter-bomber attack on a factory near Ulcinj, on the Albanian coast. Heading away from the target, the Spitfires spotted some road transport and went down to strafe. Some flak came up and Flight Sergeant W Docherty (ES306 'T') was hit and brought down. Seen to make a good crash-landing and start to run off, the Squadron was determined to try and rescue him as soon as they could arrange it. At mid-day Flight Lieutenant J Beatson, an Australian, with a section of four, escorted an ASR Cant 506B to the hostile coast, off the Gulf of Drin.

The Cant pilot proceeded to patrol up and down this section of coast but seemed reluctant to go in too close. Beatson was so annoyed at this that he fired a short burst in front of the Italian machine and forced it in! Leaving his No.3 and No.4 out over the Gulf, he and his wingman – Flight Sergeant J G Belec – went on to Rozge and circled at deck level, having seen Docherty's wrecked Spitfire there, and then Docherty himself at the river mouth, waving a red scarf. Again John Beatson flew at the Cant, firing again to force the Italian in, but the Cant pilot broke away and set course out to sea.

Totally frustrated, the two Spitfire pilots returned to the coast west of Bize, but then Beatson saw two Me109s diving down on them. He and Belec broke to starboard and he fired at one but another got behind his Spitfire (ER673 'F') and he was hit. Flames appeared in the cockpit leaving 'Shortie' Beatson (he was around 6' 5" tall) no alternative but to take to his parachute. Belec chased the 109 but it climbed away from him. Belec then returned to orbit Beatson while giving a distress call.

Lunn and his two stalwarts had taken off in W3012, and were given a course of 50 degrees from Brindisi (120 miles) – escorted by two Spitfires of 126 Squadron – in order to do what the Cant crew had failed to do. It took some time to cover the distance, but they found the circling Spitfire and then saw what they supposed was their customer, who was only about 100 yards off the southern tip of the Gulf of Drin. As they landed a gun position on the beach opened fire. The circling Spitfires immediately went in and strafed the position while Lunn, being told that the customer had been grabbed, began to taxi away to get out of range. The Spitfire attack silenced the gun, but not before Pickles was hit and wounded in the fleshy part of the upper arm, the arm that was desperately holding on to Beatson, but he did not let go. Fortunately he was not seriously hurt. Beatson explained to Lunn that he was not their original target, and told him about Docherty so they flew to where he had earlier been seen waving, but there was now no sign of him. Reluctantly they had then to head back to Italy.

The 109s were again from the Kalimaki-based JG27, this time from the 10th Staffel, and the pilot who claimed Beatson was Leutnant Holgar Lummerding – his first victory.

Back on the Italian mainland these events were about to cause the loss of two RAF pilots. Wing Commander E N Woods DFC & Bar, a former CO of 249 and now the leader of 286 Wing, of which 249 was part, took off with the new CO of 126 Squadron (also in the Wing) Squadron Leader K B L Debenham, and headed for Yugoslavia, probably intending to ambush the 109s as they headed back to Greece. Neither men were seen again, and it can only be assumed that at some point they collided and died.

The Docherty saga continued the next day and so did new searches for the two missing Wing pilots but to no avail. 249 scoured the area where Docherty was last seen and suddenly he was spotted at the river mouth. A Walrus was called up and upon arrival it landed but as it taxied into shore, everyone could see the downed Spitfire pilot wading out towards it. Unfortunately, Docherty was a non-swimmer and appeared not to have retained his Mae West, and while still 200 – 300 yards away, the Walrus grounded on a sandbank and could get no closer. The Walrus had to back off and reluctantly they had to forget rescue, leaving the lonely figure of Docherty wading back to shore. He was later taken prisoner.

Meantime, JG27 came back on the scene, with four Me109s coming down from out of the sun, but in turn they were attacked by a section of 1435 Squadron, which had just arrived, and both German fighters were shot down. Both pilots were killed, one being the same Leutnant Lummerding who had downed Beatson the day before. 1435 were on top form and went after the other two 109s, destroying both of these too.

It had been a busy couple of days. Four Spitfires had been lost, two pilots killed and one taken prisoner, plus one Walrus abandoned, while the Germans had lost five Me109s with another damaged, four pilots killed and one wounded.

The next day more searches were made because late on the 17th a pilot had been spotted in a dinghy by 1435 Squadron and he had waved back. However, nothing was found on the 18th but seven Italian refugees were spotted in a small boat 15 miles north-east of Brindisi and they were later rescued by a Walrus, a Cant and an HSL.

'Send Three and Fourpence, We're Going to a Dance'
For those not privy to old wartime jokes, this was supposed to be the result of passing a bad message over the radio. It had originally been – 'Send reinforcements, we're going to advance.' 294 Squadron recorded something similar on 22 November 1943.

Various conflicting reports were received over the telephone from 16 SOR, Navy House, in Derna (on the Libyan coast), and from the Town Major at Derna, to the effect that:
1. Two men were stranded off-shore in a schooner.
2. Two men were stranded off-shore on a raft.
3. Two men were being blown out to sea in a bathtub!

Navy House, Derna, subsequently advised the Squadron that it appeared that two army men had been washed out to sea in a bathtub by an off-shore wind. They had been rescued by someone in a rowing boat going out to them, and that no search and rescue mission needed to be launched by the Squadron.

What is not recorded is why the men were in the sea in a bathtub in the first place (were they taking a bath?) and why, as soon as they found themselves going out, did they not pull the plug!?

No Luck

Aircraft of 3 Squadron SAAF flew convoy escorts and scrambles on 28 November. A ship in convoy *Nettle* was torpedoed and damaged eight miles north of Ras Aamer at 12.50 and the Squadron were called to help. Captain Geldenhuys took off at 13.15 to direct an ASR Walrus to five sailors who had been blown off the ship by the explosion. He located four men, struggling in the water, waving for help. The Walrus returned at 17.00, the whole squadron turning out to welcome the sailors, but sadly none had been picked up, either because of the poor conditions or they had been rescued by the convoy.

Coincidences

The year of 1943 came to a close with two more Walrus rescues by 284 Squadron. Holmes and Bradley (W3012) landed and picked up Lieutenant Ken Hall of 4 Squadron SAAF on the afternoon of 22 December, returning him to Trigno. He had been eight miles east of Francavilla al Mare, south of Pescara, on the Italian east coast.

Flying on a bomb-line patrol, 1 SAAF Squadron, having received a call, detached a section to help with the search. The two Spitfires, led by Major J M Faure DFC, found a pilot floating in his Mae West off the Sangria River mouth. They orbited him until a rowing boat put out and picked him up. Another section meantime found a pilot (Hall this time) in his dinghy six miles north of Ortona and orbited him until the Walrus landed and picked him up. This was the first day 4 Squadron had operated from its new base at Trigno, and returning Hall to this landing ground, he was still 'blue with cold'.

Warrant Officers Ken Hall and M D Kelly (X9506) rescued 2nd Lieutenant Kelly, a fighter pilot from the 523rd Fighter Squadron, 27th FG, on the 30th. They had been in a fight with Messerschmitts and Kelly had wound up in the 'drink'. It was, of course, pure coincidence that a Kelly should rescue a Kelly, and so easily could a Ken Hall have picked up another Ken Hall a few days earlier.

The year ended with the Squadron's HQ and A Flight at Brindisi, B Flight at Capodichino, near Naples and C Flight at Cutella, near Pescara. In fact, the rescue on the 22nd had been the first success of the new C Flight. Thus A Flight could cover areas to the Albanian coastal areas, C Flight out over the Adriatic, while B Flight, on the other side of Italy, operated out over the Tyrrhenian Sea.

283 Squadron had now moved to Corsica, and the airfield at Ajaccio and Borgo. Ajaccio on the west side could cover the area west and north towards southern France, while Borgo on the east coast covered areas east and north-east towards the Italian coast.

Awards to aircrew of 283 at this time were the DFC for Tony Morabito and DFM for Colin Horne on 1 December 1943.

Notes from the Logbooks

The theme of this book, of course, is of successful rescues, many with individual adventures, courageous actions, and the like. However, interspersed with these for all Walrus aircrew were those missions which did not produce happy endings, or where 'customers' were picked up by HSLs. I was fortunate in being able to examine two logbooks, belonging to Lisle Newman and the late Bill Lambert, and have access to copies of those of Hamish Reid and Arnold Divers.

To illustrate unhappy endings, the following entries are noted:

1 June 1943	Search Cap Drek, 5 miles. Nothing seen but bodies.
11 June 1943	Search for Wellington Pantelleria 210°. Nothing seen.
22 June 1943	Search 008° La Sebala, 66½ miles. Nothing seen. Wrong distance given by control.
26 June 1943	Search. Nothing seen except yellow boxes, believed to be cause of call.
27 June 1943	Search for survivors of blazing ship, SE of Cap Metafusa, 10 miles. No survivors seen. Wreck almost burnt out.
2 July 1943	Seach for Warhawk pilot. No definite fix. Ribbon search 080-030°. Cap Bon, 46 miles. Only 1 mine and 1 petrol tank seen.
15 July 1943	Search 10 miles west Sembala for half barge – found bows, no bodies.
16 July 1943	Search. Nothing seen except belly tank.
18 July 1943	Search for dinghy 013° from Bizerta. No joy. Found body in Mae West which was picked up by HSL.
19 July 1943	Search 095°, 80 miles. Nothing seen except boxes, body, and 2 sharks.
3 August 1943	Search. 1 dead body 070° Palermo, 10 miles. Only wreckage seen.
6 August 1943	Mayday; search NNE of Bizerta 7 miles – no joy.
12 August 1943	Search 3749N/1023E. No joy.
15 August 1943	Empty lifeboat found.
5 September 1943	Found pilot 2 miles N of Tropea but sea too rough to land (12′ swell). Dropped supplies and arranged for HSL which picked him up later.
14 February 1944	Dinghy and pilot found but HSL only 1 mile away so becoming benevolent in my old age gave it to them on a platter. Still, I may get credit for it as we saw him first.
16 May 1944	Found dead body in position so left it to HSL.

Failing to find anything – anyone – truly gave *no joy* to the Walrus crews. Had they missed seeing anyone? Were they in the right area? More than likely there was no one to see or find. A well-known motto – "The Sea Shall Not Have Them" – was a worthy ideal to aim for, but the sea itself often had other ideas.

Chapter 4

ITALY AND CORSICA 1944

With the campaign in Italy now well on its way north, the rescue squadrons had two major seas over which to operate. The Tyrrhenian Sea to the west of the mainland, which stretched north from Sicily to Sardinia and Corsica, and the Adriatic to the east, with Italy on one side and Yugoslavia on the other. Of these, 283 Squadron operated mainly over the west, while 284 operated to the east.

At Bone, 293 were still working up, and the experienced Denny Lunn DFM, Norm Pickles and Colin Horne DFM were posted to this unit, along with Flight Sergeant Ted Holmes and Jack Berry DFM, but not before the latter had recorded their first rescue of the New Year.

January 30th saw 12 Kittyhawk IVs of 450 Squadron RAAF, led by Squadron Leader K R Sands, and escorted by Spitfires, fly out to attack shipping in Zada Harbour, Yugoslavia. A Siebel ferry was observed moving south, was bombed but missed, then the two top sections bombed two stationery schooners. One direct hit was scored on one of them, while aircraft also strafed a tug, which was left smoking. One pilot dropped his bombs on a beached naval vessel, hit it, and the tug alongside it was set on fire.

Lieutenant L Sauer, a South African, reported over the R/T that his aircraft had been hit by ground fire and he was losing engine power. He nursed his crippled fighter (FT954) towards home but half way across the Adriatic he had to bale out from 3,500 feet, hitting the tail with his right thigh as he did so. Safely down and in his dinghy, other pilots reported his position and Flight Lieutenant C W Robertson DFC remained over him until some Spitfires arrived to relieve him.

Holmes and Berry were scrambled from Cutella at 11.30 in P5718, given the position at 80-100 miles out. Despite a difficult thick haze up to 1,500 feet, Holmes made rendezvous with two Spitfire escorts and upon reaching the area saw a Spitfire circling an oil patch and a dinghy. Within minutes the South African was safely aboard and Holmes was taking off, and landed back at 13.40. Ted Holmes was awarded the DFM during February.

Lieutenant Sauer was able to return a couple of weeks later after his leg improved and went on to complete an operational tour of 191 hours on ops, as at 1 July.

On the last day of January 1944, news arrived that Flight Sergeant Arnold Divers of 283 Squadron had received the DFM. Then in February it was

announced that Norman Pickles of 284 had been awarded the DFC for his part
in various rescues including that of John Beatson in December, during which he
was wounded in one arm.

Reorganisation

Things went a bit quiet for the Walrus rescue boys now and at the beginning of
March there was something of a reorganisation in this theatre of operations.
Although 293 had been formed in England, the whole Middle East ASR set-up
had started to be reorganised following the conclusion of the Sicilian campaign.
Mediterranean Air Command wished to base two ASR Flights in North Africa
and one in Sicily, whilst one was required at the eastern end of the
Mediterranean. Accordingly, at the end of July 1943, authority had been sought
for the formation of four ASR squadrons from the existing two – each to be a
composite of landplanes and amphibians.

On 30 August 283 and 284 Squadrons were split to provide two additional
units, 293 and 294, all four squadrons to be formed to an establishment of eight
Warwicks and three Walruses. Shortly afterwards the total Walrus establishment
was raised to 20 by giving each squadron a reserve of two more amphibians i.e.
five each. In the event, the Warwick would be delayed due to some technical
defects, and did not start to arrive till late September 1943. The ME ASR Flight
became 294 Squadron at Berka on 24 September.

Now, in early 1944, 284 Squadron suddenly lost all its Walrus aircraft and
crews, who moved to 283 Squadron, together with all its motor transport. 284
re-equipped with Vickers Warwick twin-engined aircraft, under the command of
Squadron Leader J S Barnett. Flight Lieutenant Reg Hayes, hitherto in command
of 284, was sent to 293 Squadron to command one of its detachments. Then on
22 March, Flight Lieutenant R B Crampton RAAF, the flight commander of 283
Squadron at Alghero, Sardinia, was told that the squadron was changing to
Warwicks, and he was promoted to squadron leader. Finally in April, all Walrus
aircraft were transferred to 293 Squadron, although some appear to have been
returned to 284.

The arrival of the Warwick was a natural enough progression for the rescue
squadron service that was operating over large expanses of water. As had been
found around Britain, where distances were great – away from the English
Channel and southern North Sea areas for instance – a long-range aircraft could
cover more ground for longer, and faster. They could also carry radar to help
locate downed airmen. Twin-engined aircraft such as the Avro Anson and
Lockheed Hudson had already proved their worth in these circumstances. In
England, 269, 280, 281 and 282 Squadrons had all flown long hours over the sea
in search of the missing and those they had found had been mostly rescued by
High Speed Launches, while the aircraft generally had the endurance to remain
over the downed airmen till the boats arrived. They were also being equipped
with the Lindholme lifeboat, of which more later. Some American rescue units
had perhaps the best idea, as they used Catalina flying-boats that could land on
the water and take on board large numbers of survivors, although they did
present big targets for hostile fighters or coastal gun batteries.

However, there was still very much a case for using the Walrus (and Sea

Otter flying boats in the UK). It was of little use for a landplane such as the Warwick to locate men in the water, if they had no immediate – that is quick – way of getting to them. Speed was the essence as cold and exposure killed, sometimes in minutes. Knowing where they were was one thing, getting them out of the water quickly was another. Chances of survival were reduced if it took too long for a boat to arrive. There were no end of stories about races between a Walrus and a launch to get to airmen first. It was competitive stuff, but with a deadly serious side to it. By and large the Walrus, due to it being an aeroplane, got to the target first, and sometimes the HSLs were a bit reluctant to go too near a hostile coast where they might be subject to enemy gunfire a good bit longer than an aircraft.

The whole philosophy of the Walrus crews was to get the men out of the water as quickly as possible, even if they were unable to take off again. A man's chances of survival was increased 1,000 times once aboard a Walrus, with hot drinks, warm blankets or even clothes, and strong hands rubbing warmth and feeling back into the circulatory system of the body. 284 soon had a Walrus detachment back which co-operated with their bigger brothers, the Warwicks.

The First Beagle Squadron Man Rescued

Two new names appeared on the list of successful Walrus crews of 283 Squadron on the third day of March 1944 – Warrant Officers V L Prosser, an Australian, and J V Botting, operating in Z1784. They rescued an American fighter pilot from the 2nd Fighter Squadron (known as the Beagles), 52nd Fighter Group – Lieutenant James A Adams. The group was equipped with British Spitfire fighters:

I was Blue 2 of a four-plane section escorting forty-eight B.26s on a bombing mission over Italy. We took off from Borgo-Biguglia airstrip at 10.40 hours and climbed to 15,000 feet as top cover. As we approached the Italian coast, about 20 miles west-south-west of Cape Santa Marinella, my engine became slightly rough. I had noticed that the engine tended to load up, so I thought nothing of it and started to clear it by using full throttle. But the engine suddenly quit, then caught and quit again. This sequence happened about three times, then the engine quit completely.

When this had begun I had called Blue 1 (Lieutenant Ed 'Chick' Fuller) and told him I was going home and I heard him tell Blue 4 to go with me. Before I could turn, the engine stopped and I told Blue 1. He told me to glide down to about 5,000 feet and then bale out, but not to try ditching.

As I was gliding down, with Blue 4 following, I called the Controller and gave him a fix when I was at about 12,000 feet. Then I tried to drop the belly tank but it would not release. At 7,000 feet I called my escort and told him I was switching to Channel-D and that he should too. With Blue 4 now giving fixes I released my harness, rolled the trim-wheel forward and tried to roll the Spitfire over so that I would fall out, but it would not roll because of its slow speed – about 100 mph – and because I still had on the nearly full 90-gallon belly drop-tank.

At about 4,000 feet I gave the stick a hard push forward and was thrown clear of the aircraft, bashing one knee on the windscreen as I went out. I was going down headfirst when I pulled the rip-cord and the parachute opened immediately. As I drifted down I blew a little air into my Mae West and just before I hit the water I turned the parachute release. Just as I hit the sea I pushed the release button and the 'chute floated away to one side. However, the leg strap catch did not release for a few seconds, and since I was now under water, I had some difficulty releasing it. I went into the water at about 11.20, some 25 miles off Civitavecchia [situated some way north of Rome].

My dinghy was still attached to the parachute pack and it took me a few seconds to separate them under water. I finally took the dinghy out of its pack as far as I could, pulled the pin on the CO_2 bottle and gave the knob a twist. The sudden expansion of the confined dinghy caused it to burst, tearing a two-foot gash in it. Then I took out the hand pump, thinking that I might be able to tie the dinghy in the middle and inflate the good half, but the pump was entangled to the cord used to attach it to the dinghy.

I gave up with the dinghy, blew some more air into the Mae West and rolled onto my back. Blue 4 was still circling and about half an hour later he was relieved by two more Spitfires. Chick Fuller had also circled and dropped his own dinghy to me, but I didn't see where it went because of the high seas. At about 12.30 I saw the Walrus approaching. It circled me for about five minutes and then dropped a smoke pot about 50 yards from me, circled for a few minutes more, landed and taxied directly towards me. As it passed me I grabbed the starboard wheel and held on. The Walrus stopped and the two crew pulled me into it.

The sea was pretty rough, with a swell of about ten feet from trough to crest and the Walrus had now to taxi out to sea because we were being shelled by coastal batteries and could not take off in the high seas.

Although I do not remember how far it had to taxi, when the pilot finally tried to take-off, the right wing float stove in and, according to the pilot, he had to continue the take off or risk swamping. He did get off despite those waves and when we landed Dan Zoerb [who had been in the relieving Spitfire] was there to take a picture of me being helped out of it.

Lieutenant J A Adams, 2nd FS, 52nd FG

Lieutenant Dan Zoerb later wrote his report of the rescue:

Two of us were sent to continue the cover for Junior Adams. We had the two old 'co crew-chiefs' Spits. The other plane got about half way to the cover area when it had to return to base belching smoke and threatening to pack it in. My clunker had a 90-gallon drop tank attached but with no fuel in it. I took up the cover patrol but when my fuel began to get low I thought I might have to leave before the Walrus arrived. I decided to drop the empty tank before leaving so it could be used as a float and a position marker for Adams.

I began a run to drop the tank but then I saw the Walrus approaching so I started back without dropping it. The way Adams' luck had been running that day, I probably would have 'dead-centred' him with that monster tank.

In the summer of 1944 Junior Adams had a newspaper article written about him following the award of the American DFC (he already had an Air Medal with 11 oak leaf clusters, and a Purple Heart), whilst visiting his mother in Urbana, Illinois. While the article was mainly about him and three pals battling 14 German aircraft and downing 12 of them, he diverted attention by singing the praises of the RAF Walrus men who had rescued him in March:

"Those boys will go anywhere, even to an enemy-controlled beach, to save a man", he declared. "All they ask is air cover while they're doing their job. But these fellows never get a line of credit," he added with regret, "because they are not a combat unit."

Adams spoke his words of praise with the conviction born of a life and death experience, for he was severely cut on the legs as he baled out after his plane motor had stalled as he was flying an escort for a convoy of ships, and he was in rough water, supported only by a 'Mae West' life preserver, for an hour and a half before being picked up. He might have had a more comfortable stay in the sea had he not burst a dinghy when he became "a little excited" trying to inflate the rubber boat.

After the rescue, the crew of the Walrus managed a take-off at the price of a badly battered plane. "When a take-off is impossible, because of rough seas or a heavy load of survivors," Adams added, "the crews will taxi the ships to land, sometimes as much as 100 miles, with no thought of the danger to themselves or the planes."

Now 22, and a veteran of 186 pursuit pilot missions, the lieutenant began training as an aviation cadet on January 23, 1942, his 20th birthday, after completing a year in the UI college of engineering. He was employed for a year at Chanute Field while awaiting his call.

'Junior' Adams, from Bloomington, Illinois, who'd married in October 1942, had fought in the Tunisian campaign before his squadron had moved to Corsica. As the article had mentioned, he went on to fly a total of 186 combat missions, shoot down 4½ German fighters (plus two more which were unconfirmed), flying both Spitfires and later Mustangs. He retired from the USAF as a Lieutenant-Colonel after 28 years service, having meanwhile, topped 10,000 flying hours.

* * *

Four days after the Adams rescue, this time in W2788, Prosser and Botting hauled out another 52nd Fighter Group pilot, Lieutenant H S Montgomery of the 4th Squadron, but on this occasion the sea proved to be nice and calm. This was the second time he'd been rescued (see p.42).

The Future Ace

Hamish Reid and Warrant Officer J Bradley also made a successful rescue on 7 March, which involved a landing very close to the enemy, in Walrus Z1779, as Hamish recalls:

> We flew to a spot 20 miles north of the Voltorno River and a mile off shore. This was to find 1st Lieutenant Harmeyer, an American who was tangled up in his 'chute, so 'Brad' had to go over the side to cut him free. I eventually managed to pull them both back out of the water, and in through the back hatch. We had four Spitfires as close escort, which were, meantime, beating up the shore to keep the Germans' heads down. We were 16 minutes on the water, so our bottoms were twitching quite a bit!
>
> The Yank had been in the water for 45 minutes, but this shows the excellent co-operation we had with the Spitfire boys; they were really first class when we needed them. We would much rather have two or four Spitfires with us when picking up anyone beyond the front lines or near to the shore.
>
> Sometimes the American squadrons were not so keen to go in close with us, in fact, the best American squadron, was the Negro unit [the 332nd Fighter Group].
>
> Flight Sergeant J A Reid, 283 Squadron

1st Lieutenant Raymond F Harmeyer was a Spitfire pilot flying with the US 31st Fighter Group, which he had joined in October 1943. He came from New Orleans, Louisiana, and was 23 years old. Before his death in 1992, Ray Harmeyer told me:

> Shortly after take-off in mid-morning, the engine of my Spit IX failed and I could not get it re-started. We were over the water by this time, the Gulf of Gaeta, and I elected to bale out rather than ditch. As I landed in the sea, a brisk wind caused the parachute to skip along the surface, dragging me along behind it. 'Motor-boating' I believe it was called. After having difficulty with the quick-release feature on the harness, I spilled the whole 'chute by pulling on the lower risers to collapse the canopy. It worked only too well, for everything stopped – the canopy and the risers – all hopelessly entangled.
>
> My fellow pilots remained overhead until the Walrus arrived, but I don't remember how long it took. I was well chilled, completely water-logged and totally exhausted, but managed to wrap my arms around the port-side hull to wing strut and refused to leave it to paddle over to the forward hatch where two RAF guys – God bless 'em – were waiting to drag me aboard.
>
> Deducing my plight, one of them unhesitatingly jumped into that cold water and swam over to cut me free of the tentacular mess of shroud lines in which I was enmeshed. Because of my water-soaked weight, the chap in the water left me hanging on while his buddy helped him up into the

rear hatch, after which the two of them were able to lift my dead-weight (almost literally true) aboard. Those fine young men saved my ass! Thanks fellows.

Lieutenant R F Harmeyer, 309th FS, 31st FG

Ray Harmeyer returned to his squadron, which re-equipped with P.51 Mustangs in April 1944. He already had two kills on Spitfires, and by the end of his tour of duty, in May, had shot down a total of six enemy aircraft (four Me109s and two FW190s), with another probably destroyed and four more damaged. He later flew during the Korean War and served in the Louisiana and Colorado Air National Guard. His decorations included the Silver Star, two DFCs and the Air Medal with 19 oak leaf clusters.

Once back safely, Ray Harmeyer wrote up his experience in his diary:

March 8, 1944
My luck seems to be running out, and with a vengeance, for I pranged my first aircraft yesterday and damn near bought it. We had just taken off for a beach-head patrol and were a few miles out over the Gulf of Gaeta when my engine cut cold. I turned towards the beach and tried to restart the engine but in vain, so, rather than land in the water, I baled out. As I fell out of the ship, I was spinning end over end and as I pulled the rip-cord I saw the 'chute rush out past my feet. I jumped at 800-1,000 feet and was in the water before I had time to collect my senses, so didn't release the harness in time and was dragged along by the 'chute, swallowing gallons of water, some way before I spilled it. I then got out of the harness, inflated my Mae West, and succeeded in getting nicely entangled in the shroud lines, and as the parachute started to sink it dragged me lower in the water. By this time I was so short of breath that I couldn't duck under the water in order to reach my dinghy, which was tantalizingly bumping against my feet. I laboriously dug my knife out of an inside pocket, and tried to cut the risers that connected me to the 'chute, but gave it up after a while for I succeeded only in swallowing more water. My wingman, Jack Williams, had followed me down, and as I knew that he had notified the controller, I settled back to float and wait for the RAF Air Sea Rescue Walrus. My Mae West, as I learned later, had a leak in it as eventually the air all leaked out and it was only the kapok stuffing that kept me afloat, and barely so, for by the time the Walrus arrived, I was so exhausted and so low in the water that another five minutes would have finished me.

I was a sheer dead weight so the two RAF boys had a great deal of trouble loading me aboard, but in due time they deposited me at Capodichino airdrome in a semi-conscious state.

The water was freezing cold, and my hat is off to the [RAF] observer who didn't hesitate about jumping in to help me aboard. Those boys are wonderful. At the hospital, I shook for about 45 minutes, had a splitting headache and awful cramps in my stomach and legs, but within an hour I was felling pretty fit, except for the headache. I stayed overnight in the hospital, and returned to the squadron today, but will be grounded for a few days with stopped-up ears.

Ray's diary had little mottos and sayings printed on the bottom of each page. When writing the above, the saying on the bottom of one page, amusingly, was: *Paddle your own canoe, – F Marryat.* Ray would have liked the chance!

Another pilot flying with the squadron was Lieutenant John E Fawcett. He knew Ray Harmeyer as well as anyone, and once told me:

Ray Harmeyer was a friend of mine in 309 Squadron, and in fact he was my wingman for a time during that winter of 1943-44. I like to think that I helped him get started on the reputation he gained as one helluva fine fighter pilot, who came home in the summer of 1944 as an ace with six victories.

He was my wingman on the morning of February 13th over Anzio when two FW190s, flying in line abreast, cruised right under us a thousand feet below, as though they were on a sightseeing flight!

I called the break and we rolled upside down and went storming down behind them. In the process, Harmeyer, who was on my left, got about a hundred yards or so ahead of me. As we got close he turned slightly to the right in front of me, and got off a snap shot at the right hand target which immediately blew up in a great splash of black smoke, flame and scrap aluminium, which it seemed to me then, that I flew right through!

Harmeyer then immediately turned left and got off a burst at the other 190 which took fire and went down twisting and smoking, and then seen to go straight in. You can imagine my frustration in not getting one of those for myself, but the fact is Harmeyer did exactly what a sharp fighter pilot should do. They were right in front of him, I was lagging behind, so he shot them both down within about ten seconds. I was in a few air battles that winter, but never a 'turkey shoot' like that one.

Lieutenant John E Fawcett, 309th FS, 31st FG

Perhaps as a slight diversion, I can record a poem written by Ray Harmeyer at the stage, back in November 1943, he was wanting to move from the Spitfire V to the Spitfire IX. He wrote it to his B Flight Commander, 1st Lieutenant Louis A Griffing (although Ray put on the letter that it came from: '1st Lt Herman A Goebbels, Peninsular Base Sect, Way Behind the Lines'.

The B-Flight Blues

Now looka', Griff, and please heed my plea,
For I want a favor that's dear to me.
I know you'll kick and raise a fuss,
But 'till it's granted I'll be fit to bust.
So listen well and pay some mind
To the question, "When can I fly the Nine?"

Mark Five I'm called, in a spirit of jest,
But the Nine's the baby I love best,
For I figger I can't stay long alive
When I push the tit and get 285,
So I won't prang it, I'll be gentle and kind,
So how's about checking out in the Nine?

I don't necessarily want to fly it to Rome,
I'd just like to play around in it here at home.
If Lard-ass and Stech can make it around,
Why, brother, anybody can get 'em off the ground.
So unlock your heart and open your mind,
And give the new boys a chance to fly the Mark Nine.

Someone did not let the missive pass without comment, and even made a reply in rhyme:

OK, Hoiman, but first of all,
You've got to get on the fucking ball.
You've got to stop drinking that fucking wine,
Before you check out in the glorious Nine.

And it worked. A couple of days later, John Fawcett checked him out on the Nine, and as John says – "He was a damn good pilot."

* * *

Under Gunfire and the Beagles Come to the Rescue
The very next day, Wednesday 8 March 1944, Arnold Divers continued his extraordinary period with 283 Squadron, and flying with Warrant Officer P M H Graham, in the same Walrus – W2788 – rescued an injured fighter pilot off the island of Napoleon fame – Elba.

Flying Officer J W Munro RCAF of 253 Squadron had been flying wingman to Flight Lieutenant A W Watson on a sea recce mission to Elba but his Spitfire (MA691) was hit by flak and he was forced to bale out. For some reason his dinghy failed, and 'Duke' Munro was only in his Mae West, while the Germans on Elba were not helping matters by firing 88 mm salvoes as the Walrus came in to pick him up. The following account of the rescue appeared in *Mare Nostrum*, a magazine issued by MACAF (Mediterranean Allied Coastal Air Force), on 16 March.

AIR SEA RESCUE UNDER FIRE
On the 8th March the pilot of a Spitfire of 253 Squadron (F/O Munro) was forced to bale out after his aircraft had been hit by flak. He landed in the sea north of Elba, about five miles north of Porto Ferraio.
At 08.05 hours an oil patch and fluorescence was seen 10 miles south-west of the given position (42.53N/10.24E) and also a man in a Mae

West. After dropping a smoke bomb alongside the man, the Walrus landed on the sea which was rough. The engine then cut. It was restarted and the Walrus taxied up to F/O Munro who was exhausted. Whilst dragging him into position in the Walrus for take-off, the shore batteries near Marciana commenced firing salvoes of four shells each at approximately 40 second intervals.

The Walrus attempted to take off, but owing to shrapnel in the engine was unable to get sufficient revolutions. In the words of the report: "Evasive action was taken." The engine, the mainplane and the hull received further hits. Three blades of the airscrew were shot away, and rudder control severed. The pilot tried to cut the engine but was only successful after switching off the petrol and placing the mixture control in the weak position. One flame float exploded on its own due to the excessive bouncing of the Walrus.

It was decided to abandon the Walrus and the pilot fired two star red Very cartridges in the hope that the firing would cease. This produced the desired effect.

W/O Graham then destroyed the remaining serviceable equipment, inflated the M-type dinghy into which he dragged F/O Munro from the back hatch. W/O Divers destroyed the maps and inflated a K-type dinghy loading it with rations, a Very pistol and cartridges. They made F/O Munro as comfortable as possible, giving him water and rubbing his limbs to bring back the circulation. They then drifted away from the Walrus.

At 10.55 an HSL was sighted approaching from the west. The shore batteries thereupon commenced firing further salvoes of four. It is reported that they were firing 88 and 105 mm guns and that the fire was intense and accurate.

No damage was inflicted on the launch and all three in the dinghies were soon safely aboard.

Escorting fighters destroyed the damaged Walrus.

One of the two escorting pilots, in their P.39N Airacobras, was Lieutenant James J Hudson, who in later life became a well-known aviation historian and writer. In fact he was then known as Professor Hudson, and a graduate of the University of Arkansas. In early 1944 he was with the 345th Fighter Squadron, 350th FG, and his wartime service covered 191 combat missions in P.38s, P.39s and P.47s. In September 1977 he wrote an article about the P.39 in Europe, and mentions the above episode:

On two occasions in particular I had opportunity to witness the destructive power of the [Airacobra's] cannon. The first was 8 March 1944 when two of us flying P.39Ns acted as escort for an RAF Air Sea Rescue boat engaged in an effort to pick up the crew from a disabled Walrus flying-boat a few hundred yards off the island of Elba. Despite heavy coastal gunfire, the rescue was made without casualty. However, when it appeared that the Germans were attempting to seize the British plane, we were ordered to destroy it. I remember hitting the Walrus with a single 37 mm round from approximately 400 yards and was startled to see the seaplane blow up in a cloud of flames and smoke.

The Germans didn't get away with this, for also covering the rescue was the same 2nd Squadron of the 52nd Fighter Group to which Junior Adams belonged. Seeing what was going on, Captain James W Bickford led his section down and gave the guns a good working over. The 2nd Squadron of course, shared the airfield with 283 Squadron and more than appreciated their work. Arnold Divers also remembers:

What the report does not retell is the experience of being in a dinghy and the target of 88 and 105 mm shore batteries only about two miles away. We were target practice for what seemed hours until their attention was attracted by the HSL on its way to rescue us. The enemy fire was indeed intense and very accurate. Although I do feel that their first shots which shattered the propeller and hit the engine when we were in full flight about 50 feet above the sea after taking off with Munro on board was surely sheer luck on their part.

After scrambling aboard the rescue launch and still under fire, one of the three engines was spluttering and giving trouble. I was full of admiration for the mechanic in charge who with a screwdriver and hammer, nursed the faulty engine into full power to get us at great haste outside the range of the guns, and back safely to Bastia on Corsica.

I was not surprised later to learn the commander of the HSL was awarded the DSC but full marks to the coxswain for his DSM[1] and his uncanny anticipation in avoiding the accurate fire from the enemy shore. The large rum ration dished out after we got out of range was most welcome. Hard on the 'shakes' but warming to the empty stomach.

The rescue launch had been HSL 2543, a Miami Class launch based at Bastia, commanded by Flying Officer Jack Rogers, of 254 ASR MCU, and his newly formed crew. Their report stated:

. . . called to assist Walrus, which had been damaged by enemy shellfire about seven miles off north coast of Elba Island, whilst rescuing a Spitfire pilot. Rogers brought his boat in and within range of heavy coastal batteries on Elba, which opened fire on HSL. For next 30 minutes he manoeuvred towards the aircrew who were drifting in their dinghy and despite intense and accurate bombardment from the shore, succeeded in bringing three men on board and returned to Bastia. Pilots of escorting aircraft said they could not believe the HSL would survive the shelling. Rogers has previously completed many sorties in the English Channel and on African coast. The HSL had several near misses but was

---

[1] Corporal Eric Parham was the man at the wheel who received the Distinguished Service Medal, and the wireless operator had been Jack Hill, who, along with the rest of the crew, received commendations.

undamaged. Shore batteries opened fire at 11.05 – first salvo falling short; fire continued until HSL was out of range at 11.25.

In the earlier, January 1944 issue of *Mare Nostrum*, it was Rogers' story that featured, under the title of "Who's Afeard? – ASR Pick-Up in Teeth of Enemy Guns."

"They've got him! They've got him! They've [expletive] got him!" Circling above a Royal Air Force high speed rescue launch off the Italian coast, a Spitfire pilot gave this dramatic running commentary. Back at base, senior officers and AC2s alike waited anxiously for developments in this rare report by an eyewitness, and almost cheered when the tension was over.

Below the aircraft, the high speed launch weaved her way through plumes of water flung high by enemy shells. At last, shaking herself free from the clouds of spray, which at times completely obliterated her from the observer circling above, the launch leaped on to carry out one of the most heroic rescues of the war.

HOW HE GOT IT

This is the story behind the award of the DSC to Flying Officer 'Jack' Rogers, skipper of an ASR launch. The medal is a naval decoration, and although its award to a member of the RAF is not unique, it is a rare distinction.

The story begins on a blue March morning. A cold wind whipped whitecaps onto a disturbed sea. The air was clear, and from the north of Corsica the islands of Pianosa and Elba could be seen melting hazily into the horizon.

Out there, a Spitfire pilot had sent an SOS and then baled out. It was calculated that he must be in the icy water not far from the enemy coast.

A RED PENNANT

A Walrus went out first to try to locate him, followed closely by the high speed launch, of which Flying Officer Rogers was master. Fluttering on the bridge was the mascot, a red pennant bearing the Dorsetshire coat of arms and the motto "Who's Afeard?"

For'ard of the wheelhouse the decks were wet with foam, flung up as they ploughed through the waves at nearly 30 knots. Within a few minutes they received word that the pilot of the Spitfire had been found. The Walrus had landed and got him on board. For those on the launch it looked like one of those happily abortive trips.

SHORE BATTERIES

Then came another message. Shore batteries had opened fire as the Walrus was taxying to take off with the rescued airmen aboard. The Walrus had been hit – first in the screw [propeller], later in one of the mainplanes. With their aircraft crippled, the crew had sent out an SOS and taken to the dinghy, and for the second time within a few minutes the Spitfire pilot found himself again waiting for help.

More messages came, warning Flying Officer Rogers of the danger from shore batteries, and telling him from which quarter that danger was most likely to come. Above, American and British fighters took up escort. The high speed launch kept her course. The barren coast of Elba slipped by on the starboard beam.

Flying Officer Rogers was on the bridge, scanning the arc of sea ahead. They drew abreast of Porto Ferrajo, and then, just as they left it behind, there was a white puff in the water – a marking shot. Almost instantly it was followed by a salvo of five shells which burst dangerously near the craft.

SITTING TARGET

"We were a sitting target at that time", said Flying Officer Rogers. "We were simply cruising along on a straight and steady course. I felt that as they had not got us then they hadn't a cat in hell's chance."

Flying Officer Rogers gave the order, "Full speed ahead". Then, standing on the bridge, he watched the shells burst around him, and gave directions to the coxswain for a zig-zag course. The crippled Walrus came into sight, and gradually, by devious route, the high speed launch closed with it. Regardless of the fact that the Germans had obviously got the range of the aircraft, Flying Officer Rogers took his boat close in, and was preparing to go alongside, when the three airmen from the Walrus were spotted in a dinghy a short distance away.

Shells were still falling as the boat hove to, and a line was thrown out. Within a few seconds the airmen had clambered up the crash net, and seven minutes after the shelling had first started the launch turned for home, still under fire.

MESSAGE TO BASE

Before setting course, Flying Officer Rogers sent a message to base asking whether he should attempt to take the Walrus in tow. This would have meant remaining stationary under the muzzles of the enemy guns until lines had been made fast, and then setting a slow and straight course along the hostile coast. It was doubtful in any event, in the opinion of the aircrew, whether the whole plane would remain afloat much longer. Flying Officer Rogers was ordered by base not to make the attempt to tow it home.

It was about this time that the launch had its closest call. A salvo dropped just astern. To the observer overhead it looked like a direct hit – the launch just vanished in a wall of water. And afterwards the nursing orderly who had been on the companion way from the ship's 'hospital', vowed that he had got his face wet.

Flying Officer Rogers, in common with most of the RAF's old sailors, clings tenaciously to a tradition of silence comparable with that of the Senior Service. He had little to say about his exploit beyond praising the American and British airmen who escorted him.

WONDERFUL COVER

"They gave us wonderful cover", he said. "They didn't succeed in silencing the gun posts, but they did everything they possibly could in the attempt. Others remained over us, so that we had no fear of being jumped by enemy fighters. All we had to think of was the routine job of picking up the fellows in the dinghy."

When Flying Officer Rogers reached port just five minutes late on his ETA, an anxious knot of servicemen was awaiting him on the quay. They were surprised to find that the craft showed no signs of damage, although it had been under fire continuously for twenty minutes.

"It stood up wonderfully well, although the underwater battering must have been pretty terrific", said Flying Officer Rogers. "The only damage it did suffer was strain on the engines. I went in at full speed ahead, and came out after the pick-up even faster, if that is possible. The fitters who examined the boat afterwards asked me if I had been hitting the pistons with a hammer."[2]

OTHER RESCUES

Many tales could be told by the men of the ASR launches of rescues regardless of enemy aircraft, guns and minefields. Flight Sergeant Crouch, who is now Cox of Flying Officer Rogers' craft, was on one occasion strafed by Me109s.

The first burst hit a turret and tore the gun from the gunner's hands. The medical orderly was hit. Corporal C H J Gibb, wireless operator mechanic, looked out of his 'office' and saw, ". . . pieces of the ship flying around."

The steel deck curled up as a petrol tank below exploded and burst into flames. The after turret was hit and blown clean out into the sea. While some of the crew tended the injured, others fought the fire, and then turned to the job of patching up the riddled hull with wooden plugs. All three engines were out of action, but they managed to patch one up, and later got a second running.

LIMPED FOR HOME

For four hours they limped in the direction of home – the Anzio beach-head – all the time working frantically on the pumps. Finally the water got the better of them, and when they were only a mile and a half from base it rushed into the engine room and stopped the engines.

It was close on midnight, but fortunately their distress signals were seen and a sub-chaser picked them up. The boat was salvaged and is still in service in the Mediterranean. On another occasion a mine exploded near a rescue launch. A spout of water was flung up 80 or 90 feet.

UNDER OWN POWER

So violent was the concussion that the engines leaped out of their bearers. But they still kept turning, and the launch made port under her own power.

---

[2] As Arnold Divers mentioned, the engine pistons had indeed been hit with a hammer!!

Another skipper, Flying Officer R Ross-Watt, made a pick-up one and a half miles from the heavily defended port of Leghorn. "We set off just after breakfast, and thought it was going to be our last one", he said. "But nothing happened. The Jerries must have had something else to think about. They didn't even sling a rock at us."

The rescued man had been adrift, injured, in a dinghy for 27 hours and was practically resigned to being taken prisoner when he was snatched from under the enemy's nose. Now, thanks to the ASR service, he is flying again with a fighter squadron.

This was the third time Arnold Divers had been in such straits as this, having had to be towed to safety on 3 July 1943, then having to abandon his Walrus on 3 November. We shall meet Jack Rogers again, assisting in a 284 Squadron rescue in April 1944.

* * *

The third rescue for 283 in three days followed on the 9th (March), when Flying Officer Mears and another pilot, Flight Sergeant C I A Paterson, with Flight Sergeant Eric Keeble in the back (X3079) fished out a French pilot, Adjutant Jean Doudies, of 2/7 Groupe de Chasse, based at Ajaccio. It proved to be another rough-sea job and the two crewmen had to pump water from the Walrus before Mears could take off, having meantime, taxied to some calmer water. Paterson and Keeble were themselves about to become a successful Walrus team.

On 16 March, a Walrus crew went out and rescued a pilot of 80 Squadron in a dinghy. Flying Officer W J Morris had been one of four pilots on a shipping recce off the Yugoslavian coast, along the Peljesac peninsula, led by Flying Officer A K Ingle. Spotting a schooner they attacked, but Morris was hit by flak from Korcula Island. He could not make the safety of Vis Island so had to bale out of his Spitfire Vc (LZ930) half way between this sanctuary and Velaluka Bay. Ingle climbed to give a Mayday call, which soon brought rescue.

This was 80 Squadron's last casualty in the Middle East, where it had been operating since before the war. Soon afterwards it moved back to England, re-equipped with Tempests and saw out the war over Northern Europe. Sadly I have not found details of the Walrus crew or squadron.

Beagle Man Number Two
Only a couple of weeks after Junior Adams had been rescued, 283 Squadron went after another pilot of the 2nd Fighter Squadron, 52nd Fighter Group – Dick Curtis – on 18 March 1944.

I was Red 1 on a recce/strike on the Italian coast. We took off at 16.00 hours and after we completed our dive-bombing attack of factories and hangars at Marina di Pisa, we flew down the coast to the ammunition dump north-east of Cecina.

I went down to strafe a barrack-like building while the rest of the Flight orbited. Pilots of our squadron strafed similar buildings earlier in the day, causing them to burn and flare which I expected these to do. I fired from 1,000 feet and started to break away at an altitude of 500 feet, when my aircraft was hit by the terrific and unexpected explosion of the building. The explosion showed that the tempting target probably contained mines and/or artillery shells. As I had started to turn when my Spitfire was hit, I was going through the side of the plume rather than its centre, which undoubtedly saved my life. Ray McCraw told me later that the top cover aircraft felt the explosion like a kick in the pants and that the plume topped out at 4,000 feet, where they were flying!

The engine of my Spitfire immediately quit and I lost control of the machine until it emerged from the smoke and fire, at about 2,000 feet. Then the engine caught but I could not see out because the canopy was covered with soot which, however, soon blew away. I then opened the canopy because I was fairly certain that I was going to bale out.

I immediately called my formation and told them my aircraft was in pretty bad shape and I was heading for home. However, the radio was out, so I headed due west out to sea at 2,000 feet. I noticed that I had no oil pressure, black smoke was coming from the engine exhaust and both wings were riddled with holes. I had very little elevator control and could only maintain an IAS (indicated air speed) of 120 mph. I flew west until the coolant temperature hit 130 degrees and the oil temperature 110 degrees.

At 1,500 feet and with the IAS at 100 mph, it was now time for me to cut the throttle. Disconnecting everything, I stepped onto the seat, put one foot on the door hinges and shoved off. I saw the tail of the Spitfire pass by and then pulled the rip-cord. I was more or less head-down when the 'chute opened so I saw and heard my aircraft crash into the sea. Barry Lawlor also said he saw my prop stop turning before the aircraft hit the sea which shows that its engine froze and that I had flown it about as far as it would go without risking an engine fire.

I entered the water about five miles south-south-west of Cecina Marina, grabbed the dinghy lanyard and pulled the dinghy out of its cover. I became a little tired of treading water, so the brilliant idea of inflating the Mae West struck me. I then inflated the dinghy and climbed in, then noticed the escape purse in the water so I immediately paddled towards the spot and retrieved it. Meantime, the other Spitfires of the Flight flew around above me until their fuel supply was low, then one came down and buzzed me and then they all flew towards our base.

I took out the paddles and did a little paddling, trying to get farther away from the shore, but with such little success that I threw out the sea anchor instead. As there was no fluorescene pack in the dinghy I took out one from the Mae West and dipped it in the water for a few minutes.

At about 17.30 I settled down and waited for the RAF Walrus, which I knew would be on its way. I saw some Spitfires orbiting above me and heard the occasional explosion from the scene of some strafing. The wind got a little stronger producing waves with crests of two to three feet and the dinghy began to ship a little water. I was now feeling cold and so did a few exercises to keep warm.

I guess I had been in the water for about an hour when the Walrus appeared on the horizon, a beautiful sight, notwithstanding its rather ugly lines. It flew by and dropped a smoke bomb, did a 360 degree circle and ended up slightly down wind of me. I pulled in the sea anchor and drifted and paddled to the 'duck'. With the assistance of the pilot, I had no trouble getting into the front hatch. I sat down in the radio compartment, had several blankets put around me, and lit a cigarette. The sea was too rough for the plane to take off so it was taxied about ten miles towards Capriana until we hit smoother water and were able to get airborne. We got back to base at 19.45 while it was still light enough to land.

1st Lieutenant R C Curtis, 2nd FS, 52nd FG

His rescuers had been the inimitable Arnold Divers, this time with Flight Sergeant E E Smith in the back, flying W2747, who had been directed to the spot by the Air Controller until they noticed an oil patch and then the dinghy. After collecting their American customer, Divers had to taxi for 45 minutes before he found water calm enough for him to attempt take-off.

After picking up Lieutenant Curtis in the late evening close to the coast of Italy, the first attempted take-off was almost a disaster due to rough seas. Excessive bouncing as usual blew up the VHF radio set and made the ASI useless. On finding calmer water closer to the enemy coast, Flight Sergeant Smith and I were relieved when we finally bounced free and became airborne in the near dark and were heading in the general direction of Corsica. Visibility from the cockpit was limited due to salt encrusted windscreens and due to having no radio and no air speed indicator, navigation was limited. On approaching Corsica searchlights dipped south indicating we were north of Bastia. Finally arriving over the airfield (which was not equipped for night landings) ten miles south of Bastia, we found to our delight an emergency flare-path had been laid on with an odd assortment of trucks and jeeps with headlights blazing, giving the general direction of the narrow metal mesh runway. The first attempt to land was a dismal failure owing to poor visibility from the cockpit and only a vague idea of the approach speed. However, the second time round we had a rough, rattling landing, not one of my best, but at least we were firmly on the deck.

This rescue was my last successful one on 283 Squadron. Within a few days I was on my way back to the UK, twelve months after arriving in North Africa and the news that I had been at last granted a commission.

During an interview in Algiers on 6 April, the AOC MACAF, Air Vice-Marshal Hugh Pughe Lloyd, asked me if I wished to return to New Zealand as I had completed three years attached to the RAF. I indicated I wished to fly Mosquitoes on operations prior to returning home. On returning to the UK I was for a time personal pilot to Air Vice-Marshal Leslie Hollinghurst and General Gale, as part of 38 Group, prior to the airborne landings at Arnhem. A short time later, much to my surprise, I was posted to Harwell to do a conversion course onto Mosquitoes and then transferred to 140 Wing, 2nd Tactical Air Force.

Although I enjoyed my stint with 283 Squadron, being trained in NZ as a twin-engined bomber pilot but transferred to fighters in the UK, I felt my true talents had not been fully exploited by the RAF. As a low level night intruder bomber pilot I had finally reached my ultimate.

Apart from flak damage over Bremen and again over Hamburg, I was half way through a second tour on Mosquitoes when the war in Europe finished in early May 1945. My last operational trip was on 2 May, over Bremen with 487 Squadron RNZAF, based at Melsbroek, Belgium.

                                                       Arnold Divers, 283 Squadron

By the time Arnold Divers left 283 Squadron, he had well over 1,000 flying hours in his flying log book, and well over three and a half hours dinghy time!

Bob Curtis, from New York, had joined the 2nd Squadron in Tunisia in May 1943, staying with it during the Italian Campaign until September 1944. He shot down his first German aircraft in February 1944, then the Squadron changed from Spitfires to Mustangs. By the end of his combat tour he had shot down 14 enemy aircraft and won the DSC, the Silver Star, two DFCs and 19 Air Medals, having also been in command of the 2nd Squadron from May 1944.

                                            *   *   *

South Africans to the Fore

There was a rescue on the 19th, although I haven't been able to find out too much about it. 1 Squadron SAAF had scrambled two Spitfires at 17.25 to look for a missing B.17 Fortress crew. Sent on a course of 060 degrees out to sea, for 25 miles, and then given various vectors by the Controller, Captain S A 'Bomb' Finney (his No.2 was Lieutenant Sam Schneider) saw a dark object underwater, going deeper and giving off bubbles, possibly the sinking bomber.

Shortly after that, they located two dinghies, close together, and an orbiting Spitfire. A fix was taken and then a Walrus (call-sign Spongebag 4) was duly vectored to the scene. The light was now so bad that Finney could not see the Walrus, but Control ordered him to fire off a Very flare to attract its attention. As fighter pilots do not carry Very pistols, Finney used instead two hand-held distress flares from his Mae West and this enabled the Walrus pilot to home in, locate the dinghies, and effect a successful rescue.

Bomb Finney was promoted to Major a couple of days later and given command of 2 Squadron SAAF.

The day after the B.17 crew rescue, it was a South African pilot from 2 Squadron SAAF who was in trouble. They had been operating out of Yugoslavia and on the way back, the engine of Lieutenant W J Geeringh's Spitfire cut out three times. He tried to make Vis but went down and had some difficulty in getting out, only leaving the machine at about 300 feet. For some seconds Geeringh was caught half in and half out of the cockpit, his head striking the aerial mast but he eventually kicked himself free. Moments later he hit the sea, ten miles east of Trigno, and about 20 miles east of Penna Point (Punta delia Penna). ASR was incredibly quick off the mark, a Walrus picking him up just 25 minutes later, which landed him back on his airfield thirty minutes after that.

It has not been possible to find records of some of these Walrus rescues, and the author has assumed that they were probably the work of B Flight of 284 Squadron, as it appears some of their Forms 540/541 did not reach the main squadron headquarters and have not, therefore, been bound with the rest of the records. These may well include rescues made on 19 March (B.17 crew), 20 March (Lt Geeringh), 25 March (Lt Homer), and 2 June 1944 (Lt Gannon), and P/O Davies on 25 January 1945.

March 1944 was proving busy. On the 25th two 1 SAAF Squadron Spitfires were flying an early morning weather recce to Antrodoco, and returned in thick cloud. Lieutenant A W 'Ash' Homer, watching his leader and not his instruments as they spiralled down in the dense pea-soup, lost sight of him, then lost control of his fighter, so baled out.

Lieutenant Derek Gilson, meantime, came out of cloud, having heard Homer say he was taking to his parachute, and immediately searched for him, located him, and orbited for a fix, then stayed overhead till relieved. A Walrus duly arrived and took Homer back to Trigno. The Walrus crew were taken in to breakfast, and then a gale sprang up which stopped flying for the rest of the day.

* * *

Although 283 Squadron had been told of their change of aircraft to the Warwick, the Walrus actually came back to form one flight. 284 and 293 were still operating Walrus aircraft and although it was rumoured that Warwicks would also be going to 293, it too would keep Walrus detachments at Capodichino, on the most southerly point of the heel of Italy, and Cutella, with its metal-strip runway, a couple of miles south-east of Trigno.

> Our 283 Squadron became 293 Squadron in April 1944 and I went back to 284 in Sardinia. So from May 1944 I found myself on Corsica, kept my hand in doing air tests on Spitfires for the MU, and even took a Spitfire to Maison Blanche in North Africa; must have been round the bend! Later we went on detachment to the south of Sardinia, to Elmus, in July.
>
> Flight Sergeant J A Reid, 293/284 Squadrons

Final Rescues by 283 Squadron

The last two rescues by 283 came in early April 1944. Pilot Officer L H Newman, now commissioned, and Flight Sergeant S R Prouse, in W2747, picked up an American P.40 pilot – Lieutenant J R Donahue, from the 65th Squadron, 57th Fighter Group, on the 2nd, while Paterson and Keeble (Z1784) rescued a Spitfire pilot on the 7th.

On the latter sortie the Walrus became grounded in shallow water off the Corsican coast and HSL 2600 (Flying Officer S D Browning commanding) came to their aid. The launch, being unable to get in close, sent two men with a rope across in a dinghy, and were therefore able to haul the seaplane off.

The rescued pilot is believed to have been Flight Sergeant Day of 253 Squadron. He had been part of an escort to 24 American B.26 Marauders bombing the railway bridge at Incisa. Day had been flying a borrowed Spitfire from the US 2nd Squadron (Beagles), which, as we have seen earlier were not the most reliable. He crash-landed on the beach at Borgo after take-off due to technical failure and 283 were sent out to bring him back.

The first Warwick rescue by 283 was recorded as 23 July, a 185 Squadron Spitfire pilot being found in his dinghy and the Warwick crew dropped a Lindholme lifeboat to him. The rescue was completed by the arrival of a HSL. The Spitfire pilot, a South African, Lieutenant R J Lowe, had been attacking a Ju188 and had been hit by return fire. The enemy gunner also damaged a second Spitfire. However, the Junkers did not get back to its base.

294 Squadron

The Air Sea Rescue Flight finally became 294 Squadron on 24 September 1943 under the command of Flight Lieutenant S A M Morrison, who had previously been with 277 Squadron in the UK. It was not spectacularly busy, the war having moved on, but the Squadron's first rescue came two days later.

Six Hurricanes of 213 Squadron were flying a fighter sweep west of its base at Paphos, on the west coast of Cyprus. Sixty miles to the west-south-west, Pilot Officer P T P Temple-Murray (HV444) was forced to bale out due to a bad glycol leak. He lost his dinghy pack but Flight Lieutenant G Carrick, the Australian leader of the mission, and Pilot Officer G Steinberg RCAF, successfully dropped theirs, one of which was recovered by the downed pilot.

Flight Lieutenant D J Harcourt, Sergeant A J Christian and Pilot Officer C R Berry, in W2709, were scrambled at 10.00 hours, and sent out from Lakatamia, near Nicosia, Cyprus, where the Squadron had a detachment, on a course of 280 degrees, 25 miles from Paphos. They made the pick up and returned the pilot safely to his base.

In October – the 17th – 294 Squadron made a rescue following the loss of a Beaufighter off Cape Pamos, Cyprus. 227 Squadron had sent out four Beaus at first light to patrol over convoy code-named 'Nostril' but in the event, they did not meet it.

The Beaus had flown out from Nicosia at 04.50 and at 09.45 the crew of 'W' (JL735) radioed that fuel pressure was falling and running low. They were obviously leaking petrol and then both engines promptly stopped. The pilot, Sergeant J R Reid, made a good landing on the sea, tail down, but the tail appeared to snap off as they hit. The other Beaufighters circled making distress calls but they could only see one man in the water in his Mae West, in the centre of a fluorescene patch. A dinghy was dropped to him and he was seen to clamber in, then one Beau flew off in order to make certain help would soon be forthcoming. The other two remained over the dinghy, a reassuring sight to a man alone in a lonely ocean.

At Lakatamia, a Walrus of 294 was alerted. Warrant Officer F E Tutton, with Warrant Officer C W Batten and Flight Sergeant R D Drake (W2709 again), took off, and with the help of a Hurricane fighter, located the dinghy. They landed and picked up Reid, who was bruised but otherwise unhurt. His navigator, Sergeant Harold Cameron Seymour, from Perth, Scotland, had gone down with the broken-off rear fuselage section.

* * *

We end this chapter with two further rescues carried out by 294 Squadron, which was still operating at the western end of the Mediterranean into 1944. On 30 March, 16 SAAF Squadron had two of their Beaufighters up on a practice formation flight. One of them, piloted by Captain K G Muir and Lieutenant Strydom as navigator, was unable to gain height after an engine cut, and before he could reach land, he was forced to ditch one mile out from the shore, 20 miles from Benghazi shortly before noon.

Captain Barrett in the other Beau saw the crew safely clamber into their dinghy, the downed aircraft sinking in 27 seconds. He called a Mayday which was picked up by the RAF base at Berka III on VHF, and within 30 minutes a Wellington and a Walrus were on their way.

Two other Beaus, one from 16 SAAF and another from 227 Squadron, also joined in to help but the Walrus, crewed by Flight Sergeants H G C King, J M Frater and J Welsh – Z1782 – was soon on the scene. They quickly spotted the two flares fired off by Muir, landed on the choppy sea and moments later they were flying their customers home.

This is possibly the only such rescue of a SAAF Beaufighter crew as both 16 and 19 SAAF Squadrons which flew these aircraft, usually operated far out of reach of any help in the bitter mini-war over the Aegean between 1943-45; a fierce, private and almost unknown little war.

Almost a month later, 29 April, a Ju88 of 2/(F)123 was shot down off Cyprus by Spitfires, and a Walrus was sent out to pick up survivors. Pilot Officer J S Turner, Warrant Officer J D Ormesher and Flight Sergeant G R Lowe in W3013, located a dinghy eight miles off Cape Gata, landed and picked up Oberleutnant Helmut Jonas and his crew.

Chapter 5

IN ITALIAN WATERS

The final year of the battle for Italy provided much activity for the two main ASR Walrus Squadrons, 284 and 293. The former squadron was still based on Corsica, while 293, which had just started operations now that 283 Squadron had merged with it, still had detachments on the mainland, at Pomigliano, Capodichino and Cutella. Detachments moved to other bases over the year as the war gradually moved northwards.

One new pilot with 293 was Alexander Stevens:

When I joined 293 in the late spring of 1944, the squadron HQ, together with one flight of Warwicks (carrying droppable lifeboats) was stationed at Pomigliano, near Naples, and a detachment of Warwicks was also based at Foggia. The Squadron CO was Squadron Leader Richard Pye who was succeeded in the autumn by Squadron Leader Gellatly, a New Zealander who later joined Fairey Aviation as a test pilot.[1]

There were three Walrus detachments, two on the Italian mainland, based on the most forward available airfields on the east and west coasts respectively, and one on Corsica. After a pleasant time converting to the Walrus (i.e. mainly practicing water landings in the Bay of Naples), I joined the west coast detachment at Nettuno.

The Anzio beach-head broke through and Rome fell very early in June, and air resistance in Italy became pretty slight thereafter. This, of course, resulted in a much-reduced demand for ASR. From Nettuno we moved up to Tarquinia, Piombino, Rosignano and eventually to Pizzo on 1 October where they remained when I left the Squadron on Boxing Day, 1944.

When I joined the detachment, Reg Hayes was flight commander and the other two pilots were Ted Holmes and Gordon Brown. All of these went tour-expired about the end of June 1944. I know little of the other two detachments except that late August/early September (for about two weeks) I took a relief aircraft to the east coast because two of their kites

---

[1] Wilfred Ronald Gellatly OBE AFC MRAeS, RNZAF 1940-45; RAF 1947-55; Chief test pilot and Group Chief test pilot, Fairey Aviation to 1976, and later Sales Executive for Westland Helicopters.

had had to return to Squadron HQ for engineering work. They certainly had a busier time than we had on the west side. I joined them at Chiaravalle and after a few days moved to Piagiolino. My crewman was a Canadian Wop/AG, Pilot Officer Johnnie Clarkson.

To show that not all searches ended happily, we were scrambled to a position off Ancona and diverted subsequently to a position off Cattolica on the day that it was re-taken. A naval vessel out at sea was firing away at a shore position and we landed to pick-up a Spitfire pilot. Regrettably he was dead but whilst getting close enough to establish his condition, his parachute lines became ensnared in our tail wheel. I stopped the engine and Johnnie went overboard to disentangle them but we were unable to get the body on board.

Pilot Officer A G Stevens, 293 Squadron

Cutella Detachment, April-May 1944

The Cutella detachment of 293 Squadron made the first of a string of rescues on 3 April. Flight Sergeant E J Holmes DFM and Warrant Officer J R Berry DFM RNZAF (Z1813) were scrambled to Ortona, on the east coast, where a P.40 pilot had gone in. Flight Sergeant H E Eaves, an Australian with 450 RAAF Squadron, had been dive-bombing a railway bridge over the River Saline.

Eaves' Kittyhawk (FX644) had been hit in the engine by 40 mm flak, causing a glycol leak and after three minutes the engine caught fire. He baled out and landed in the sea, climbing into his dinghy. Then a rowing boat put out from the shore, collected him and brought him to the beach.

As the Walrus crew arrived and saw what had happened, they called base for instructions and were told to pick up the pilot if at all possible. The Walrus landed near to the beach whereupon the pilot was ferried from the shore, out to the aircraft, and flown home.

The next day Warrant Officer G F Brown and Flight Sergeant C S Taylor (Z1813) were sent out following the report of a Wellington having come down 30 miles out. The Wimpy (JA511 'Y') was a machine from 40 Squadron, which had been on a night raid against the Manfred Weiss Works, in Budapest, Hungary. Moderate to intense flak had been met, with searchlights and even night fighters. The skipper – Flight Sergeant L J Redden, an Australian, was on the bomb run as the starboard engine stopped, probably hit by a stray lump of shrapnel from a bursting AA shell. Nevertheless, he continued on to bomb, hitting a large building in the centre of the target area.

Making his way home, the bomber gradually lost height over Yugoslavia and finally, once over the sea, was forced to ditch off Termoli, on the east coast of Italy. Everyone got out and into the dinghy, but Redden was injured in the crash, having broken his shoulder, elbow and forearm.

Spitfires of 1 Squadron SAAF found the dinghy – Lieutenants E F 'Ernie' Harriss and J O 'Ozzie' Newton-Thompson – and then the Walrus (Spongebag 7) appeared, landed and picked up the five men, before starting to taxi to Termoli where an ambulance was waiting. Brown was still unable to take off as his wheels would not retract, so he taxied to the beach at Vlasto, where he finally became airborne and flew home. Prior to this, and to the amusement of the South

Africans of 1 Squadron, they saw the Walrus chugging by their coastal base at Trigno long after their two pilots had landed. Newton-Thompson himself was rescued on 1 May 1944.

It was at this time that the detachment crews were informed that a tour with the squadron would now constitute 200 operational flying hours or one year, whichever came first. So one must assume this was the same for other ASR units.

The Liberator Survivors

Messrs Brown and Taylor – Spongebag 7 – were out again on the 6th (in Z1813), picking up five survivors from an American B.24 Liberator from the 761st Bomb Squadron, 460th Bomb Group. Again they found Spitfires circling some wreckage, landed and picked up the five airmen. And again it was 1 SAAF Squadron fighters that were overhead. Lieutenants S J Richards, and – of course – Ozzie Newton-Thompson (Hotspur Black) – had been in on the search, finding the Liberator circling men in the water, clinging onto oxygen bottles.

Talking to the orbiting B.24 over the R/T, Dick Richards was able to satisfy the American pilot that the two Spitfires had the men in sight, because he was low on fuel and needed to leave. Then, leaving Ozzie to orbit the scene, Richards went off to look for the Walrus, which he found and guided to the spot.

After it had alighted he directed it to the various survivors. Then Hotspur Red section arrived to relieve Hotspur Black. Red leader, Lieutenant D S 'Dave' Hastie was on his last operation of his tour, and he saw two launches coming out from the direction of Vis at high speed. This worried the Walrus crew, now much too heavy to take off, and they asked Hastie to investigate. They turned out to be friendly and he guided them to the pick up area, where they picked up more Americans.

The Americans were all exhausted and the two rescuers had some trouble getting them aboard. The men had no dinghy and were all spread about an area covering two miles. Later, two Motor Torpedo Boats came along and following their search over a wider area, two more men were found. Being unable to take off, despite a long take-off run, Brown had to taxi over to the boats so that four of the Americans could be transferred over to them. Much later the Walrus took off and brought back one injured man for medical treatment.

With the light now fading, Hastie and his No.2 had to leave for their nearby airfield, and long after darkness had fallen, the South Africans heard the Walrus "lumbering overhead, on its way to roost!"

Gordon Frederick Brown and Cyril Sidney Taylor were both awarded Distinguished Flying Medals soon afterwards.

* * *

Liberator Crew Rescue

On April 6, 1944, our plane, a B.24 Liberator – 761st Squadron, 460th Bomb Group – stationed in Spinazzola, Italy, was part of a 15th Air Force formation headed for a target area around Zagreb, Yugoslavia. After completion of the mission, on our way home, we developed mechanical

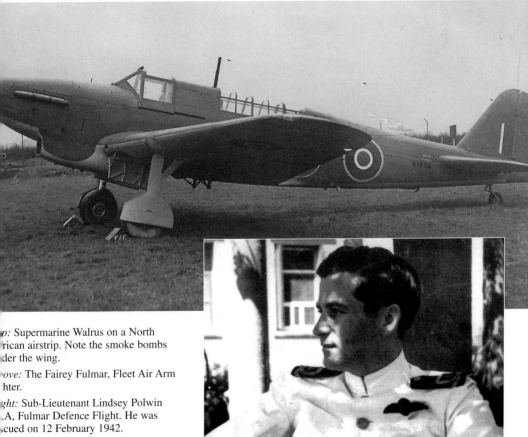

p: Supermarine Walrus on a North
rican airstrip. Note the smoke bombs
der the wing.

ove: The Fairey Fulmar, Fleet Air Arm
hter.

ght: Sub-Lieutenant Lindsey Polwin
A, Fulmar Defence Flight. He was
cued on 12 February 1942.

Top left: Sgt Denny Lunn DFM flew with 277 Squadron in England, and with 283 Squadron North Africa, 1943.

Top right: Norman Pickles DFC was another who flew rescue missions in the UK and in the Mediterranean.

Above: An American Mitchell fr the 12th Bomb Group after ditching on 2 January 1943 on it way back from Crete. Note one the crew standing on the tail, midway between the two rudders

Left: Sergeants Colin Horne DFM Frank Bettridge and Arnold Dive DFM, 283 Squadron. Bettridge was lost on a rescue mission, 27 May 1943.

Right: Walrus 'F' being refuelled on Taher airfield, Djedjelli, Algeria, 1943. Code on tail appears to be either D or 26.

Middle left: Squadron Leader Walter Sterne DSO, OC 283 Squadron.

Middle centre: Flying Officer A B Morabito DFC RCAF, 283 Squadron.

Middle right: Sergeant W S Lambert DFM, 283 Squadron.

Bottom: Personnel of 284 Squadron. Back: ground crews. Front, from left to right: Denny Lunn; Cyril Taylor; Norm Pickles; Dick Eccles; Bradley and Ted Holmes.

Right: Dick Eccles, 284 Squadron, marking this Walrus' fourth 'saint' insignia, denoting four successful rescues.

Middle left: Flight Sergeant Ernie Smith, 284 Squadron.

Middle right: Lieutenant Paul G McArthur, 79th Fighter Group, rescued off Pantelleria by 283 Squadron, 10 June 1943.

Bottom: Lieutenant Gordon Rich, 309th Fighter Squadron, 31st Fighter Group, rescued by 283 Squadron off Pantelleria, 11 June 1943.

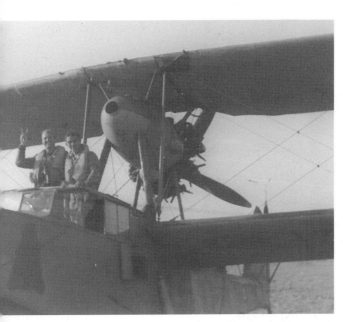

Top left: Lieutenant Matt Morey, 31st Fighter Group (left), who guided Colin Horne (right) to Lt Rich on 11 June 1943.

Top right: Martin Barnes, 112 Squadron, rescued by 284 Squadron, 14 August 1943.

Left: Walrus aircraft, Algeria, late 1943.

Bottom left: Lisle Newman, 283 Squadron.

Bottom right: John C Kelly, 86th Squadron, 79th Fighter Group, was rescued by 284 Squadron on 31 July 1943 after having spent all night in his dinghy. He is pictured with a section of his parachute, shortly after being brought home by the Walrus crew.

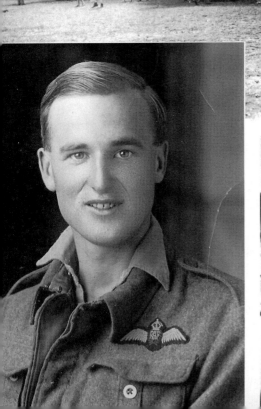

Top left: Flight Officer Clifford W Nelson, 309th Fighter Squadron, 31st Fighter Group, rescued by 284 Squadron on 21 September 1943.

Top right: Arnold Divers, 283 Squadron, after an air test in FD-L.

Left: Flight Lieutenant S A M Morrison commanded 294 Squadron as it progressed from ASR Flight ME in September 1943. He had previously flown with 277 Squadron in England.

Bottom: Walrus W2706, ASR Flight Middle East, used in the rescue of a Wellington crew on 28 June 1942. Taken at Mersa Matruh, 1944.

Top: Walrus Z1780 FD-W, 283 Squadron.

Left: Ted Holmes, on fuselage, helping Sergeant Ritchie from the Walrus after landing at Triolo, 20 October 1943.

Bottom: Walrus X9506, 284 Squadron, landing at Triolo on 20 October 1943, with Sergeant H Ritchie on board, sole survivor of a 14 Squadron Marauder.

Top left: Wing Commander W G G Duncan Smith DSO DFC, 244 Wing, rescued by 284 Squadron 2 September 1943, despite the intervention of several enemy fighters.

Top right: The crew of a Mitchell from 82nd Bomb Squadron, and the 283 Squadron crew who picked them up, taken aboard the hospital ship which eventually rescued them as the Walrus was lost. From left to right: Arnold Divers; Eric Keeble; Lt Steinberg; T/Sgt Stevens and Lt Paul Devlin. Kneeling: Sgt Keyes and Lt Bill McGonigle.

Right: Walrus FD-S, 283 Squadron, in flight from Salerno to Naples, 14 October 1943.

Below: Walrus FD-W of 283 Squadron, Palermo airfield. Note wrecked Italian aircraft, and the mass of petrol drums on the left.

Top left: Divers and Keeble after the rescue; note the American trousers – and cigars!!

Top right: Lieutenant J A Adams, 2nd Fighter Squadron, 52nd Fighter Group, with his Spitfire V at Palermo. 'Junior' Adams was rescued by 283 Squadron on 3 March 1944.

Left: Ray F Harmeyer, 309th Fighter Squadron, 31st Fighter Group, rescued by 283 Squadron on 7 March 1944. He went on to become an ace on Spitfires and Mustangs.

Bottom: 'Junior' Adams being helped out of the rescue Walrus at Borgo airfield, 7 March 1944.

Top left: Warrant Officer James 'Hamish' Reid, 284 Squadron.

Top centre: Flight Sergeant 'Sticky' Glew DFM, tragically killed by strafing Thunderbolts on Cutella airfield, 29 April 1944.

Top right: Lieutenant D T Gilson, 1 SAAF Squadron, rescued by 293 Squadron, 24 May 1944.

Middle: Smoke float. An essential aid in keeping anyone in the water under observation.

Bottom: Rescued!

Top left: Lieutenant Richard C Curtis, 2nd Fighter Squadron, 52nd Fighter Group. He was rescued by 283 Squadron on 18 March 1944. His crew chief, S/Sgt Lloyd Gilbert is in the cockpit. Bob Curtis became an ace, ending the war with 14 victories.

Top right: Flight Officer Mansdorf (co-pilot), 1st Lieutenant Fred Smith (pilot) and 2nd Lieutenant John Schwartz (bombardier), officers of the B.24 from 761st Bomb Squadron, 460th Bomb Group, rescued by 293 Squadron, 6 April 1944.

Bottom: The Liberator crew. Back, from left to right: Sgts Wilson; Forbes; Breckenridge; Skrzynski and Demers. Front, from left to right: Schwartz; Budriunas; Mansdorf and Larscheidt.

Top left: Major Bert Sanborn, CO of 2nd Fighter Squadron, 52nd Fighter Group, was rescued by Lisle Newman, 11 April 1944. The 2nd Squadron's Beagle motif can be seen on the cowling.

Top right: Lisle Newman photographed after landing Bert Sanborn at his base.

Left: Men of 283 Squadron, from left to right: Flight Sergeants P M H Graham and Lisle Newman; groundcrew member Arnold Divers; groundcrew member.

Bottom: Walrus Z1777-S, 283 Squadron, Salerno beach-head.

Top left: Flight Lieutenant Arnold Divers DFM RNZAF in 1945.

Top right: Captain J O Newton-Thompson, 1 SAAF Squadron. Having been on escort to several ASR missions, he had finally to be thankful to a Walrus crew from 284 Squadron who rescued him after he had baled out on 1 May 1944.

Bottom left: Trevor Humphrey who included Capt J O Newton-Thompson amongst the men he rescued in 1944.

Bottom right: Trevor Humphrey by a Walrus.

Top: Liberator #15, 484th Bomb Group, that collided with another Lib over the Aegean on 3 May 1944.

Middle left: B24H #21. After the collision Bill Abbey (seen on the wing) flew his ship back to base at Torretta, Italy, despite the loss of 12 feet of wing.

Middle right: Trevor Humphrey also rescued Flying Officer G C W O'Neil MM RAAF, of 451 Squadron, 7 June 1944.

Bottom: Walrus ZE-P of 293 Squadron, Italy. Note the securing attachments to the wing floats to stop the machine tipping over in a high wind.

Top: Some of the crew of a B.24 of 726th Bomb Squadron, 451st Bomb Group, rescued by 293 Squadron, 10 June 1944. Back, from left to right: Lts Pickard, H Guiness, Bird and Schwab. Front, from left to right: enlisted men Flint; Gardner; R J Anderson; McPeek; Wathen; Loglais and Schuler. Guiness, McPeek, Wathan, Loglais and Anderson were on the fateful mission, Flint W Gardner and Robert Anderson being the two lost.

Middle left: Marauder crew from the 444th Bomb Squadron, 320th Bomb Group, whilst training. All were rescued by 293 Squadron and a HSL, on 5 November 1944, except Chapman, who did not go overseas. From left to right: Charles Kamanski; Leland S Ford; William Beebe; Peter Greco; Kelly Friel – and Chapman.

Middle right: Marauders of the 320th Bomb Group over the target.

Bottom left: Ray Veitch, 260 Squadron, who had to be rescued three times in April 1945, with 293 Squadron helping with the pick-ups.

Bottom right: Lt K B Walker SAAF and F/Sgt W Burnett, 293 Squadron, 1944-45.

Top left: Although rescued, Burdick and his rescuers, Walker and Burnett, had to be taken off the Walrus by a destroyer after a night adrift at sea. The picture shows the men being brought back to the destroyer by one of her boats.

Top right: Three Walrus aircraft of 293 Squadron at Pisa, Italy, early 1945. The middle one of this trio, W2757, was involved in at least six rescues.

Middle left: Lieutenant Greg Burdick, 2nd Squadron, 52nd Fighter Group, rescued by Lt K B Walker and

Flight Sergeant W Burnett, 9 December 1944.

Middle right: The Vickers Warwick used to carry an airborne lifeboat to anyone in the water and awaiting rescue, either by boat or amphibious aircraft.

Bottom: A Lindholme lifeboat lands on the water having detached its parachutes. Provided the man/men in the water were physically able to get to and into the boat, all would be well. If however, they were wounded or unable to reach it, it was useless.

engine problems, first one engine, then a while later, a second engine conked out. At this time, we were alerted to prepare for a ditching. When the third engine malfunctioned, we were rapidly descending towards the Adriatic Sea.

We hit the water at 90 mph (over stalling speed) with a blinding crash. Nine members of the crew successfully got out of the plane. The tenth, Sergeant Raymond Demers, ball-turret gunner, did not escape and unfortunately went down with the ship when it sank within a few minutes.

We never got our dinghy out since the plane's structure was so warped, the release mechanism failed to work. Our Squadron CO Major Spear, circling above, attempted to drop his dinghy, but on ejection it fouled up with the protuberances on the rear of the plane and became damaged. If the dinghy had hit the twin stabilizers, he might have been in the water with us.

Waist-gunner Orris Forbes was unable to inflate his Mae West because it was damaged, so he hung onto some floating oxygen bottles for as long as he could, but finally he slipped under and away. Waist-gunner and radio operator Sergeant Walter Skrzynski tried swimming to what appeared to be land in the distance, tired, took in water and could not be revived when picked up later by an MTB. Tail gunner Sergeant Anthony Larscheidt received a severe injury to one leg, lost lots of blood, and he too succumbed when picked up later by the MTB.

Considering the lapse of time (three-four hours) before being located the crew tended to drift, straying away on normal tide, which undoubtedly accounted for the spread of survivors.

When the Walrus arrived, there was no way for it to be able to remove eight water-logged men. It took off with one man, Sergeant Herbert Wilson, who appeared to be suffering from a serious head injury. The rest of us – seven – awaited the arrival of some MTBs. Eventually when a boat neared me, I latched onto it for dear life and would not let loose until a British sailor assured me I was safe. I released my handhold and was hauled aboard. In true British naval tradition I was given a portion of rum that without doubt quieted my chattering teeth. We were taken to the Isle of Vis, off the Yugoslav coast, occupied by British Commandos, American Rangers and Yugoslav partisans. Here, Sergeant Larscheidt and Sergeant Skrzynski were buried. We spent the night in what appeared to be a cavern and returned to Bari the next day aboard an LCI [Landing Craft – Infantry]. From there, we were driven 40 miles by truck, returning to our base.

In all, there were six survivors of our crew: Pilot, 1st Lieutenant Fred Smith, co-pilot Flight Officer Harry Mansdorf, navigator 2nd Lieutenant Bronislaus Budriunas, bombardier 2nd Lieutenant John Schwartz, flight engineer Sergeant Herbert Wilson, and nose gunner Sergeant Harry Breckenridge.

We were all sent to the Isle of Capri for a week's rest, and resumed combat flying upon return to our base. On a subsequent mission over

Ploesti, Rumania, Sergeant Breckenridge received a shattering plexi-glass injury to his eyes and was permanently grounded. Now only five remained of the original crew, four officers, and Sergeant Wilson, plus five replacement gunners whenever we were scheduled to fly.

The ditching incident was our third mission and on our 28th on June 16, 1944, we were set afire by anti-aircraft fire and brought down over Vienna, Austria. Only three survived; myself, Mansdorf and Wilson. Pilot Fred Smith, navigator Lieutenant Budriunas and our five new gunners all perished.

After eight months as PoWs, Mansdorf and I were part of a repatriation movement in an exchange of wounded prisoners and we arrived stateside in February 1945. We did not know Sergeant Wilson's fate until we returned home, learning that he too survived and was a PoW somewhere in Germany.

I will be eternally grateful to two British doctors in Stalag 17A, Kaisersteinbruck, Austria, who ministered to my burns and to Mansdorf's ugly knee wound with a very limited supply of medical equipment as provided in prisoner of war camps. One doctor was English and the other from India; unfortunately I never got their names.

2nd Lieutenant J Schwartz, 461 BS, 460th BG

From the records of the 460th Group, came the following reports:

The crews, with loads of 20 cluster frag bombs, headed for the airdrome in Zagreb, Yugoslavia, on 6 April. Four aircraft from the 460th attached themselves to the 461st and dropped their bombs with them, but most crews jettisoned their bombs in the Adriatic due to the target being overcast. On the return flight, Lt Frederick B Smith lost altitude and speed until the plane disappeared over the Adriatic. Major Robert L Spear, flying with Captain Crossey, turned back to give Smith air sea rescue procedures and to radio their position (just off the coast of Bisevo Island) to 15th AF. He saw the tail of the ditched plane go under and counted nine survivors. Since no life rafts could be seen Spear decided to drop his, but when the rafts broke free from the plane they became entangled, destroying the radio antennae and badly damaging the empennage. Spear continued to circle the area until relieved by a Spitfire. The first message said that seven survivors had been picked up, but actually there were only six: S/Sgts Demers, Forbes, Skrzynski, and Larscheidt had drowned. The remainder of the crew returned from Bari the next day.

761st War Diary – 6 April 1944

Nine crews from the 761st took off with the formation – only seven came back over the mountain and landed. Each ship noted while in the traffic pattern, it was discovered that the Squadron Commander, Major Robert L Spear, flying with Flight Commander James Crossey, was missing. The other missing aircraft had been piloted by 1st Lt Fred B Smith, Flight

Commander of D Flight. The interrogation soon told the story.

The mission had been unsuccessful. The primary and alternate targets were overcast and no bombs were dropped. On the route back Lt Smith, in the last ship in the formation, had slowly lost altitude and speed until he finally disappeared. When it became apparent that Lt Smith was about to ditch his a/c, Major Spear turned back to give air sea rescue procedures to the straggler. His radio operator began immediately to send the position (just off the coast of Bisevo island) to Air Sea Rescue Division, 15th AF. Nine survivors could be counted but no rubber dinghy could be seen. Major Spear dropped some life rafts. As the rafts broke loose from the plane, they became entangled with the radio antennae and the tail. When the rafts finally came free from the ship, it was discovered that all radio antennae had been destroyed and the empennage badly damaged. Major Spear continued to circle the scene of the accident until he was relieved by a Spitfire. He then returned to the base with an account of what had happened. Soon after his landing, a message was received which reported that seven (sic) survivors had been picked up.

During the mission to Vienna on 16 June, the name of their B.24 was General Nuisance, and an eye witness to them being shot down took an air-to-air photograph of their Liberator in flames. The photograph shows flames pouring from the waist and bomb bay. Then followed an explosion, which sent bodies and wreckage into space. Three parachutes were observed, but one of these seemed to have become entangled in the tail assembly. In 1946, John Schwartz recorded what had happened inside the bomber that day.

We were in the process of usual turn away from the target when anti-aircraft fire made contact with the ship. As bombardier on board, my station was in the nose of the ship along with the navigator and nose gunner. In this position I was hit with several minute pieces of flak about the legs. Receiving no alarm over the inter-phone, naturally I assumed the plane wasn't mortally hit. . . . However, a few seconds later I glanced back through the tunnel, and noted flickering motions. I unhooked my oxygen equipment and crawled back to investigate. The entire bomb bay was a blazing inferno.

I scurried back to the nose, shed my flak suit, hooked on my parachute chest pack and kicked the navigator, Lieutenant Budriunas, in the knees to draw his attention. He immediately went through the same procedure after releasing our nose gunner, Sergeant Weldon Carter, from his turret. I was in the process of re-hooking the inter-phone to inform the pilot, Lieutenant Frederick Smith and other crew members of the existing danger, when the ship suddenly lunged to one side. Because of the centrifugal force, we were hopelessly trapped since the plane was either violently spinning or in a very deep spiral. Fire raced up into the nose and un-used rounds of .50 calibre ammo started bursting. From here on out, I found myself floating through space.

Automatically I pulled the rip-cord and the 'chute opened. I landed some two hundred feet from a German hospital in Austria, where I was immediately carried to and given first-aid for third degree burns of the face, hands, legs and backside.

* * *

On the afternoon of 7 April 1944 a section of Spitfires – again 1 SAAF – located a dinghy 18 miles east of Ortona and began to orbit. Picking up a distress call from a P.38 pilot, one of the Spitfires, flown by Ernie Harriss, flew off towards Sangro but only found fishing boats, which, it was hoped, had picked up the American.

Meanwhile, Lieutenant J R Spencer watched a Walrus arrive to pick up the occupants of the dinghy. It was Holmes and Berry (Z1813) who made the rescue, picking up ten men from a B.17 Flying Fortress, from the 774th Bombardment Squadron, 463rd Bomb Group. The Group had not long been operating out of Celone airfield, Italy. Heading out from Penna Point on the afternoon of the 7th the Walrus crew had been told that P.38 Lightnings were circling 'seven' men in a dinghy but they failed to find them. Then they saw two P.38s heading for Italy but these were replaced by two more who then directed the Walrus to the men, who were now being covered by Spitfires. Collecting the men aboard, Holmes taxied to Ortona Harbour, where he handed Lieutenant S L Florsham and his crew over to the Navy.

* * *

Flying Officer Trevor Humphrey and Sergeant Heseltine arrived at the Cutella detachment from Corsica on 8 April. Humphrey had already been active with 278 Squadron in England and saved many lives. He had joined the RAF in the summer of 1940 and once he had passed through OTU went to the newly formed 136 Squadron, flying Hurricanes. Just as the war with Japan was about to begin, 136 was assigned for overseas service. Being a married man, it was decided he should remain in England.

He then moved to 278 and later 277 ASR Squadron, and then in February 1944, the niceties of being married or not faded away, and he was sent to Algiers and then on to 283 Squadron.

Trevor Humphrey made his first Italian Front rescue on 13 April, with Heseltine, in Z1813. The downed P.38 Lightning pilot, Captain Ronald E Ashmead of the American 48th Squadron, 14th Fighter Group was in the water not far from the island of Vis off the Yugoslav coast. He had been on a mission over the nearby mainland. The Walrus collected an escort of P.38s who took him straight to their fellow pilot, and they picked him up without difficulty. Trevor thought the man had been on a special mission, for he said little about it on the way home, but the next day a packet of 200 cigarettes arrived for the two Walrus men. 1 SAAF Squadron also helped with this rescue mission.

> Operations from Corsica, to anywhere along the western seaboard of
> Italy, became a veritable happy hunting ground for us at this time. There
> were some nine aerodromes on Corsica, from which flew Spitfires,
> Kittyhawks, P.38 Lightnings, P.47 Thunderbolts, as well as a couple of
> B.26 Marauder squadrons. A lot of potential work for us.
>
> Flying Officer T H Humphrey, 293 Squadron

The South Africans were once more in evidence on the 17th but with less
successful results. 1 SAAF, along with 4 SAAF, had been escorting six Italian
SM82s dropping supplies near Kazanti, and Lieutenant F C 'Jock' Hamilton had
to take to his parachute on the return flight. The sea was rough and searches
failed to find him.

Next day a morning search by 4 SAAF Squadron located him and he waved
up from his dinghy. Another search that afternoon could not re-locate Hamilton
and on the 19th 4 Squadron led out a Walrus but found only an empty dinghy.

Trevor and Heseltine were at it again too on 18 April (in W2747), this time
searching for Lieutenant Kenneth G Haydisx, a Mustang pilot from the US
307th Squadron, 31st Fighter Group. They had only recently exchanged their
Spitfires for P.51s and were now operating out of San Severo, one of the many
Allied air bases north of Foggia. The 31st Group were flying cover for P.38s
strafing targets at Larariano and Aiello. Some Me109s had engaged them and
three 109s were claimed destroyed, with two more probables and one damaged.
However, Major Garth B Jared of the 308th Squadron had baled out and so too
did Lieutenant Haydisx. Two more Mustangs were lost on the way home due to
bad weather.

> As I recall, this chap had turned back without an escort – which was
> unusual – and he didn't make it. Because there was no escort we didn't
> actually know where he was. All we'd been told was a given bearing, so
> I decided to fly along this bearing and look for an oil slick. He was
> fortunate in that the sea conditions this day weren't at all bad and we did
> spot the oil patch, which hadn't dispersed or disappeared.
>
> We then calculated the wind direction, flew in that direction and
> spotted the pilot where his parachute had deposited him. He was only 12
> miles out from Termoli but he had been lucky. Fortunately too, we were
> able to see better on a calm day, so we found him easily once we'd found
> the oil. We had been told he was in trouble and had a 500 lb bomb hung-
> up, so he couldn't ditch and was going to have to bale out. We taxied back
> towards Termoli and took off in calmer water near the beach.
>
> Flying Officer T H Humphrey, 293 Squadron

Not You Again!
It was not too often that a squadron picked up the same pilot it had rescued on
a previous occasion, but it happened to 293 Squadron on 20 April. Brown and
Taylor were scrambled at 12.10 pm (in Z1813), and after leaving Penna Point

saw a Spitfire diving at a dinghy, making sure the Walrus crew could see what he was diving at. They saw the man and landed, picking up the same Flight Sergeant H E Eaves whom Holmes and Berry had brought home on the 3rd! Again the target for 450 Squadron RAAF had been a railway bridge, and Eaves had been hit whilst heading back to the coast of Italy. Smoke had poured from his Kittyhawk (FX599), but he'd nursed it back to the coast before ditching.

The Australian's full report read:

I was flying White 1. We were briefed to bomb the railway bridge just south of Chervelli, about nine miles west of Ancona. After bombing and pulling away, I observed a twin-engined aircraft on Falconera landing ground. I obtained permission to strafe same from Leader; my No.2 and myself climbed into the sun and dived down to the deck, strafing, but could not set the aircraft alight, although I obtained strikes. I pulled up and when at 2,000 feet over some sheds near the coast, light AA was thrown up and I was hit somewhere in the engine. The windscreen was immediately covered in oil and then the glycol temp. went off the clock. Engine cut and kept picking up spasmodically, except that by this time white and black smoke was pouring out. I jettisoned my long-range tank and headed out to sea, turning with the coast around Ancona. Nursing my aircraft, I managed to reach a point about five miles west of Ancona when the engine went dead. I was still at 2,000 feet and decided to ditch (as on 3 April I'd already made one successful ditching) and radioed the Leader to this effect.

Another thing in favour of ditching was a calm sea. I tried to jettison my hood but it stuck and had to be punched out, it then twisted and struck my head, tearing the earpiece and side out of my helmet. I put 15° of flap down and could not estimate the direction of the wind (as it happened I ditched downwind). The aircraft glided gently onto the sea at 110 mph and I had to look out of the side of the cockpit as the windscreen was still covered in oil. Aircraft settled on the water fairly smoothly but immediately nosed down. By the time I'd loosened harness, both wings were covered and the engine was below the water. I lost no time in jumping out into the sea, and inflated my Mae West.

I had no trouble in releasing my parachute and detaching my dinghy and was aboard it in a few moments. I could see our aircraft doing turn abouts above me and when two Spitfires took over, I thought I was sitting pretty. Three US Lightnings appeared from the river mouth where we had done our bombing. I noticed them jettison their long-range tanks or bombs. One of these three 'friends' decided he didn't like me as he put a burst from his guns about 100 yards from where I was peacefully waiting to be picked up. No doubt he was warming his guns up for his attack on the Spits. The Lightning climbed up to the Spits and one made an attack, which he broke off as the first Spitfire identified himself. Another Lightning carried out his attack on the second Spitfire with a burst, which looked nearly head-on, and white smoke poured out of the Spitfire as I saw him head for home.

Several times I thought the Spit had lost me and felt very much alone, but he knew his job and he guided the ASR Walrus straight to me, when it appeared. After dropping a flare, the 'duck' alighted on the sea and turning towards me, it gave me another ducking as it brushed by. I once again had to thank the boys who'd wasted no time in fishing me out and we were soon on our way back to base.

Like me, they were in a mighty hurry to get out of the area and I don't blame them. I was soon back with the squadron and felt none the worse for my second forced swim in the Adriatic this month.

Eaves' luck ran true to form three days later. He crashed into another Kittyhawk on the ground and injured his right hand.

What he wrote about the mix-up overhead was quite true. The Spitfires of 1 SAAF Squadron relieved the Kittyhawks circling above Eaves, the position of which they noted as being six miles south-east of Ancona, near Sirolo. The two Spitfires were repeatedly attacked and one had to break away and make a crash landing (Cat 3), its pilot badly wounded. The other Spitfire pilot stuck to protecting the dinghy and keeping it in sight, and by skilful evasion managed to avoid damage and also to control himself into not retaliating, especially after his companion had been hit.

Eventually the American pilots left and 7 Squadron SAAF Spitfires arrived with the Walrus. The lone 1 SAAF pilot headed away with fuel tanks down to their last few gallons, but he was pleased to hear over the radio that the rescue had been successfully accomplished.

Capodichino Detachment – April 1944

The aircrew members here were Reg Hayes, Hamish Reid, Tony Morabito, W/O Bradley, G F Brown, Denny Lunn, Norm Pickles, K G Hall, Warrant Officer M D Kelly RAAF – and Sticky Glew. Hamish Reid and Morabito made the first rescue, on the evening of the 10th in Z1777.

Flight Sergeant A G Newman RNZAF in Spitfire JG109 had flown a mission at 18.00 hours, led by Captain J C Bolitho SAAF, six aircraft patrolling Terracina. Newman's Spitfire developed engine trouble and he had to bale out. The others kept station over him until the Walrus arrived, the crew finding him safe and well despite some facial injuries. Just over a month later, Newman shot down a FW190 and was commissioned.

Newman's location was within the horns of the bay, south-east of San Felice Point, south of Anzio. He was about seven miles off Terracina. It was coming on for dusk and there was a six-seven foot swell, and a 30-knot wind, which was at 45° to the swell. Both were taking him inshore.

We had passed an ASR launch, about eight-ten miles to the south, but it obviously wouldn't reach the man before it got dark, or the alternative was that he would be blown ashore. So we took a calculated risk to land.

We got down all right because you could always land a Walrus in a much greater sea than you could get off again, and six-seven feet is just about the optimum you can take off from. We found he had banged his face on the Spitfire's tail, but he was cheerful enough and we pulled him in. We attempted to take off, which had to be done into wind, which, of course, threw us 45° to the swell.

We were just about getting airborne when the seventh wave of the seventh wave smashed the port float and we were lucky it didn't cartwheel us into the sea. Obviously that was the end of that!

Tony got out onto the starboard wing, as did our good pal Newman, so I attempted to taxi away from the shore, playing a wee bit at being a submarine – while firing off red Very flares. Eventually the Walrus began to sink under us so we got into the big dinghy – probably the best-equipped crew for a rescue you'd ever seen! We had more red flares, and tins of water, food, etc, and could have lasted for a week.

The HSL spotted us and picked us up in due course, filled us full of rum which 'didn't touch the sides' as it went down and took us over to Ponza Island, where we spent the night with the radio crew. The next day the HSL returned and took us back to Naples.

Flight Sergeant, J A Reid, 293 Squadron

This, as it happened, was Tony Morabito's last rescue, for he was tour expired on 13 April.

Beagle Pilot No.3 – the Boss
Back on Corsica, 284 Squadron had been kept busy in April. On the 10th, the Borgo detachment, with Walrus aircraft, and aircraft from 283 Squadron, merged to become 284 Squadron detachment, under the command of Flight Lieutenant G M Gallagher. The next day, they had their first rescue under this 'new management', carried out by Pilot Officer Lisle Newman and Flight Sergeant E E Smith (Z1784).

The pilot turned out to be a neighbour of theirs, Major Bert Sanborn, commanding officer of the 2nd Squadron (the Beagles), 52nd Fighter Group.

On the day I was shot down we had made a sweep up the coast just looking for something to clobber. I was flying a Mark XII Spitfire, the only one on the squadron. It was very light coloured, some called it white, and I had been told that it was known and considered a good target by the other team. I had taken it for my personal plane. When he delivered it, the ferry pilot said I shouldn't let a green pilot fly it but he wouldn't tell me just why. Needless to say I tried it out and found what he meant. On the day of the mission I had with me a new pilot and I was going to show him how to do things. Boy did I show him!

We dived-bombed a rail yard outside Leghorn and then proceeded to shoot the place up a bit. On my first pass I wasn't touched and should have quit – the intelligent thing to do. However, someone called in that all the quad-20s were giving me full attention. I guess that after two years overseas I was getting a bit short tempered (and stupid) so I went back after the guns. I was right on the deck and as I opened up on one crew, they did the same and from what I could see it was a draw.

I was hit under and behind the engine. That resulted in all sorts of improper odds and ends coming into the cockpit. I was not hit myself in any way but I thought it was better to head out to sea. I headed away from land, and called the D/F station. An officer named Rocky, from Muleshoe, Texas, always manned the radio when I flew. When I decided the engine had had it, I tried to jettison the canopy which would not co-operate, so I forced one side open and the slipstream completed the job.

Next, my seat-pack decided to jam, so instead of just popping out, I slid down the fuselage. Again, with more luck than skill, I missed the tail. I'd always wanted to know if you could find the D-ring by sight if your hands were burned and unable to feel. You can't, and I guess I shook a few others up with the delay.

It was also my first flight without my personal 'chute, so the slack fit was an interesting experience! No problem from there on. I just sat in my dinghy, dodging bottles, cigarette cases and other high-speed missiles my friends tried to drop to me. I was rather close to the coast but as the other side had shelled a Walrus a short time before [and been strafed for this temerity], I gather they decided taking a shot at the CO was not in their best interests. I also had a couple of fighter-bomber flights sitting overhead, which seemed to get their interest. A PT boat was sent after me, I understand, but the Walrus arrived first. I had met the pilot before this, and his first remark as he pulled alongside, was, 'What are you doing up here?' I believe I replied, 'fishing' and asked if he'd brought any bait!

My 'new boy' wrote that we were flying level at 3,000 feet when the flak started breaking around us and he shot his way out with guns blazing. Did you ever hear of a pilot shooting his way out at 3,000 feet with 'guns blazing'? To make it better he said he did it at other times. I have been caught in light flak at low altitude a number of times and I always just hit the deck and fly the hell out of there – wide open. It was 'his' guns blazing that were of great interest to me as his leader, plus the seat of my pants as I left the area!

Major B S Sanborn, 2nd FS, 52nd FG

Sanborn had baled out eight miles from the coast and one by one his pilots had to leave the area of the dinghy and return to base. The last to leave were Dixie Alexander and Jim Varnell Jr (Sully). I was in touch with Dixie Alexander – a former Eagle pilot with the RAF – before his sad passing in 1993. He also sent me a copy of his book *They Called me Dixie* from which he gave me permission to quote. Of this episode he recorded:

On the 11th, Major Sanborn, the CO, led a dive-bombing raid north-west of St Vincenzo. We were after a railway bridge over which the Germans passed a lot of supplies. I don't believe we seriously damaged the bridge, but we certainly weakened it and made it impassable for several days. We then strafed two trains and a bunch of trucks. Sandy was hit by flak on the way out and I was hit by small arms fire. I saw the round come up through my starboard wing, and at the same time heard the 'plink' and smelled the cordite. It's funny how you always get that certain odour, even if it's a small round.

Sandy, however, was severely hit. He took his airplane as far as he could and then baled out about eight miles off the coast. At first we had six aircraft orbiting the spot where he had gotten into his dinghy, but after a while only Varnell and I remained. I was usually able to conserve my gas better than most pilots, and I always tried to tell the guys, especially in my flights, that when on a straightaway, reducing manifold pressure and r.p.m. would stand them in good stead. Anyway, we had alerted base by way of the first two returning aircraft. Varnell and I were relieved by a section of four Spitfires. Sandy was picked up by the Walrus and brought home in good shape.

Lisle Newman:

There was an amusing incident with Major Sanborn's rescue. When we landed beside the smoke float we couldn't immediately see him at all. I thought, good God, have I landed on top of him? Where the hell is he? My first thought then was that I would have to take off again in order to locate him. Then he suddenly came shooting up over a trough.

We got him aboard in about two minutes and in, then we were going down again. I told Smithy to hang on; no time to put up his seat. Then he hit his head on the roof and fell back in a crumpled heap on the floor. I went to throttle back and then I thought if he is hurt he must be flown back as quickly as possible. So I continued the take-off – another four bangs – and we were off.

Luckily the Major was not hurt and came up just rubbing his head a few minutes later.

By this time Squadron Leader Sterne had put me forward for a commission while on Corsica, which was approved. This served me well because I got down to Egypt later and finally Iraq for two more years.

Pilot Officer L H Newman, 283 Squadron

Bert 'Sandy' Sanborn had stayed with a burning P.38 earlier in his career and spent 18 months recovering from his injuries but then rejoined the squadron in Tunisia. He remained in the USAF after the war, retiring with the rank of Lieutenant-Colonel.

Another Squadron Commander
Lisle Newman and Flight Sergeant E E Smith, still with 283 but attached to 284, rescued another American CO on the 15th, this time it was Major William P 'Red' Benedict 'boss' of the 66th Squadron (P.47 Thunderbolts), 57th FG, 9th Air Force. He was some way off the Corsican coast – 42.45N 10.35E, and they fished him out at 12.20 hours. Lisle Newman remembers little of this rescue although he vividly recalls that the Major was a large individual, well over six feet tall, and it took Smithy all his strength to get him into the Walrus.

On the 24th, Gallagher and Smith picked up another 57th Group pilot, Lieutenant James A Eaglen from the 65th Squadron. It was Eaglen's second recovery from the sea. The 57th Group was operating from Alto, Corsica.

Another HSL Co-operation

Four days after this rescue, on the 28th, Flight Sergeants Colin Paterson and Eric Keeble (X9471) were ordered up by Borgo Control at 16.15 hours to search for a downed Liberator crew. Seven men had apparently baled out of it, so a search was made for Mae Wests. Spotting one, they landed and picked up 2nd Lieutenant P F Rabne, who'd been wounded, then taxi-searched, finding another man, Lieutenant P W Magmuson half an hour later. He was so exhausted and distressed that it took an hour for the Walrus crew to get him into the aircraft. With nobody else in sight they then had to taxi back to the coast where they handed their customers over to medics at 19.30, but not without some difficulty as we shall read below. Still unable to take off, they then had to taxi to Bastia Harbour, some 50 miles away, escorted by an HSL, reaching it at 01.30 in the morning.

Once again HSL 2543, commanded by Jack Rogers, was in on the rescue. His report says:

At approximately 16.40 Regional Flying Control informed us that another pilot had been found two miles north-west of first airman and that two aircraft were covering positions. Was also informed that the sea was unsuitable for the Walrus to land. At approximately 17.00 I heard via VHF that the Walrus had landed and picked up two airmen but was unable to take off. A third airman had been found. I decided to pick up the third airman and then return to the Walrus and take off their two survivors.

Aircraft now reported they had lost contact with the man in the water but would continue to search. During this time I returned to the Walrus to transfer the survivors. I arrived at aircraft at 17.45 and communicated with them through VHF asking if I could take survivors from them. I received: 'No. Water too rough. I'm going to beach the aircraft at the nearest point. My engine is not too good – please stand by.'

I then asked of the pilot what type of beach it was and offered to tow the aircraft rather than risk beaching the craft. The pilot had decided to beach aircraft and for me to take survivors from him. The Walrus eventually beached at 18.45. I informed Control of the position and requested an ambulance to proceed there at once.

I was unable to contact Walrus so returned to search for third airman at the same time, informing Control of my intentions. During this time, ambulance had been unable to make contact with the aircraft, the nearest road being a considerable distance from the beach – some four miles. At 19.23 I was ordered to return to the Walrus and take off survivors. At 19.27 I recovered a fighter dinghy in position 42.08N/09.45E. Control informed me this had no connection with present search.

I arrived back at scene of beaching at 19.50 and found aircraft attempting to become waterborne. On succeeding he taxied very near the HSL. It was impossible to communicate with the flying boat and the craft was beached again. This operation was repeated three times. By this time four men had arrived at the beach, presumably the ambulance party and the survivors were handed over to them. The Walrus again became waterborne and attempted to take off but without success.

It now appeared that the aircraft needed my assistance and the crew communicated with me by means of semaphore. They desired me to lead them to harbour. Course was set at 20.30 and Walrus moored up at 01.30 hours.

* * *

A Tragic Waste
Towards the end of April, the 29th, the Air Sea Rescue service lost one of its long-serving air gunners in a stupid and tragic way. Warrant Officer R C 'Sticky' Glew DFM had been with the Walrus squadrons for three years both in England and the Mediterranean, and was at Cutella landing ground on this day.

He had just flown into Cutella with Hamish Reid and was hammering in tent pegs for a billet. Suddenly a gaggle of P.47 Thunderbolts from the 325th Fighter Squadron, (assigned to the 306th US Bomb Wing) way off course, spotted the strip and decided it was enemy and four, in line abreast, came down to strafe it. Several aircraft were hit on the ground, Spitfires, P.40s and P.47s, and one bullet went through the tent. On one side stood Hamish, on the other Sticky Glew. Glew was hit by the bullet and died instantly. He was buried at Termoli, a brief ceremony officiated by the 293 Wing padre, following a memorial service. Four other people on the ground were injured.

Later an American Thunderbolt pilot came to the detachment to apologise and it was understood that he was then sent back to the States.

Go For Five, Get Six
May 1st saw four aircraft from 1 SAAF Squadron, led by Captain A J 'Tony' Biden, take off at 06.00 am on a weather recce to Sulmona, Spoleto, Perugia, Cattolica and Ancona. He attempted to fly inland at one point but the cloud was right on the deck, so he continued up the coast. Cloud over the sea was 9,000 feet but it gradually lowered till the four aircraft were right down at sea level by the time Ancona was reached.

Off Roseto, Captain Ben Odendaal saw a flare on the sea, reported it to Tony Biden and the four pilots went to the spot and located a dinghy and five men, who waved up at them as they flew by. Biden reported the find to Control and then orbited the spot until two more Spitfires arrived. Had the South Africans left, it would have been very difficult for anyone to have found them again in the choppy sea.

At 07.50 Lieutenant Jimmy Landman and Ozzie Newton-Thompson were the two pilots sent off to relieve the four aircraft over the dinghy, the four having then to return to base. Soon afterwards a Walrus hove into view, and landed on the rough sea, which damaged its hull, but it taxied to the dinghy and got the five men aboard.

The Walrus, from 284 Squadron (W2747), was piloted by Trevor Humphrey, in company with his Yorkshire gunner, Heseltine. Their customers were Americans, the survivors of a B.17 crew, one of two bombers lost over the Adriatic on 30 April.

The Americans had been in the sea for some while for bad weather had prevented flying, with high winds, heavy rain, and so on. However, a weather-Spit, out on a recce, spotted a dinghy and off we went on a sortie which was to last five hours, ten minutes – most of which was spent on the water!

It was a very heavy sea and I put the nose of the Walrus through an eight-footer instead of over the top of it. The men didn't look in a good way – there wasn't much waving going on – so I had to go down for them. The huge wave smashed the side cockpit window and bent the nose round, popping a lot of rivets on the outside (we were in a metal Walrus) but luckily got away with it.

We hauled these chaps on board and just as we were just getting the last one in, Hesletine said, 'I think we've got another customer!' 'What?' I asked. 'Well, there's this chap coming down in his parachute.'

Looking up, there indeed was one of our Spitfire escort, having baled out due to his engine cutting out. We weren't too far off the coast, but we got him aboard, which made a total of eight bodies. There was just no way of getting off, so it was going to be a matter of taxying to Ortona, which was at least two to three hours away. This we managed and just outside Ortona a boat came out as we began to receive shellfire from the coast.

The chap on the boat was indicating to me that I should go further south in order to get out of range of the guns and to find a place to beach. However, I had now a 500 mag. drop on the port magneto and a 250 drop on the starboard one, so all the taxying had oiled up the plugs, which wasn't helping either.

So, with 88 mm shells splashing all about us, we headed south and away and finally beached. The Walrus was a write-off after that for I'd really strained the metal one side where the rivets had popped, and concertinaed the nose forward of the front hatch. Whether it was ever rebuilt I don't know but as far as the squadron was concerned, it was a write-off.

The Spitfire pilot had been Lieutenant J O Newton-Thompson, a South African. After the war the MCC went to South Africa and amongst the teams they played was one from Cape Province. I read that a certain Newton-Thompson had made 77 not out and I thought, that name seems familiar, so on spec, I wrote to him and asked if had been one of my customers? He wrote back and said 'yes', and that, thanks to me, he was able to live to tell the tale and had no qualms about scoring so heavily against the MCC!

Flying Officer T H Humphrey, 284 Squadron

Newton-Thompson's engine had cut after an hour's flying, but no red warning light had come on to indicate that the fuel in the long-range tank was running low. He had tried to switch to main tank but the engine failed to pick up, so he had to bale out. He was at 600 feet as he did so, and after the parachute opened, he only swung once before he hit the water. As he came to the surface he saw a plume of water as his Spitfire went in. Jimmy Landman watched – chuckling – as Ozzie got into his dinghy and hoisted its little red flag.

The 'Spongebag' call-sign used by 284 Squadron had been changed this same morning to 'Brainstrust', which Jimmy Landman mistook for 'Brainstorm' and used this several times in radio conversations with both the Walrus crew and with Control. The latter became confused at one point and started using 'Brainstorm' too.

However, Landman successfully directed the Walrus to the dinghy's position, and as Newton-Thompson reported, it took 4$\frac{1}{2}$ hours to taxi back to safety. Trevor Humphrey finally beached at San Vito, and despite the damage, was able to take off again next morning. John Oswald Newton-Thompson was promoted to Captain in September 1944 and transferred to 4 SAAF Squadron and received the DFC the following year.

In 1 SAAF, Newton-Thompson had been the dinghy officer, a job that occasioned him to lecture on emergency dinghy-drill. He was now able to talk from first-hand knowledge and experience.

The rescued Americans had been Lieutenants W A Hoffman and E T Betz, and Staff/Sergeants G Aletsee, O McCullers and L Fornia, from the 773rd Bombardment Squadron, 463rd Bomb Group, operating out of Celone air base, Italy.

More Americans, and some Italians
The Walrus men made three rescues on 3 May. 284 Squadron's Gallagher and Smith went out to help in the rescue of a downed Mitchell crew during the morning, finding and picking up 1st Lieutenant H Beebe and his crew. Two attempts at take-off with this load failed and so a rendezvous was arranged with a HSL, and the customers were transferred, allowing the Walrus to get airborne. Beebe's crew were 2nd Lieutenants W H Martin and N J Lunmark, Staff/Sergeants I S Escher, Korzeriowiski and Sergeant R Sinclair.

Shortly after noon, Paterson and Keeble took off in Z1784 and rescued four Italians from a raft, ten miles off the island of Pianosa, half way between Corsica and the mainland. They were escaping from the Germans who were conscripting islanders for forced labour battalions in Germany.

Meantime, 293 Squadron's Brown and Taylor took off late morning to fly to a spot three miles north of Pianosa Island too. They were escorted by two P.39s from the 347th US Fighter Squadron, 350th FG – Lieutenants Sharek and John P Jerue. Upon arrival, they saw a Liberator circling, then saw fluorescene patches and a dinghy which apparently the circling Liberator crew had dropped to men in the water. As the Walrus crew arrived, they spotted one man without a Mae West, swimming towards the dinghy. Landing quickly, the Walrus had just reached the dinghy as the man arrived.

Taking the man on board, the Liberator then buzzed them, indicating another crew member in the water some way off. Obviously the downed crew had baled out, hence the spread of bodies. Brown taxied over and picked this man up, and then taxied north another three miles to where the Liberator crew were doing sterling work, having now found yet another crewman, dropping a smoke float to indicate his position, and then helping to guide the Walrus to him.

With three men aboard, and no more to be seen, Brown attempted to take off, but with a five-six foot swell he was finding it difficult. Therefore he taxied some 20 miles and finally, finding calmer water, was able to get off after three more attempts. The rescued airmen, Lieutenants Rutter and Manhart and Staff Sergeant Schneider, were from the 824th Bombardment Squadron, 484th Bomb Group.

In 1995, Bud Markel, President and founder of the 484th Bomb Group Association, wrote to me concerning these events of 3 May 1944:

> On this date the 484th Bomb Group flew a practice mission to re-acquaint crew members with formation flying and to practice pin-point bombing. While this type of mission could not duplicate combat conditions exactly because there was no opposition, and live bombs were not used, it was a method of increasing the crews' proficiency.
>
> The crew led by 1st Lieutenant William Abbey, in a B.24 (No.21 *Rum Runner*) were returning after dropping practice bombs (100 lb thin steel sand-filled bombs with black powder in the nose to give off black smoke) on the small island of Pianosa.
>
> According to Forrest Nance, Abbey's B.24 had asked for permission to fly closer to Ship #15 – *Ramp Rooster*, flown by Forrest Nance, so that in-flight photos could be taken. Nance was leading a six-plane formation that day. Abbey's plane approached from its right side bringing it parallel with the left side of Nance's aircraft. The two ships collided, Abbey's plane losing about 12 feet of the right wing. Because the command pilot on a B.24 sits in the left seat, a close-in approach from the right would be awkward, as the pilot would have to look over his right shoulder and over the co-pilot, through the opposite window. From later discussion on the ground, Nance accused Abbey of sloppy flying and continued to tease him from time to time so it has to be assumed that Abbey was flying at the time of the incident and not the co-pilot. After the war, when Bill Abbey was sick, probably at the time he was suffering from the onset of cancer, Nance went to visit him and apologised for all the ribbing. Abbey died sometime after the visit.
>
> On impact the three crew members, 1st Lieutenant Myron Manhart – navigator, 2nd Lieutenant Sheldon M Rutter – bombardier, and Staff/Sergeant Bernard R Schneider – nose gunner, all in the nose of the aircraft, baled out quickly through the nose wheel door after seeing parts of Abbey's plane being swept away. There is some thought that the bale-out bell may have sounded. The rest of the crew were pinned down as the aircraft went into a flat spin shortly after impact, and could not bale out.
>
> By adding full throttle on number three and four engines and pulling power from one and two engines, Lt Abbey was able to break out of the

spin and fly carefully back to the airfield at Torretta, Italy, (near Cerignola) and was able to make a difficult landing using full aileron for lateral control. Nance's aircraft sustained damage to the number one engine's oil line, causing the crew to feather it. They were then able to fly back to base safely.

Meanwhile, Sergeant Schneider fell deep into the water and was trapped under his parachute. Using a pocketknife he was able to cut a hole in his parachute and swim through it. His life vest inflated immediately and he opened the sea marker cartridge. The bright yellow dye was visible from the air and another B.24 (possibly Nance's aircraft) spotted three crew members in the water and flew in a circular pattern around the downed men at low altitude and possibly dropping several extra Mae Wests and a dinghy.

One source quotes that several Me109s may have flown over to investigate and saw what was going on, but did not attack and flew off. The Me109s were normally based at Udine, in northern Italy. The circling B.24 was able to direct a Walrus to the general area. The three crewmen were spread wide apart. Lieutenant Manhart, reported to be an accomplished swimmer, was trying to swim back to Italy. The circling B.24 directed the Walrus to taxi to each man where rescue was effected.

By this time the sea had become too rough to take off so the plane had to taxi to smoother water and after three attempts to break free of the ocean's surface it finally took off and brought the men back to Italy where they were put up in a British Field Hospital at San Servo. The men by now were quite sick due to swallowing a lot of seawater. They were put up in a malaria ward that was full of suffering British soldiers. They were picked up the next day by Major Fairbanks of the 824th Squadron and driven back to the airfield in a staff car.

Lieutenant Rutter was not a regular member of the crew; he had replaced the assigned bombardier, Leonard Jorgenson, who was left back in the States because of illness. On this day Lieutenant Rutter was not wearing a life vest and had to swim to the Walrus.

I pieced this story together from several sources including telephone interviews with Lieutenant Nance and Sergeant Schneider, and Edwin Turner, the crew chief of *Rum Runner*, so the events may not be historically correct in fine detail, but the incident did happen basically as described.

Tech/Sergeant John L Hahan, the flight engineer, who landed with the aircraft was not wearing a parachute harness on this day either. He would have gone down with the plane if everyone had had to bale out.

The crews were:

Rum Runner		*Ramp Rooster*	
1st Lt William A Abbey Jr	pilot	Capt E Forrest Nance	pilot
1st Lt Walter G Price	co-pilot	1st Lt Layton W McDonald	co-pilot
1st Lt Myron A Manhart	nav	1st Lt Jack Glitterman	nav

Rum Runner		*Ramp Rooster*	
2nd Lt Sheldon M Rutter	bomb	1st Lt Reinhold Rickert	bomb
T/Sgt John L Hahn	eng	T/Sgt Andrew J Beard	eng
T/Sgt David H Wolfe Jr	radio	T/Sgt Robert J Dixon	radio
S/Sgt Bernard R Schneider	nose gun	T/Sgt John P Hensel	nose gun
S/Sgt Albert K Borcharding	ball gun	S/Sgt Eugene La Pierre	upper gun
S/Sgt Scott W Larson	tail gun	S/Sgt Melvin I Albert	tail gun
S/Sgt Joseph E Pemental	upper gun		

Rum Runner was repaired by the service squadron and returned to duty. It is doubtful that this aircraft survived the war as at one time, because of severe losses, the 824th Squadron was reduced to just five aircraft. Normal complement was 12, but often was as high as 20 aircraft. *Ramp Rooster* was damaged by flak and fighters on 17 December 1944, and salvaged a few days later. On average each original aircraft was replaced three times in the one year the 484th Bomb Group was operational.

Success Never Guaranteed
Mention of the Airacobra pilots of the 347th Fighter Squadron, 350th FG, who escorted several rescue missions, gives the opportunity to show how it was not always possible to complete such sorties with happy endings.

In mid-April 1944, Lieutenant James T Madderra, a popular 'Red Ass' (347th FS) pilot was shot down by flak along the Italian coast whilst engaged on a dive-bombing mission. He was seen to bale out of his P.39, land in the water, inflate his dinghy and wave to his brother pilots as they flew low over him.

Because of his nearness to the occupied Italian mainland as well as the dangerousness of heavily mined waters in his vicinity, it was impossible to send air sea rescue planes or launches to bring him in. Jim Madderra had been with the 347th since June 1943 and ended up as a prisoner of war.

Chapter 6

TOWARDS ROME

293 Squadron's first rescue by its detachment at Pomigliano came on 12 May 1944, when they saved a Liberator crew from the 485th Bomb Group. This was carried out by Flight Sergeant E J Holmes and his New Zealand gunner, Jack Berry. Walrus X9506 'C' was scrambled at 14.10 pm and told to fly to position 40.41N/14.21E where two dinghies had been sighted. Arriving at 14.28 they saw two American fighters and a Boston circling the two rubber rafts with nine men in them.

Landing safely, Holmes taxied to the dinghies and took on board most of the men but all nine bodies could not be fitted in. The engine was stopped and a passing ferryboat was signalled to come alongside and take some of the airmen. Seven were transferred, the most seriously wounded one, plus one other, remaining in the Walrus. Now able to take off, Holmes took his two passengers back to base.

The Lib had come from the 830th Squadron of the 485th Bomb Group and consisted of Lieutenants Martin, Strandord, Connolly Jr, Flight Officer W S Lee, Sergeants Knight, Mungier and Maxton, Corporals Longo and Hughes. Unhappily, the tenth crew member, Sergeant Haymer had gone down with the aircraft.

You Can't Win Them All
Four days later (the 16th) Reg Hayes and J W Bradley were scrambled in the same Walrus to rescue a P.40 fighter pilot down in the sea off the coast north of Gaeta Point, near a heavily defended spot covered by German AA gunners. Taking off at 17.50 pm, Hayes was over the spot at 18.15 and was extremely pleased to see four Spitfires orbiting the position. Unfortunately, two people from the shore had swum, or waded out to the airman's dinghy and pulled him in. The Walrus crew could see the man on the beach with his two rescuers.

The pilot was Lieutenant P E Duncan of the 314th Fighter Squadron, 324th Fighter Group, operating on a late afternoon mission from Pignataro Maggiore, Italy. He was reported missing and presumably ended up as a prisoner of war.

The Spitfires were from 601 Squadron which had been scrambled to the spot, and finding four P.40s circling over a dinghy a mere 75 yards off shore, relieved them. At this point, Lieutenant P D Pote SAAF (JF746) reported that his engine was running rough. Others saw his machine begin to stream glycol and the South African quickly decided he would have to take to his parachute. Fortunately there was an American destroyer in the vicinity – the USS *McKinley* – so two of the Spitfires escorted Pote to it, where he baled out and was picked out of the water after 15 minutes by the warship.

Meantime, Flying Officer C St.C Yarnell RCAF had stayed above the P.40 pilot, whose dinghy had drifted almost to the shore where men could be seen waiting for him. Yarnell's aircraft was then hit by light AA fire, just before he heard that the Walrus was heading in. Once the Walrus came in sight, Yarnell dived down and fired a short burst into a nearby lake to attract its attention, then called Hayes to tell him that the P.40 pilot was now on a jetty, advising Hayes to land and taxi alongside it.

Reg Hayes obviously felt that this was a bit risky considering the presence of what must be assumed to be enemy soldiers on or near the jetty, and especially with the likelihood of more hostile gunfire.

Hayes circled low over their heads, while preparing a note to drop, instructing the pilot to make an effort to put back to sea in a small rowing boat that they could also see just along the beach. Circling round for the third time, automatic small-arms fire was encountered; the natives were decidedly unfriendly. One bullet entered the cockpit through the windscreen, and wounded Hayes in the left arm. Nevertheless he continued to circle but noted that the three men had moved off inland and taken cover. Hayes informed the fighters what had happened and that he had no choice then but to return to base.

At this stage a call came that a High Speed Launch was approaching, its skipper announcing to the aircraft that it had just been shelled from Gaeta. Yarnell flew towards it and directed the boat towards the jetty but more shells fell close to the HSL and its skipper decided enough was enough, and as the missing pilot was now nowhere to be seen, the HSL turned away for home.

Hayes was the first man in 293 Squadron to be wounded in action. He was later to receive the American DFC, similar decorations being received by other Walrus pilots, Squadron Leader Walter Sterne DSO and Colin Horne, both of 283 Squadron.

Oranges for Lunch

On the 19th Holmes and Berry were back in action, again in X9506. Again the area of search was off Gaeta Point but a good look round failed to produce any sightings. Then an aircraft was noticed circling further out to the west. Holmes flew over and found a dinghy two miles west of Gaeta, and a mile off shore. He landed immediately and picked up 2nd Lieutenant Steven Molner of the US 315th Fighter Squadron, 324th Fighter Group, and returned him to his squadron's base at Capua. The 315th had been on a mission to Fondi that morning, meeting heavy AA fire, which brought down Molner and Lieutenant A J Harnet (still missing) both of whom had baled out.

Twenty-five minutes after returning from this sortie, Holmes and Berry were sent off again to make another rescue, taking a few oranges with them as their lunch. This time the search area was five miles south of Terracina, but they only found a floating mine.

From this spot they flew to a second Mayday position – 41.13N/13.37E, but again found nothing. Radio calls were continually made with base and this brought a new position. On the way to this one, the Walrus was met by a P.39 fighter and guided to a dinghy 15 miles out from the Volturno River mouth. Holmes landed at 15.45 and rescued a man from a dinghy and four others who were hanging from its sides. Taking the men aboard, they taxied one mile to the east and picked up a lone survivor floating in the sea.

The aircraft now had six passengers and two crewmen, so Hayes started to taxi towards the coast. Three miles off the beach two HSLs came along and the six injured men were taken off and onto HSL 133. The Walrus took off at 16.05 and was back home 20 minutes later. The survivors came from a downed B.24 from Cerignola airfield.

Corsica, May 1944

In April the Borgo detachment with Walrus aircraft and aircraft from 283 Squadron had become 284 detachment under Flight Lieutenant Gallagher. On 12 May, Warrant Officer J A 'Hamish' Reid, and Tony Morabito (the latter tour-expired but still operating), were sent off late in the day – 20.40 – to rescue a downed Spitfire pilot north of Cap Corse.

Eight pilots of 328 Squadron, Free French, had been flying an armed-reconnaissance mission between La Spezia and Livorno. Attacking a trawler they found off the coast, Lieutenant de Saboulin's engine had suddenly stopped, causing him to ditch into the sea. The Frenchman suffered leg and facial injuries in the crash which hampered the Walrus crew's efforts to get him into the amphibian, but they did so. They were not helped either by the darkness nor by the fact that a nearby airfield on the coast was suffering a heavy air raid attack.

Getting the injured pilot safely away from the coast, Reid later met up with HSL 2597 – Flight Lieutenant T H Lindsell – which took de Saboulin aboard, allowing Reid to taxi home via Bastia harbour, which they reached at 00.25 am.

> By the time we had transferred the Frenchman to the HSL it was too dark for us to attempt a take-off in the open sea, so we decided to taxi back to Bastia and the HSL skipper promised to arrange that we would be guided into the harbour when we eventually arrived. So we set off on a course to reach the coast, not particularly worried, for the minefield we knew we would have to pass over was set at 12 feet and we could use our Aldis lamp to keep far enough away from the coastline to prevent running aground.
>
> Happily chugging along, we heard some aircraft fly overhead and then spotted some activity on the horizon, roughly on our heading, but about 20 miles away. Then some bastards started shooting at us!
>
> Our wake and the exhaust ring of the Pegasus engine which would be glowing red hot were a give away, so someone had decided to get in a bit of target practice on their way to their real target. I quickly shut everything off and waited until things seemed quiet ahead. Tony had the worst job, as he had to hand-crank the inertia starter so that we could continue our journey into Bastia.
>
> We were met later and the trickiest bit was avoiding the partially sunken ships in the harbour. When we eventually got back to our base we

found some stuff had been dropped on it, mainly small stuff, but
fortunately with no casualties.

Warrant Officer J A Reid, 284 Squadron

Shortly afterwards, the two ASR boys were the guests of the Wing in which 145
Squadron operated, at a 'bash' at the Victor Emanuel Palace at Caserta. This was
due to their rescue of Flight Sergeant Newman, on 10 April. They ended up
being presented with a highly polished Alfa-Romeo propeller blade, which they
stuck up outside their tent and used as a shaving mirror.

Three days later – the 15th – Paterson and Keeble, in L1784, took off during
the morning in company with HSLs, to rescue a downed B.25 crew off Elba.
Trevor Humphrey and Heseltine, in X9471, stood by and were later called to give
support. Humphrey and his usual gunner, Heseltine, had recently returned to the
squadron having requested a return to Corsica from 293 Squadron, on 6 May.

The rescue area was south of Elba, where the Walrus arrived at 10.40 to find
that the three men spotted in Mae Wests had been lost sight of by three patrolling
fighters. In company with the escort, everyone began a fresh search and after 15
minutes, one airman was sighted. Paterson landed and picked him up and then
taxied about, spotting a second man and picked him up as well. Still chugging
round the third man was finally discovered and rescued.

The three men had baled out and the remaining missing men were known to
be in different positions, so the Walrus took off and landed at base at 12.10.

One of those rescued had suffered flak wounds to the body, the second man
a torn hip, and all three men were chilled. The rescue had been hampered
because their life vests lacked fluorescene. Paterson and Keeble had done an
excellent job, as they discovered they were taxying through a minefield and
some of the mines had broken free and were floating around on the surface. Yet
they stayed for half an hour on the water, even going to within 50-100 yards of
Elba in order to pick up all three men.

Humphrey and his gunner, having been sent out later, were recalled once
HSL 2595 – Flight Lieutenant James F Lang – picked up three other men,
including the captain, Lieutenant Simpson. All came from the 446th Bomb
Squadron, 321st Bomb Group. Lang received the DSC and his Cox'n, Flight
Sergeant J Edwards BEM, the DSM.

A Different Sort of Rescue?

Paterson and Keeble were involved in a very strange rescue on 21 May, being
sent off at 12.25 by Borgo Controller, which had been told that two dinghies had
been spotted off the coast, with four men in one, and one in the second.

Paterson reached the area at 13.05 and found the dinghies without any
difficulty. The sea was quite rough in the area of the singleton, so he landed by
the others where conditions were better. Picking up the occupants, he took off
and returned to Borgo, while two P.39s guided a HSL to the solo man, and took
him on board. Altogether there had been six US P.39 Airacobras giving help and
cover, Lieutenants Miller, Sharek, Heckenkamp, King, Franek and Weida, again
from the 347th Fighter Squadron.

It was soon found that the men were not survivors in distress. A British soldier amusing himself in a dinghy, had drifted out to sea as the wind became stronger and seeing him, four American soldiers had tried to reach him in another dinghy, but they too could not regain the beach. Still, it ended happily and all helped with the head-count of bodies picked-up.

Two Springboks

Two South African fighter pilots were the next men collected by 293 Squadron towards the end of May. On the 24th, Denny Lunn and Warrant Officer Kelly (Z1779) went off at 09.30 and just over an hour later brought back Lieutenant D T Gilson of 1 SAAF.

Derek Gilson had been one of eight pilots from Sinella landing ground who had escorted 12 Marauders up the east coast of Italy. Near Rosetto he noticed his engine temperature had risen to 100 degrees and was still rising. He turned, escorted by Colin Shaw, his No.2, and climbed to 16,000 feet. Glycol fumes were now streaming from the engine, and then, while some way north-east of Pescara, the engine burst into flames; the time had come to leave.

He had some difficulty getting rid of the canopy but once this was done, he rolled over and pushed the stick forward. Out he popped, and seeing the aircraft fall away below him, rapidly deployed his parachute. Drifting down he attached the dog lead from his dinghy to his Mae West and within minutes he had splashed down into the sea.

Nearing the water he had turned the release buckle, hitting it as he touched down, the parachute collapsing clear of him. Inflating his Mae West with the CO_2 bottle, he then hauled in the dinghy, but he found it difficult to get it out of its pack, so remained supported by the Mae West. The fluorescene patch was easily spotted by his wingman (although Gilson was forced to swallow several mouthfuls of it as the waves broke over him), whereupon he climbed to transmit a fix. Within 40 minutes of ditching, the Walrus arrived, landed and brought him home. It will be recalled that Derek Gilson helped in the rescue of his wingman back on 25 March 1944.

On the 26th, Hall and Kelly (Z1779) brought back Lieutenant R G Bosch of 4 SAAF Squadron, from Sinella LG, in time for a late breakfast. 21-year-old Bosch was one of four Spitfire IX pilots out on an armed-recce of the roads up along the east coast of Italy to Ancona and Fabriano, flying at 10,000 feet. They found and strafed some MT but Bosch's engine began to give trouble and he had to bale out over the sea, 12 miles north of Pesaro. Within the hour Hall and Kelly had him out of the water and heading for safety.

293 Squadron's Detachment at Nettuno

In late May 1944, 293 Squadron set up a C Flight detachment at Nettuno, at Anzio, only about 35 miles south of Rome. Anzio had seen the Allied landings on 22 January, being heavily defended by the Germans until mid-May, and now the 'Eternal City' was about to be occupied by the Allies in early June.

The detachment was living underground and had little or no stores. Luckily 43 Squadron, based nearby, was helping out. The sea party arrived from Naples on the evening of 24 May. The usual crowd of envious Americans collected around the Walrus aircraft, asking questions, most of which were: 'How old are they?' or 'What do they do exactly?'

One American that found out was Lieutenant Gordon A Bell of the 84th Fighter Squadron, 79th Fighter Group – a P.47 pilot – on 6 June. While in northern France this day saw the invasion of France along the Normandy beaches, Gordon Bell was flying a sortie north of Rome. His mission ended in a dinghy 30 miles up the coast from the mouth of the River Tiber, but G F Brown and C S Taylor fished him out just a few hundred yards from shore at 15.00 and brought him home.

Gordon Bell, from Tacoma, Washington, was a veteran pilot by mid-October 1944 but his luck ran out finally on the 12th, following his 153rd combat mission. Captain Bell, as he was by then, died in a landing accident at Jesi air base, Italy. His death was recalled by Lieutenant-Colonel Herbert L Speas Jr for me back in 1995.

> I was his wingman on that mission of 12 October 1944. We were flying P.47 fighter-bombers with the 87th Squadron, 79th Fighter Group out of Ancona, Italy. Our target was a railway bridge at Compasanto, north of the Po River front line with the German army.
>
> Before reaching the target, Gordon called on the radio that he was having engine trouble and then headed back to base. We dive-bombed the bridge and formed the flight back together, heading south for base. Gordon called again and said he was losing power and could not maintain altitude, but thought he could make it across the front line to friendly territory. He kept getting lower and lower, but did make it across the front line. Gordon called that he would have to crash land and I told him that I would follow him down and mark his location to send help.
>
> He opened his canopy and made a wheels-up belly landing in what looked to be an open field, but turned out to be an orchard with mid-sized trees. He made a good landing and skidded through the orchard, knocking trees down and finally came to a stop as a wing hit a tree and spun the plane round. I pulled up and made several passes over his plane but he was still sitting in the cockpit.
>
> I flew back to Ancona and reported what had happened to Major Ben Cassiday. He jumped into a jeep with one of the other pilots and took off north to check on Gordon. Unfortunately he found that Gordon had died in the crash landing. He had forgotten to fasten his shoulder harness tight and hit his head on the gunsight just above the instrument panel.
>
> Gordon was a fine man and it was a sad occasion to lose him after he had completed 153 missions and had been awarded the Silver Star, DFC, and Air Medal with two oak leaf clusters. It was a tough business, for over the course of the war, our squadron lost about 25% of its pilots, but many survived the war as PoWs, and some were rescued or made it back to friendly territory.

Losses on the Ground

293 Squadron lost an aircraft on 22 May on Borgo airfield. A P.40 Warhawk of 5 SAAF Squadron swung on take-off due to engine failure and crashed into

Walrus P5718, wrecking it completely. Sergeant Drew of 293, sitting in a lorry close to the runway, was visibly shaken as the Warhawk had narrowly missed him as it careered to one side before slamming into the amphibian. The Walrus was replaced by K8549 flown in from North Africa on the 28th. This machine had been built in 1936 and following service at Lee, Gosport, on the carrier *Argos*, it was returned to the RAF in late 1943 and then shipped to Casablanca. It did not survive 1944, having its wheels ripped off at Rimini on 19 October, and was struck off charge.

Gannon Hits the Silk

Bell Airacobras of the 347th FS, 350th Fighter Group often helped search and rescue sorties from their base on Corsica and Sardinia during this period. The following is an extract from the 347th's history:

> 'When you gotta go, ya just gotta,' said Lieutenant Jack Gannon, 2 June, when he baled out over water after the engine of his P.39 froze and completely locked. Rapidly losing altitude, he tried to ditch his plane only to be knocked back into the cockpit by the force of the wind. He eventually threw himself clear but lost his seat dinghy in the attempt. His 'chute opened at about 600 feet. Gannon remained in the icy water for about 30 minutes. His wingman, Lieutenant Maurice Brasch, circled the swimming pilot and directed a rescuing Walrus crew to the spot. Gannon suffered no ill effects from his chilling experience.

Gannon, from Nashville, Tennessee, had joined the 347th in April 1944, and he later served with Headquarters, US Air Transport Service. Maurice Brasch, from Muskegon Heights, Michigan, later served with the 12th Tactical Air Force.

* * *

Back at Nettuno on 6 June, a Spitfire landed at the airfield in the evening and was hit by a Thunderbolt, which ran over it. Many of 293 Squadron's lads ran to help, along with others, and were caught as the Spitfire's guns let off a short burst of fire. Many casualties resulted, among them was LAC Ken Taylor, who had been with the Squadron in England, who was killed, and LAC Day, who died the next day. LAC Brown was also slightly injured.

On the 11th, the detachment retired one of its long-serving Walrus machines – X9506. She had nearly 30 'saints' painted on her (each representing a man rescued), proof that the Squadron had not always been as slack as it had recently become.

The detachment was now 100 miles behind the front line but permission to move north had been refused when requested by Flight Lieutenant Hayes. On the 13th, a Walrus was pranged on the east coast, flown by Flight Sergeant Brown and Flight Sergeant R Barnes, both of whom ended up in hospital.

However, things were about to change. In late June the detachment was sent to Tarquinia, 40 miles north of Rome, on the coast, and another went to Sinello, on the opposite east coast, south of Pescara.

* * *

On the day Gordon Bell was rescued, 284 Squadron also marked European D-Day by rescuing yet another South African, this one flying with 242 Squadron RAF.

The team of Paterson and Keeble were again on hand (Z1784), taking off at 15.40 pm. Six Spitfires of 242 Squadron had been on a fighter sweep over Florence but nothing had been seen and heavy cloud cover caused the mission to finally be aborted. Lieutenant P J S Louw, flying as Blue 2, reported that his engine temperature was rising and Red Leader told Blue 1 and 2 to return home immediately. Not long afterwards, Peter Louw's engine caught fire and he baled out, 1½ miles east of Grosseto rocks, on the west coast of Italy. His No.1 circled the spot until two P.39s arrived with a 'Digit' aircraft – the Walrus.

Louw was in his dinghy waving his little red flag as the Walrus touched down and safely hauled him aboard. However, things did not go too smoothly. The sea was rough and in landing the hull was damaged and a lot of water washed into the Walrus as the waves crashed over it. After getting the South African aboard, both he and Keeble had to pump all the way to the Isle of Grosseto, where there was calmer water for take-off.

As they approached the island, some men on a lighthouse appeared to be handling a 20 mm cannon and upon seeing this, Paterson veered away, but their escorting Spitfires made a couple of passes at the lighthouse and suddenly the men appeared to lose all interest in their gun.

Attempts were now made to take off but each one failed and then the hand pump packed up and the Walrus began to take on more water and began to sink. The three men had no choice but to climb into an M-type dinghy and await a HSL, which had been called for. Sitting in the dinghy the men watched the Walrus go under but they were soon rescued by Flight Lieutenant Lindsell and his HSL 2597 (who had helped Hamish Reid the previous month) and were taken back to Bastia.

Louw, also known as 'Dutch' by his RAF companions, was lost on 28 July 1944 during a two-man standing patrol. For unknown reasons (possibly oxygen failure as he was flying at 24,000 feet), his Spitfire suddenly plunged down in a headlong dive and crashed into the sea.

Confirmed Member of the Late Arrivals Club

On the 7th, Trevor Humphrey and Heseltine (R6549) were scrambled at 11.50 am to rescue a downed Spitfire pilot of 451 Squadron RAAF, Flying Officer G C W O'Neil MM RAAF. Everything went to plan and after picking him up, they flew him to his base at Serragia on the east coast of Corsica.

Wing Commander E J Morris DSO RAF (a South African) OC 251 Wing, led the twelve aircraft on this armed-recce, starting out at 10.05, with Flight Lieutenant E E Kirkham flying a fluid six as top cover. They attacked some road motor transport in the Tarquinia-Viterbo areas, one being set on fire by O'Neil. As they headed away, moderate small-arms fire from Vitralla hit O'Neil's coolant system (Spitfire IX MH769). Of interest here is a report, which O'Neil later made out, containing advice for those in a similar situation:

As I crossed the Italian coast I noticed the radiator temperature gauge playing games, rising and falling, from 110° to 130°. Called formation leader and throttled back to 198 mph, and +2 boost. Called 'Blacktop' on Channel 'B' and got them to fix me and give me a vector, and just as a precaution, gained angels to 4,000 feet. Oil temperature normal and engine quite smooth and I thought maybe just the gauge was u/s, but continued to keep in contact with Control on Channel 'B'. Asked them if they required further fix on Channel 'C' but they were quite satisfied.

I frequently pressed radiator control button to try and keep temperature down but unsuccessful. Rising temperature continued to increase and rose to 180°. Called Control on 'B' and informed them my 'cockerel' was in distress. Temperature rose even more and started on second time round the clock. The engine commenced to vibrate and glycol came from the starboard side. Immediately called Control, informed them and told them I may have to leave aircraft at any time. Got them to fix me again and turned onto a course of 270° to make the coast as quickly as possible.

Continued using radiator control button in attempt to keep temperature down, but it continued to rise and fall. Engine got rougher and glycol came from starboard side each time temperature reached a peak – about 90° on second time round the clock. Realised I could not possibly make the shore. Informed Control and screwed R/T switch sufficiently to leave in 'on' position. Temperature was fluctuating up to 80° on second time around the clock and engine was failing. Glycol now coming from both sides. A fire started and went out on starboard side and shortly afterwards, started again. All this time I was contacting Control and told them I was about to leave aircraft. Gave a Mayday and left R/T on. Undid straps, R/T plug and oxygen, cut switches on engine, goggles over the eyes, opened hood and side door, held aircraft steady with right hand on stick, left hand on port side of hood. Got airspeed to 120 mph and stepped on the door hinges. Dived down and out, passed trailing edge of port wing, and cleared aircraft OK.

As soon as 'chute opened, threw off gloves, helmet and heavy boots, inflated Mae West by bottle on descent and turned 'chute release to ready position. Pressed release just after striking the water and got clear of 'chute as quickly as possible, with dinghy in possession. Had a little trouble finding CO_2 bottle to inflate dinghy and it inflated inverted. However, it was no trouble to set right and get aboard. Fluorescene had dyed water considerably by this time, so I pulled it into the dinghy to conserve same, and baled out what little water was in dinghy. Dipped fluorescene in water from time to time to spread the dye (note: the fluorescene will not last over 30 minutes if used continually).

Pull in dinghy cover which contains signal lights, rations, etc. (I did not do this.) If picked up by Walrus and its wheels have not come down on landing on water, dinghy may become entangled and it is very awkward, especially if dinghy cover is still trailing over the side. Let the ASR people help you aboard the Walrus and strap yourself securely for take-off. Get aircraft from [your] formation to orbit you if sufficient fuel and get a relief sent out from base to carry on the good work. It's good for morale.

Note: See your oxygen is on and use it if any glycol is coming back into
the cockpit, using plenty when necessary.

Flying Officer G C W O'Neil, 451 Squadron

The Wing Commander and his No.2, Flying Officer E J Sidley, had circled
O'Neil for as long as their fuel lasted. Flying Officer E C House took off at
11.45, re-located the dinghy and helped guide in the Walrus. Once O'Neil had
been picked up, House dived down and destroyed the dinghy with gunfire.
George O'Neil went on to complete his tour in July.

O'Neil's was a fairly simple rescue. A good position was given by
Control, good controlling as well, telling him when to bale out, etc., and
we only took one hour, 25 minutes from take-off to the time I landed back
at base, having also landed at his base at Serragia to drop him off.
I dropped smoke floats and landed in a moderate to heavy swell – it
was a lovely summer's day I remember.

Flying Officer T H Humphrey, 284 Squadron

George Connor Watson O'Neil had been a sergeant-pilot at the beginning of
1943, with 450 Squadron. On 13 January of that year he had come down behind
enemy lines in the western desert but managed to get himself back four days
later, for which he received the Military Medal. Then on 25 July he came down
near Namman with engine failure but again found his way back to the squadron.
Now, nearly a year later, and an officer with 451 Squadron, he had been rescued
from the sea – a true member of the 'Late Arrivals Club'. He received the DFC,
Gazetted in November 1944.

* * *

Sergeant Heseltine was in on a rescue a week later (14 July) but this time his
pilot was Flight Lieutenant Gallagher, along with Sergeant K R B Jones –
X9503. 154 Squadron had been out on an armed-reconnaissance to the Florence
area, led by Group Captain P H 'Dutch' Hugo DSO DFC and Bar, CdeG, a
veteran of the Battle of Britain. Some MT had been shot-up but Flying Officer
D C Dunn's Spitfire IX (MJ677) had been hit by some light flak which damaged
his CS unit in the engine and he had to bale out 20 miles off the Italian coast.

It had been an evening mission, and 284 were scrambled at 20.45 as dusk
was setting in. Escorted by two Spitfires of 328 FF Squadron, they reached the
position at 21.25 and the occupant helped by firing off a two red star cartridge
flare. Setting down was easy, and Dunn was picked up, but getting off proved
more problematical. Gallagher made four attempts at it, failing each time to get
un-stuck, so began to taxi back. Later a HSL arrived to take the Walrus in tow,
bringing them safely into Bastia the next morning.

On the 15th, Humphrey and Warrant Officer R G Hale, in R6549, rescued an
American fighter pilot off Cap Corse, on the northern tip of Corsica. This was
2nd Lieutenant R L Johnson of the 66th Fighter Squadron, 57th Fighter Group.
Heading out at 06.50 am to a position at 42.56N/09.32E, they found two
Spitfires orbiting the dinghy.

This rescue was right up north, hardly any wind at all. They'd sent out a HSL from Bastia Harbour, but I beat them by a long way; I was quite happy about that!

Flying Officer T H Humphrey, 284 Squadron

On 20 June, 284 made the last rescue of the month. Squadron Leader J S Barnett, along with Sergeant Jones and Warrant Officer Hale (X9471) were scrambled at 13.20 to rescue a P.47 pilot found in a dinghy. Quite why it needed three crew is unclear, for in the same way that Gallagher had been unable to get off the water on the 14th, so Barnett failed too once he had rescued Lieutenant Marril of 2/3 French Squadron at position 42.55N/10.23E near Elba. Spitfires from 328 FF Squadron had been over the dinghy (Lt Rebière and Sgt Hivers). A call for help brought HSL 2595, commanded by Flight Lieutenant J F Lang DSC, which towed them back to Bastia.

293 Squadron's Detachment at Sinello

While all this had been going on around Corsica and off the Italian west coast, 293 Squadron had set up a detachment at Sinello in June, and on the 10th it made its first rescues from the new airfield.

First was a Wellington crew picked up by Denny Lunn and Norm Pickles (in L2170) early in the morning, 15 miles out from Penna Point. The five-man crew had gone down the previous night after a raid but Lunn found them, picked them up, and presumably due to calm water, was even able to take off again with the full load despite the weight. The five men were all NCOs, Flight Sergeants Slade and Briscoe, with Sergeants Barber, Taylor and Best.

At 11.20 Brown and Barnes were off in the same Walrus ('Z'), but no sooner had they become airborne than the engine cut out and they crashed into a field near the airfield, the Walrus being written-off. Brown suffered a broken jaw, a lacerated arm, plus cuts and bruises. Barnes was shaken but back with the Squadron four days later, although unfit to fly immediately.

The sortie was taken over by Lunn and Pickles, who took off in another Walrus ('W') at 11.25 and headed out from Ortona on a course of 045°, for 15 miles. They located survivors from an American Liberator in the water. Landing, the crew found it hard work to get the men aboard, Pickles having to jump into the water to swim to the dinghy in order to secure a rope to it. They finally got seven men aboard and then taxied back to Ortona Harbour. The B.24 came from the 726th Bombardment Squadron, 451st Bomb Wing, 15th Air Force. Herbert A Guiness was the pilot, who wrote in 1995:

> Thanks to the RAF Air Sea Rescue service I am living an active life in beautiful California. Our mission that day was the Porto Marghero oil refinery in northern Italy. Our Squadron, the 726th, was at the tail of the 15th Air Force formation. By the time we reached our target area, German and Italian anti-aircraft gunners had found our range and altitude, and we were struck by flak hits several times, which knocked out our two port engines (No's 3 and 4) as well as flak penetrating the fuselage and severing hydraulic lines and control cables. We lost all

hydraulic pressure and had to feather both port engines.

It was an enormous job to keep the plane flying in a straight line, and myself and my co-pilot, Lieutenant Bird, both had our right feet pushed on the starboard rudder pedal to keep her straight.

We fell out of formation due to greatly reduced speed, and we gradually lost altitude, even though we pushed the remaining two starboard engines to their limit. I believe we were at about 24,000 feet over the target, so we were able to gradually lose height safely. A single P.38 fighter flew escort with us to protect us from the enemy aircraft – the Germans loved to pick on bomber drop-outs.

As we headed back towards southern Italy over the Adriatic ocean, we gradually lost altitude. It became obvious that we could not make it back to our base outside Foggia, and even if we could have made it, our landing gear, flaps, etc, were doubtful due to the complete loss of hydraulic pressure. Therefore, bale-out or ditching seemed to be our only alternatives. I opted not to order a bale out over the sea; it was better to stick together.

The ditching, when it came, was very difficult. We could not get the flaps down (cables severed I guess), and we hit the water pretty hard. The top turret gun assembly crashed into the rear of the cockpit, instantly killing our flight engineer. The plane went under the water and then floated up to the surface after it stopped its forward motion.

It floated for about two minutes, as I recall, and then started to sink. We were able to deploy one of the rubber life rafts from the wing by releasing it externally. We all swam for it, but Sergeant Robert Anderson, our ball gunner, evidently drowned before we could get to him. I was rather bloodied up with a lacerated nose and hand from a cracked windscreen, and I cannot quite remember too much of what happened in the raft, but I do remember the Walrus setting down and taxying over to pick us up. I also remember the long taxi ride back to the coast of Italy.

On this mission, my regular bombardier, Lieutenant Schwab, did not fly with us. Lieutenant McDowell, who suffered a badly broken leg in the ditching, and who very bravely helped deploy the life raft despite his injury, had replaced him.

I recall a British doctor bandaging me up, and being given a British woollen shirt, which itched like hell, and then being taken by ambulance to the 15th Air Force hospital in Bari, where I remained for about three weeks. I then returned to my squadron and flew one more combat mission before being rotated back to the USA.

I am eternally grateful to the unknown P.38 pilot who stayed with us all the way to the ditching, and to the Walrus crew for their timely rescue.

Prior to the mission that day – which was my 32nd – our crew and my plane, named *Lonesome Polecat*, were on several missions to the oil refineries at Ploesti, Romania.

1st Lieutenant H A Guiness, 726th BS, 451st BG

Lonesome Polecat – serial # 42-52114 – arrived in Italy with the Group, its crew chief being George M Hansen. Its original pilot had been Lt W L Bias, with Guiness as co-pilot. On 30 March 1944 it suffered battle damage through fighter attack, including one very large hole in the left wing. A direct 20 mm hit in the nose had killed the nose gunner.

On the 10 June mission (Group Mission # 63) the crew had been: 1st Lieutenant Guiness, 2nd Lieutenant Bird, co-pilot, 2nd Lieutenant McDowell (bombardier), T/Sergeants Langlois and Whitlow, S/Sergeants McPeak (gunner) and Wathen (tail gunner). The two lost had been Robert J Anderson (ball gunner) and Flint W Gardner (nose gunner).

It had had a close call on 30 March during an attack by German fighters. A large hole was blown in the port wing and it took several 20 mm cannon hits. One hit the front turret and killed the gunner.

* * *

On 19 June 1944, this 293 detachment moved to San Vito, 15 miles south of Pescara, then to Tortoreto, 30 miles north of Pescaro, ten days later.

From San Vito, on the 25th, Hall and Kelly, in K8459, were scrambled at 17.30, heading out six miles from Farno. They rescued Flying Officer J Johnstone of 241 Squadron. Taking off the port float was damaged but they got away with it and returned safely to base.

241 Squadron had Johnstone (Spitfire IX JF701) make out the following report of his 'day out':

> I was No.3 of Blue Section – four aircraft – escorting 12 Baltimores to bomb marshalling yards at Rimini. Took off 14.12. On bombing run, the bombers split into two sections, each of six aircraft. Blue 1 called up and asked me to look after the second six, meanwhile the first six bombers with Blue 1 and 2, were so far ahead that I lost sight of them and never saw them again. Myself and No.4 stayed above and behind the second section, about 600 yards, and followed them out to sea and then due south-east. I was approx. 14,000 feet, my ASI approx. 240 mph. Lost sight of No.4, so called him up on the R/T and he replied but I did not understand what he said.
>
> I noticed an aircraft behind and took it to be No.4, then turned slightly to have a better look and noticed it had a long-range tank and a white spinner. Before I could do anything I was hit in the port wing and liquid poured out on fire. Engine stopped and debris flew around in the cockpit. Lost control of aircraft and removed R/T plug, oxygen and Sutton harness. Regained control and flames now extinguished. Opened hood, rolled over to the right and pushed myself out of the aircraft with left hand and both feet, my right hand firmly clamping the parachute release. There was a loud bang and pain in my crutch and I found myself dangling in mid-air and the aircraft spiralling down to the sea. Must have baled out at about 10,000 feet, at approximately 15.45.
>
> Descent seemed very slow and I could not judge my height above the water, so after falling for some time I removed my helmet and dropped

it, noticing that it took some time to hit the deck. Later I dropped one glove and the second glove hit the water very quickly so I turned the parachute release box and pressed it as soon as I entered the water. The Mae West would not inflate but I was able to remain afloat easily, so got the dinghy out and inflated it (no hand pump required), clambered aboard in the approved manner and set sail for the coast; my position approx. 20 miles north of Ancona.

My wristwatch had gone, therefore I only had a rough idea of the time. After some time had elapsed, two Spitfires flew nearby and I tried to attract their attention with a signal cartridge but it did not function. I then picked up my gloves, which were floating in the sea. Two more Spitfires flew directly overhead and again the signal cartridge was a failure.

I then noticed a rowing boat about half a mile away and set course for it, and on reaching it, climbed aboard and found two oars inside. Also pulled on board my dinghy and sail. I took off my battledress top and boots and socks to dry, and kept on my khaki slacks and shirt. Two more Spitfires then appeared and I tried the remaining signal cartridge, which went off with a loud report and shot out of my hand, into the sea!

However, the Spitfires noticed me and remained in the area, circling me. They in turn were relieved by six Spitfires and while they were in the area, a Walrus arrived and picked me up. (Time approx 19.30). I ripped the dinghy and let it sink; the boat was left on the surface. My escape kit was u/s having sea water in it and the First Aid kit was lost in the sea as it was only tucked inside my battledress blouse and must have slipped out. Arrived back at base at 21.00 hours. No injuries sustained.

Johnstone's wingman, Pilot Officer D G English, did not return either and was reported missing. The pilot who found Johnstone in his boat was Flight Lieutenant A H Harland of 241 Squadron. Johnstone had landed eight miles off Pisaro following the attack by a Messerschmitt 109 fighter, and it is understood both Spitfires were shot down by 109s, 39 of which the Luftwaffe had in the air around Rimini that afternoon.

July 1944

Air activity increased during July evidenced by the flurry of rescues carried out by 284 Squadron. It began on the 1st when Trevor Humphrey, along with Sergeant Burnett, picked up an American of the 57th Fighter Group, Lieutenant T E Wright. The Group had attacked bridges and then spotted at least ten Me109s with four more way above. The Americans attacked the top four and claimed all of them shot down, two by Lieutenant Howard W Cleveland. In the fight however, three P.47 Thunderbolts were damaged and Wright baled out of one of them after almost making his way home.

However, they were not 109s but five Italian Fiat G.55s and six Macchi C.205s. The Walrus must have been scrambled in anticipation for by the time Humphrey arrived in the area, having taken off at 11.10, he saw a parachute descending towards the sea five miles east of base. Within minutes the pilot was on board and heading home.

The rescue of Lieutenant Wright was a copybook one. The American Controller gave me a line on him all the way. I was told he was OK for gas and OK for flying, but he had a 500 lb bomb hung-up under one wing and his hydraulics had been shot to pieces so he couldn't pancake at base. I was told they were going to get him to orbit out to sea at a nice safe distance until I saw him and as soon as I had him in sight, he was going to be told to jump. And that is exactly what happened. I saw him, told the Controller, saw him bale out, saw his Thunderbolt hit the water and he hadn't even time to get out of his harness before we'd got to him. It was a lovely day for doing it too. The sea was nice and smooth, no wind, and it was all over in half an hour.

Flying Officer T H Humphrey, 284 Squadron

Within a few days it was Howard W Cleveland himself who had to be rescued, he who had shot down two fighters on the 1st. The 57th Group had been on another fighter-bomber mission and Cleveland got his damaged P.47 to within 36 miles of Corsica before he went into the sea.

Lieutenant K B Walker SAAF and Warrant Officer D P Devery RAAF, in X9503, were off at 07.50, found the American in his dinghy, and had him back to his base at Alto by 09.20. Five days later, on the 11th, Trevor Humphrey led the detachment to Elmas, on the southern part of Sardinia, just inland from Cagliari.

Complicated and Prolonged

284 Squadron were involved in a prolonged rescue over the two days of 11th and 12th of July, which despite all the problems, ended in success, but it took a lot of time and a lot of aircraft.

On the 11th, Sergent/Chef Courteville, of 326 Free French Squadron was one of four pilots on a dawn recce flight, again led by 'Dutch' Hugo DSO DFC, but Courteville had run into trouble and had to leave his Spitfire V. He came down between Leghorn, on the Italian west coast, and Gorgona Island, in exceptionally rough seas.

At 09.45 four Warwick aircraft of 284 flew out, one carrying an airborne lifeboat. They began a creeping line ahead search, while Spitfires of 326 Squadron provided air cover, which it continued to do throughout the day. The Warwicks were just beginning the last leg of their search, which they discovered later, would have brought them over the dinghy, when they were diverted to another position further north, off the island, but nothing was seen and they then had to return to base to refuel.

Just as a course was set, they received a message to go to another spot to the north-east of the island, one aircraft being able to fly to the area. Upon reaching it, the Warwick crew found an American Catalina flying-boat and a Spitfire circling a dinghy. At 12.47 pm, the Warwick dropped its Lindholme gear but it failed to deploy. The wireless-operator then radioed for further aircraft, as the sea was so rough it was considered impossible to ask for HSLs to attend. The Catalina crew were also reluctant to try and set down.

Throughout the afternoon, further attempts by the Warwicks to drop a

Lindholme boat to the Frenchman failed. On one drop a parachute failed to
collapse and it dragged the boat away from the dinghy, and on another drop the
wind was so strong it carried the boat away before the pilot had a chance to reach
it. This was the problem with the Lindholme idea. It was fine if conditions were
nice and calm, and if the man/men in a dinghy, or just in the sea with a Mae
West, were fit enough, not wounded, etc, but any severe conditions made it
virtually impossible for anyone to get to the live-saving boat. The longer the
survivors were in the sea, the less likelihood of them being physically able to use
it anyway.

Meantime, while all this was going on, a succession of Spitfires, Warwicks
and Beaufighters took it in turns keeping the man in sight as the afternoon
progressed. Smoke floats and fluorescene were dropped continually in order to
keep the dinghy in vision. When a third Lindholme drop failed, the rescue had
to be called off till the next morning as the light began to fail, although
Beaufighters remained over the dinghy till dawn.

Finally the Walrus amphibians were called out. The first only found one of
the drifting lifeboats so returned. A second Walrus crew – Squadron Leader
Barnett and Flight Sergeant Mann RAAF – found the dinghy at 07.10, with a
Spitfire above it, and the Frenchman was still seen to be very much alive despite
a stormy night. They dropped a smoke float and then discussed the conditions.
However, with waves rising up to ten feet high, the Walrus could not land, but
then HSL 2601 (Flying Officer R Ross-Watt) managed to battle its way to the
area and the Walrus guided the boat to the dinghy. They soon had him aboard
following his 26-hour ordeal.

This same day a letter was sent to Air HQ by the French air commander:

From: French Air Commander on Corsica. Ajaccio, 12 July 1944.
To: Brigadier-General L C Craigie USAAF,
Commanding 63rd Fighter Wing.

Dear General,
   I have to express to you my feelings and my gratitude for the rescue of
our French pilot, Sgt/Chef Courteville on 12th July 1944.
   I know perfectly well the most abnormal and dangerous circumstances
which accompanied this sea rescue.
   I can tell you but little of the comforting feeling our pilots receive from
the always available help of the ASR people, who, whatever may be the
risks never think of anything but their salvation mission.
   Will you please transmit my personal thanks to the organisation who
took part in this rescue, including the Royal Navy who nearly lost a ship
in that action, if my information is exact.
   Please believe me, yours most gratefully,

Colonel Paul Gérardot.

* * *

Two more American P.47 fighter pilots were rescued a few days later, both by the South African, Lieutenant K B Walker and his Australian gunner, Warrant Officer Devery. First came Lieutenant Louis J Pernicka of the 66th Squadron, 57th FG, during the late afternoon of the 15th, and then Warrant Officer Sylvan L Kapner of the 527th Fighter Squadron, 86th Group, in the early afternoon of the 17th. Kapner had injured himself as he ditched his Thunderbolt, and ended up with a broken nose and several teeth knocked out. On the latter sortie the Walrus crew spotted a HSL heading for the target, but they landed and picked up the Yank before they arrived.

Let's Pretend

Trevor Humphrey was involved in a very different sortie on 19 July, as he relates:

> The Italians, recently 'liberated' from the Fascist yoke, were anxious to do something non-combatant, and they did have a number of spare aeroplanes. Amongst them was a Cant Z1007 which they painted white and put red crosses on it, to indicate the manner of their planned missions. They said they'd like to be air sea rescue, to give them something to do.
>
> My orders were to stage a mock rescue which we thought should be as realistic as possible. I flew out with Burnett and one of our fitters, Corporal Trumble, who wanted a ride. At a given spot we were to drop a dinghy and give a Mayday call, but when we chucked it out, it caught in the slipstream and wrapped itself around the tailplane!
>
> I suddenly had no aileron control and very little rudder movement. I went down in a gentle diving curve and hit the sea with rather a smack. As soon as we hit, the dinghy fell off and having been ripped in the process, it promptly sank. Burnett gave a Mayday, but Malta Control, of course, were expecting one from us!
>
> I didn't fancy my chances of taking off again in this heavy sea, but I began to make attempts, but the waves made it difficult and I kept repositioning Burnett and Trumble up and down the fuselage in the efforts to find the right balance. Finally we literally bounced into the air off the last wave and had sufficient revs on the engine to enable us to miss the next wave.
>
> So much for our undertaking to see what the Italians could do. They did fly out to the spot given them by Malta Control but never found us and I don't think they really had a clue where to look. I felt certain they had flown to the spot given, looked straight down, saw nothing, so went home again. This was later confirmed to me by a ground officer who had flown out with them. They flew to the exact spot, saw nothing on the sea, shrugged in typical fashion, and flew out, giving no thought to a proper search!
>
> Flying Officer T H Humphrey, 293 Squadron

293's C Flight Moves to Fermo

During July 293 moved its Tortoreto detachment to Fermo, mid-way between Pescara and Ancona on the Italian east coast, which was only about 20 miles up the coast. Sergeant P F Lydford and Warrant Officer J A Slater, in L2223, were scrambled at 13.35 on 8 July to collect survivors from an American bomber crew, 58 miles out from Fermo on a course of 045 degrees. A second Walrus was also flown out once it was realised there could be up to ten people to rescue, this one flown by Second Lieutenant J V Peters SAAF and his gunner Flying Officer Morgan.

Ten men were indeed found in dinghies, the two crews sharing them equally between the two aircraft. L2223 was able to get airborne, but the other Walrus didn't make it, so had to taxi home. These men may have been survivors from one of three B.24s of the 464th Bomb Group lost this date, although it seems highly likely the men were from a B.17 outfit (see also details on 21 July below).

Denny Lunn DFM and Norm Pickles DFC both became tour-expired on the 12th and left 293 soon afterwards, quickly followed by Colin Horne DFM two days later. Between them they had vast experience of ASR work but there was plenty of new blood taking over.

One crew 'taking over' was that of Peters and Morgan. They picked up a 601 Squadron pilot on the 20th – Flying Officer H G Proudman. Proudman (in MK481) had been in one of four Spitfires dive-bombing a road junction west of Pissaro. Medium to heavy flak fire was experienced over the target area and Proudman's machine was hit. Heading out over the sea he was forced to bale out a couple of miles away from the coast at Fano. Peters and Morgan were off at 07.10 and had their man back with his unit and then returned to base by 09.15, despite having to take off towards Fano (into wind) which was still occupied by the Germans.

The next day this duo were off again on an early rescue mission, this time to pick up 2nd Lieutenant Eastman recorded as being from the 537th Fighter Bomber Squadron, although no such unit existed in this theatre. It was more likely the 527th FBS, 86th FG.

Later this same day, a badly shot-up B.17 Fortress made an emergency landing on 293's airfield, the pilot and crew being the same men the squadron rescued on 8 July. The pilot gave the ASR boys a grand compliment by saying that he was no longer afraid to ditch as he was confident 293 would bring him home again!

* * *

The detachment were off for the third day in a row on 22 July. Lieutenant A G Riley SAAF and Flying Officer A A O'Dell (in W2757) were sent off at 12.30 to rescue an American Thunderbolt pilot seven miles south-west of Cape Portafino. They found two P.39s from the 346th Fighter Squadron orbiting and by 14.15 they had landed and picked up Lieutenant Taylor from the 526th Fighter Bomber Squadron, 86th FG, which was operating out of Grosseto. A smooth operation, the Walrus was back and down by 15.30.

Chapter 7

UP NORTH

By August 1944 much of the ground fighting was rapidly moving north, and most of the air actions by Allied aircraft were well north, into Tuscany and Romagna.

On Corsica, the Borgo detachment of 284 Squadron moved to Calvi while the Elmas detachment went to Borgo. Following this game of musical chairs, there were no rescues until 19 August. On this day, Hamish Reid and Warrant Officer Rawding, in X9503, were sent off to find survivors from an American Mitchell, which was reported as ditched in position 42.13N/09.38E, just off the north-west coast of Corsica.

They soon found three men in the water, in just their life vests and a half inflated dinghy. Reid landed and swiftly had the men aboard, then headed for the island. For once, the sea was too calm for take-off – you can never win! Flight Lieutenant D D Browning's launch HSL 175 came out to meet them, and having made rendezvous, took off 1st Lieutenant Farnnan, 2nd Lieutenant Evarts and Corporal Flynn of the 487th Bombardment Squadron, 340th Bomb Group. This was Reid's last rescue. On the 22nd he almost got three chaps from a B.26 but a HSL beat him to them.

> 283 Squadron had become 293 in April 1944 and I went back to 284 in Sardinia. So from May 1944 I found myself in Corsica and kept my hand in on Spitfires by doing air tests for the Maintenance Unit; took a Spitfire over to Maison Blanche on one occasion – must have been round the bend!
>
> Went down on detachment to the south of Sardinia, to Elmas, in July 1944. By this time we were getting new pilots in and I was doing a bit of training, until the end of August, when I was tour-expired.
>
> My commission eventually caught up with me after I found myself as Station Warrant Officer at RAF Turnhouse, Edinburgh. I was then posted to the south of England.
>
> Hamish Reid

There were a lot of changes at this time. As from 16 September 1944, B Flight of 284 Squadron became E Flight of 293 Squadron. During this period – 10 April till 16 September – B Flight had been responsible for 41 live rescues and

picked up one dead body, sharing the honours with the HSLs of 254 Air Sea
Rescue unit on several other occasions.

Flight Lieutenant James became CO of 284 Squadron on 23 September, with
flights at Bone and Elmas. Squadron Leader Barnett, formally OC 284, now OC
293, became tour-expired on 27 September. Flight Lieutenant G M Gallagher
also left and by 1945 was OC 624 Squadron, which used Walrus aircraft for
mine spotting from various Italian bases, plus other bases in Greece and Malta.

Rescuers 1, Germans 2

293 Squadron appears to have become the main ASR Walrus unit now, and on 5
August 1944, the Squadron had the unique, but unfortunate experience, of
carrying out a successful rescue but losing two of its aircrew. It happened like this.

Red Section of 241 Squadron was on a shipping patrol and spotted two
aircraft flying low when they were returning. These in fact turned out to be
another section (Yellow 1 & 2) from their Squadron, out on a dinghy search.
However, before recognition confusion reigned, and Yellow 1 proceeded to
chase Red 4, who had detached himself from the rest of the section. All of a
sudden Yellow Leader saw this aircraft crash into the sea.

As Yellow 1 circled he saw the pilot pop up and shortly afterwards, clamber
into his dinghy, and recognised it as a RAF type, which was his first intimation
that he had been chasing an aircraft from his own side. At least he then had the
good grace to call in a Mayday, which alerted the Walrus boys.

Red 4 had been Sergeant K Etchels (Spitfire VIII JF351) who with the others
of Red Section had taken off at 06.15 that morning. 293 scrambled Sergeant P F
Lydford and Warrant Officer J A Slater (L2223) at 07.40, who some time later
arrived over the dinghy, landed, and took on Sergeant Etchels, who was about
ten miles north of Rimini. The sea was against both take-off and taxying and
rather than drift about out to sea and risk a probable break-up of the Walrus,
Lydford decided to head for the enemy shore and beach it.

Meanwhile, an ASR launch from Ancona was on its way to rescue the men
and to tow the aircraft away, but as the Walrus's radio had become u/s through
seawater, Lydford was unaware of this and continued towards the shore. The HSL
was only about four miles away by this time, and despite warning shots ahead of
the amphibian by the Spitfire pilots, who could see the boat in the distance, the
Walrus headed in and beached beneath the cliffs just north of Pisaro.

Shortly afterwards the HSL arrived and stood about 50 yards off shore,
hoping the three men would swim out. It later transpired from Etchels, that
neither of the Walrus crew could swim, and although they launched a dinghy,
heavy surf prevented them from getting off the beach. Etchels tried to persuade
them to throw themselves into the sea in their Mae Wests as it was more than
probable that the HSL crew would throw them a line and drag them to the boat,
but they apparently did not have the confidence to try it.

During all this time, the HSL was being engaged by gunfire from the cliff
tops, the crew replying with bursts of fire from their turret guns. The covering
Spitfires too joined in and made enemy soldiers on the cliffs keep their heads
down with strafing runs. Eventually, Etchels, saying it was madness to wait any
longer, stripped and put on his Mae West, then struck out for the launch, and

although the soldiers fired some 30 rounds at him, he was not hit, and made the launch without difficulty.

The skipper of the launch decided to send a man ashore to rescue the Walrus crew but just then the enemy fire intensified and so he quite rightly felt that discretion was the better part of valour, and unable to risk his boat or men any longer, backed off and made his way back down the coast to Ancona. With this, the Spitfires made another pass, this time shooting at and destroying the stranded Walrus. Lydford and Slater were taken prisoner, ending up in Stalag Luft 7 at Bankau, near Kreulberg, Upper Silesia.

* * *

Messers Peters and Morgan, in L2170, were again in the picture on 22 August, picking up Flying Officer G L Garnham of 241 Squadron, three and a half miles off Fermo, in the early morning. He had been out on an early morning shipping recce off Rimini, led by Captain E R Dixon SAAF, and had been forced to bale out of his Spitfire (JF339) off Fano due to lack of fuel, following flak damage whilst strafing some motor transport just inland.

Captain Dixon, who called in the Mayday, and remained overhead until relieved by two more Spitfires, which 241 had scrambled, covered him. Garnham was rescued after an hour in his dinghy and brought safely home.

241 Squadron lost another pilot the next evening, Flight Lieutenant D M Leitch. Hit by flak or debris during a postponed, last sortie of the day, he was forced to bale out five miles out to sea two to three miles south of the River Po estuary. A Walrus was scrambled but then it was realised that it would be dark by the time it reached the area, so it was recalled. Two Spitfires did continue on, found the man as he fired off a red distress flare, but that was all the two pilots could do. They would try at first light on the 24th.

Lieutenant Peters, this time with Flying Officer Bradley, were away at 05.45 the next morning (in L2170), flying on a heading of 360°, 50 miles from base. Two Spitfires had been sent out at first light to try and locate the man, if indeed he was still there, and spotted him in roughly the same position after a 20-minute search, hampered by a sea haze, which reduced visibility to three miles. By this time the Walrus and two more Spitfires had arrived and everyone saw the man's distress flares.

Peters landed and picked up Leitch, who was none the worse for his night at sea, although he was hungry, and brought him home to Falconara at 08.10. Leitch was to report that he had had a rather restful night, which was interrupted once by the appearance of a surface craft. Leitch, thinking it was a HSL, fired off two distress signals, which were replied to by a very large white flare. This aroused his suspicions so he did not make further efforts to show his position. He was waiting and hoping to hear English voices, but there were no further sounds.

The 24th proved a busy day, for no sooner had the excitement of the Leitch rescue subsided, than Sergeant Newsome and Warrant Officer Kelly were scrambled at 12.40, following Sergeant Bickle and Flying Officer Bradley who had gone out ten minutes earlier. The two Walrus machines were escorted by Spitfires of 145 Squadron.

An American bomber crew had come down 50-55 miles due east of 293's base at Falconara, and upon arrival at the area, five men were seen in the water. Both Walrus aircraft landed, one taking on board four men, the other the fifth. Neither aircraft were able to get airborne so began to taxi back. A launch was despatched and it met the two amphibians and took all five men aboard.

Newsome and Kelly finally got themselves unstuck off Senigallia, landing at Chiaravalle at 19.10, very much the worse for wear. Bickle and Bradley could not get off at all and had to be towed back by the launch, finally mooring in Ancona Harbour at 21.20.

The Spitfires of Neville Duke's 145 Squadron had flown to Falconara that morning for a bomber escort mission, but the weather was so bad it was postponed. Therefore, two sections flew as cover for the rescue sortie. Duke noted in his diary that the men were survivors from a Liberator. The survivors were listed as 1st Lieutenants Mills and Fritts, 2nd Lieutenant Dionne, and Corporals Marchese and Nichols, from the 465th Bombardment Group.

These rescues were covered in issue No.51 of *Mare Nostrum* due to the fact that it marked a special occasion for 293 Squadron:

CENTURY UP

On the 24th August, 293 Squadron passed the 100 mark in the number of lives saved. The first rescue effected by the Squadron was on the 3rd March 1944. A description of the Squadron's work on the day on which it topped the century gives a good idea of its successful operations during the past six months. Ten lives were saved on this day alone.

Lt Peters and F/O Bradley were airborne from Falconara at 05.45 hrs with Spitfire escort. They flew north-west for 85 miles along the enemy coast and found a British Spitfire pilot about one mile south of the River Po estuary. Lt Peters landed, picked up the pilot and flew him to his base.

A Warwick took off from Foggia the same morning, captained by F/Lt Hayward. Two Spitfires and a Catalina joined them in the search for the crew of an American Fortress, who had baled out in the middle of the Adriatic, almost due north of Foggia. The Warwick located three survivors in their Mae Wests, three empty dinghies and an empty Mae West. The Catalina located a further two survivors. An HSL was homed to the position and directed alternately by the Catalina and the Warwick, till all five were picked up.

Shortly afterwards, F/Lt James was ordered to go to a position some 30 miles off the Italian coast in a Warwick from Foggia, carrying an airborne life-boat. The sole survivor of an American bomber crew was found in his Mae West, being circled by two Spitfires, and no launch was in sight. F/Lt James then made his run and dropped the lifeboat about 70 yards down wind of the pilot. The boat worked perfectly, parachutes developing smoothly, buoyancy tubes inflating and rockets firing correctly. It was unfortunate that the pilot was too badly injured to reach the boat, but an HSL was homed in by the Warwick, and this arrived soon after to rescue the wounded man.

Two Walrus aircraft piloted by Sgts Newsome and Bickle, with W/O

Kelly and F/O Bradley, left Falconara at midday for a position 55 nautical miles north of their base. The crew of a Liberator were sighted and these also were in the water in their Mae Wests. The sea was rather rough for landing a Walrus, but the survivors were in obvious distress and it was known that no launch was near at hand. Both aircraft landed, Sgt Bickle picking up four men and Sgt Newsome one. Neither aircraft could take off, owing to the state of the sea and they both taxied back towards Ancona. The rescued men were later transferred on to a HSL, which came to meet them.

Flight Lieutenant A I James of 293 Squadron, mentioned above as piloting the Warwick, was about to take command of 284 Squadron and be promoted to squadron leader.

Is Someone Trying to Tell me Something?
The first rescue by 293 Squadron in September came on the 11th, and it again involved Newsome and Kelly. Captain M Lawton SAAF, flying with 92 Squadron, had received his captaincy promotion this same day, but he celebrated it in a very different way than he would have intended.

Six Spitfire VIIIs were dive-bombing a bridge in the late afternoon, scoring one direct hit and one near miss. On the way back they strafed some tanks moving south along a road about four miles north-west of Cerora. Some ground fire came up and hit Lawton's Spitfire (JF704) which forced him to bale out five miles east of Rimini. Lawton later wrote:

> As I hit the water I released my 'chute, wriggled free and inflated my dinghy. After about 20 minutes I saw the Walrus, and after it had landed, I paddled to the flame float it had dropped and waved it about to indicate my position. I had no trouble in boarding the Walrus, through the back hatch. The machine had to taxi back as it could not take off. About 45 minutes later it was mistaken for a German E-boat and was fired upon and set on fire by two Royal Navy MTBs. The three of us dived into the water and swam away, with the aid of our Mae Wests. 15 minutes later we were picked up by the MTBs. At about 10 o'clock in the morning, the MTB hit a mine and had to be towed back! I was then taken on board another boat and taken to Ancona.

The Walrus crew had been airborne at 19.30 (X9529), escorted by a Beaufighter from 600 Squadron in case its radar might prove useful. They found their man, and although the light was failing, Newsome landed safely and picked up the South African, and as darkness fell, he was being taxied back south. The sea was calm and there was no anxiety. That changed at around 21.00 as the crew heard the engines of a small boat or launch, and to their utter amazement, were suddenly fired on by one of two motor torpedo boats, who failed to recognise the outline of the Walrus, assuming it to be, of all things, a German E-boat (i.e. the equivalent of a British MTB!) out on a mine-laying mission.

Despite a two-star distress cartridge being fired off, and an interrupted SOS call – interruption caused by the necessity of dodging tracer bullets – the firing continued so all three men were forced to abandon the now burning Walrus and dive headlong into the sea. Within a very few moments the amphibian sank and after about five minutes in the water, all three men were picked up by MTB 633, where (they later confirmed) they were well treated. (One would hope so!)

The night's adventures, as Lawton has already described, were not over as the boat was then ordered out on an E-boat hunt during which the MTB struck a mine and was badly damaged. None the worse for wear, the three airmen were put ashore in Ancona Harbour on the morning of the 12th following a more than memorable night. Back with 92 Squadron, Captain Lawton at least got something out of it – the squadron doctor prescribed a spot of leave to Sorrento.

* * *

The Rescue of a Minesweeper Crew

Alex Stevens, after his brief period with the 293 detachment on the east coast, was back with the west coast detachment, and on Friday 13 October, was involved in the rescue of a minesweeper crew, whose ship had hit a mine. This resulted in Alex being awarded the DFC, having received his commission soon after the rescue. They had been sent out at 06.55, returning at 08.50, then scrambled again at 10.20:

> We had been out earlier looking for a Beaufighter crew reported missing overnight but had only found an oil patch. We returned to base (Pisa) and were scrambled again, late morning I think, to search for survivors from MMS 170, which had disappeared on passage from Sardinia to Leghorn during the previous night.
>
> We were flying a vector, given by control, which was taking us to the north of Isola di Gorgona and on route we passed over a HSL which had come out from Leghorn. We tried to make contact but his VHF was unserviceable, so we proceeded on our given course and soon sighted a number of men on two rafts. They were some 16 miles out from Gorgona, on a bearing of 040 degrees, which in turn is some 25 miles to the WSW of Leghorn. It is, or was at that time, uninhabited, and in most parts it rises sheer from the sea and is something like a mile across.
>
> Because of the number of bods on the rafts, and the sea conditions, I decided to make another attempt to contact the launch, so returned to the area where we had last seen it. It was nowhere to be seen and we later learned that it must have been under an overhanging cliff whilst doing a circuit of Gorgona in case survivors had got ashore.
>
> We therefore assumed that the launch had gone off to an unrelated job, so returned to the rafts and landed. There was a substantial wind coming from the south and quite a swell running. With some difficulty my Wop/AG Roy Barnes and I got nine of the dozen seamen packed into the Walrus, by which time – miraculously – the launch appeared, and collected the remaining three men.
>
> Take-off was out of the question so we started to taxi towards Leghorn,

but the heavy swell and strong crosswind made this almost impossible. Gratefully I accepted a tow from the launch who safely delivered us and our nine survivors to port where we moored up to a buoy.

                                     Pilot Officer A G Stevens, 293 Squadron

Stevens and Barnes were driven back to Pisa by lorry and the Walrus (W2179) was flown back the next day.

    Concerning the citation for his DFC (see Appendix A), Alex Stevens mentions that it is not totally accurate. The wireless in the launch was u/s, not the one in the aircraft, and there was no shortage of petrol. As he comments: 'I may not have been the world's most experienced pilot but I knew enough not to stay in the air beyond the aircraft duration!' He was also sorry that Roy Barnes was not mentioned in relation to the rescue.

*   *   *

The war on land had now reached northern Italy and the final rescues by 284 and 293 would be made in the northern waters of the Ligurian Sea and in the Gulf of Venice. Meantime, two more Walrus men had been decorated. Colin Ian Peterson, now a Warrant Officer, received the DFC, while his crewman, Eric Keeble, received the DFM. In addition, Reg Hayes received a Bar to his DFC.

    A note in the Pisa airfield control tower log for 1 October confirms that the Walrus boys were usually there with the main action. At this time, Pisa was the closest airfield to the bomb line on the west coast of Italy, and aircraft from other bases used Pisa for emergency landings. The log records:

> First day of operation. 416th NFS [night fighter squadron] came in. Detachment of 346th FS came in. Two Walruses came in from 293 Squadron. 10 October:
>   [Call sign] – PLANESONG – 293 RAF Sq, Air Rescue – Walrus.

A new name appeared on the list of successful Walrus pilots on 16 October 1944, this being Flying Officer H F Burditt who teamed up with Flying Officer I Morgan. They set off in L2266 at 16.30, flying 15 miles to the north of Rimini, in order to find their customer below an orbiting P.47, five miles off shore. They could see a man in the water in only his Mae West, so quickly landed and hauled him aboard. He was Lieutenant Jack L Slatton from Anderson, South Carolina, flying with the 85th 'Skull' Fighter Squadron, 79th Fighter Group, hit by flak over Ravenna and forced to ditch.

A Tragic Story

This same crew were in the frame again on the 21st. Again using L2266 their target was a man in the water 20 miles out from Venice on a course of 180°. The historian of the 459th Bomb Group Association, Lyle McCarty, gave me permission to quote from his work on the 459th as well as sending me an excerpt from the Group's War Diary which he had edited:

On October 20, 1944, Lieutenant Arthur Hartman, a 758th Squadron pilot, ditched in the Adriatic Sea on the return from a raid to Munich. Hartman's aircraft appeared to be under control as he left the Group formation as it crossed the Italian coast and headed over the Adriatic.

Inexplicably, Hartman headed toward Yugoslavia rather than towards the Italian peninsular; from that point, Allied-held territory in Italy was no farther away from Nazi-occupied Yugoslavia.

Details of what happened next are missing, but Hartman ditched his aircraft in the sea off Venice. The 758th Squadron Diary contains the following entry for October 23, 1944: 'Sgt [Paul E] Estep of Lt Hartman's crew came back today. The rest of the crew were drowned or killed when their plane crashed in the Adriatic Sea. Sgt Estep had a tragic story to tell of his experience.

He and five others escaped from the plane and clung to the [floating] nose wheel. One by one they dropped off and drowned due to the choppy sea. Estep did the best he could to hold on to each one of them and when the last man went down, he went under twenty feet with him, but couldn't hang on. Estep was rescued 24 hours later by a PBY[1].'

In the rather sketchy information file in the Missing Air Crew Report, Estep indicated that all crew members were aboard the plane when the ditching occurred and that none were injured by prior action. He described the touch-down by Hartman as 'perfect'.

Only one crew member out of ten survived this ditching, but six managed to exit the aircraft, five of whom later drowned as they bobbed in the sea hoping for rescue.

On 21 October, one of the pilots on the raid made out the following statement:

I, First Lieutenant Thomas D Rutherford, 0862975, state that on 20 October 1944, I was flying in a B.24 type aircraft, on a heavy bombardment mission over Munich, Germany. Captain Walter L Gates Jr, of the 758th Bombardment Squadron, 459th Bombardment Group, was flying as pilot of the aircraft I was flying in. We were flying in the Number 1 position of A Flight. Lieutenant Hartman was flying in Number 7 position of A Flight. We had experienced some very accurate flak on the way to the target and also on our return trip. We were about half an hour from northern Italy when I noticed the aircraft that Lieutenant Hartman was flying in veer away from the formation towards Yugoslavia. We were very short of gas ourselves at this point and later had to make a forced landing and re-fuel. Lieutenant Hartman seemed to be in no difficulty inasmuch as all four of his engines were running smoothly and the ship was flying level under control. It seemed very funny that Lieutenant Hartman should fly a course to Yugoslavia, when the Italian coastline was just as close. The last I saw of him, he was flying along the coast of Yugoslavia on a southerly heading.

---

[1] Although noted as a PBY, which was the usual term for an American Catalina flying boat, it was a RAF Walrus which picked up the survivor.

The Liberators were based at Giuilia #1, Cerignola, Italy and had left for the mission at 14.20. Hartman's bomber was a B.24J serial number 42-52010 and the crew were as follows:

2/Lt Arthur Hartman	pilot	from Sequin, Texas.
2/Lt Donald G Smithey	co-pilot	Grandview, Missouri.
2/Lt Arthur E Fierman	navigator	Philadelphia, Pennsylvania.
2/Lt Donald Collins	bombardier	Fort Dodge, Iowa.
Sgt Don Kearney	eng gunner	Bellflower, California.
Sgt Theodore E Scott	eng gunner	Stewart, Ohio.
Sgt Harvey R Sorensen	arm gunner	American Falls, Iowa.
Sgt Richard I Oldenburg	gunner	Oakland, California.
Sgt Harold H Lauck	gunner	Hood, California.
Sgt Paul E Estep	radio	Mount Union, Pennsylvania.

Hartman, Collins, Kearney, Scott and Lauck, were all married men, as indeed was Paul Estep.

Estep later confirmed that Hartman, Smithey, Collins and Kearney did not escape from the Liberator, and that Fierman, Oldenburg, Scott, Sorensen, Lauck and himself were in the water from noon until darkness fell.

Paul Estep had the sad and unenviable task of writing up the reports on his dead comrades, each on a 6-3861, AF form. Apart from those who did not survive the ditching, who had all been in the front section of the bomber, Estep noted that flak had indeed come through the machine and he and Sorensen laid on the extra life raft, and it appears that Lauck had been slightly wounded in the face. Those hours in the water must have been harrowing for Estep.

He and Collins were on the rear flight deck when the plane hit the sea, and Collins drowned first on the wheel. He was injured in the ditching, thinking his ribs might be broken. Unable to keep his head up, and affected by the cold water he slipped away. Sorensen died in Estep's arms, mainly from the cold. Estep also had an arm round Fierman till about 10 pm when he too died. Lauck seemed stunned or dazed, then all at once he struggled away from the wheel and went under about ten feet from the wheel. Last to go was Scott. He was holding onto Estep's Mae West and pulled him under as he went down. Estep managed to break free and swam back to the surface.

These are harrowing things to relate, but I have done so to illustrate what the fate of many other men would have been like had the courage of the air sea rescue men been less than what it was.

Anymore for the Skylark?
As if one rescue was not enough for Burditt and Morgan, they had no sooner picked up Paul Estep than they were told of another man in the water.

Captain Arthur William Meikle DFC of 7 SAAF Squadron (known as 'Heinkel' Meikle), was leading a sortie to dive-bomb a gun position, but then received a radio call that some tanks had been reported. Vectored to the given location he found nothing so continued to the original target, obtaining hits on the gun position. Two cars were also spotted and destroyed, and a third damaged, in strafing runs north of Lake Commacchio.

Meikle's aircraft was then hit, quite possibly from ricochets from his own guns. As he headed away, glycol began to stream back but he made the coast and flew out to sea. About 15 miles out he finally had to abandon the aircraft but two pilots had stayed with him – Lieutenants Symons and Van Diggelen, who radioed for help.

While this was happening, Sergeant A W Jones of 112 Squadron was out on another mission, led by Squadron Leader A P Q Bluett DFC. During an attack on some barges and trains, Jones' Mustang (HB925 'Z') was hit by flak and he too baled out over the sea, seen in the water swimming with just his Mae West.

Fighters from 3 SAAF Squadron were scrambled to help locate an airman reported in the sea 20 miles south of Venice and if they found him they were to orbit until they reached PLE (Prudent Limit of Endurance) – i.e. covering the man until either he was rescued or the fighters were down to just enough fuel to get them home.

The fighter pilots did indeed locate the airman, who, it was discovered once a fix had been made with base, was just five miles from Venice's harbour mouth. Failing to contact the promised Walrus the fighters flew south, located the amphibian and led it back to the spot.

Burditt and Morgan arrived in the area, joined by a Warwick aircraft from the Squadron, and found two Spitfires and a Mustang. Landing, they took on Captain Meikle but they were never going to be able to take off again. The Warwick crew meantime, had found Jones and directed the Walrus towards it. Taxying over, they lifted Jones into the back with their other two guests. By this time, the Walrus was starting to attract attention from the shore, gun batteries beginning to lob some shells over.

Sergeant Bickle and Flying Officer Bradley now arrived on the scene, ordered out with all this 'trade' in the offing, but by this time the sea was becoming too rough for a safe landing, not to mention the shell fire. As if there wasn't enough going on, some Spitfires and Me109s started to have an air fight way above, and the Warwick crew saw a pilot drifting down in a parachute. They flew over him after he hit the water, dropped their Lindholme dinghy to him, and watched with some satisfaction as he climbed aboard. (He turned out to be a Spitfire pilot.)

Later still, an American PBY Catalina arrived and although it landed some way from the Walrus, it taxied close and the three survivors were transferred to it and it took off. Burditt called the other Walrus crew saying he and Morgan would stay with their machine till the next morning. The next day search aircraft were sent out but there was no sign of the missing crew. Both men did not survive the night on the sea, and became prisoners of war, Burditt languishing in the famous Stalag Luft 3 at Sagan, while Morgan was reported to be in Stalag Luft 1, Barth.

November 1944

The month of November 1944 started off quietly enough for 293 Squadron, but by the end of the month they were pulling men out of the water again. The Squadron's new(ish) E Flight was now at Calvi, Corsica, under the command of Flight Lieutenant K W J Topley.

Persistence Pays Off

Mike Gallagher made what was probably his last rescue from Corsica on 5 November, flying with Warrant Officer V Udburg in W3048. Five men were reported in the sea ten miles south of Cape Corse. A B.26 Marauder guided them to the spot where two dinghies were found, each containing one man. Before landing, the Walrus made a sweep of the area but only wreckage could be seen. Finally, Gallagher landed and picked up Lieutenants Kamanski and Ford from the 320th Bomb Group. Taxying around, the search was continued for other crew men until a HSL arrived and both men were put aboard it, then they took off for another look round.

North of an oil patch, Gallagher and Udburg spotted a third man, swimming around in a Mae West, and Udburg signalled to the man that he had been seen, but then a fourth man was located about 100 yards away, also in a Mae West. He was also waved at. Still not giving up, Gallagher circled once more and was rewarded by finding the fifth man clinging to a half inflated dinghy.

The Controller was informed of these developments and soon the HSL was motoring up, Gallagher finishing the mission by guiding the launch to all three men who were soon enjoying a reunion with their crewmates.

By this time Gallagher was finding the Walrus a bit unsteady in flight and so force-landed on the sea, but declined the HSL skipper's offer of a tow. Instead he taxied to Bastia, arriving at 18.25. The Squadron riggers could find no faults with the machine and could only surmise that the water rudder had not been fully unlocked prior to take-off after putting the survivors aboard the launch.

Leland S Ford recalled in 1997:

> We started out on the mission as a spare aircraft, but one plane dropped out of formation due to engine trouble and we took its place. Our target was the Rovereto railroad in the Brenner Pass, connecting northern Italy with Austria and Yugoslavia. On the bomb run approximately 12 to 15 German planes attacked our formation. The attached Intelligence Report of the mission records the description of the German aircraft and their method of attack.
>
> My plane, #84261, lost an engine shortly after we dropped our bombs on the target, also the fuel booster pump in the bomb-bay was hit and it was leaking fuel into the bomb-bay, making us almost a flying bomb!
>
> We were accompanied by three planes from our Group and crossed the coast of Italy just south of Genoa and headed for Alto, Corsica, where our airfield was located. Our one good engine started heating up and losing power, and soon we were down to 3,000 feet, where we finally decided to bale out. At that time our three companions escorting us back radioed our position to the air sea rescue boys in Bastia, Corsica. The rest is history.
>
> Kamanski and myself gave our pilot wings to the fellows who rescued us when we transferred to the launch. They gave us dry clothing and a hot cup of rum. We were all very grateful to those two men who rescued us.
>
> On this particular mission I was co-pilot and Charles Kamanski was the pilot. Lieutenant Beebe was the bombardier, Sergeant Peter Greco was

the engineer/gunner, and Sergeant Kelley Friel our radio man/air gunner.

The rescue took place on my 19th mission, and I went on to fly 39 more over France and Germany, for a total of 58 combat missions. I retired from the Air Force in 1969, having later flown F-86s, F-89s and F-102s.

1st Lieutenant L S Ford, 444th BS, 320th BG

The raid report:

ROVERETO RAILROAD FILL, ITALY

At 09.55 hours, 18 B.26's took off. No B.26's returned early. One B.26 lost prior to target: A/C Battle No.1 was hit by enemy aircraft fire at Garda, F-4470, at 11.28 hours. It slid out of formation, pilot evidently fighting for control. Three chutes emerged, and one minute later the right wing came off. Aircraft then turned over on its back, and crashed into a mountain, exploding at F-6091. 17 B.26's were over the target. 15 B.26's dropped 111 x 500# Demolition bombs (1/10 & .025 second delay fuses) and five x 500# Demolition bombs (six-hour delay fuses) on the primary target at 11.33 hours, from 10,600' to 9,600' on an Axis of 06°T. 20 x 500# Demolition bombs (1/10 & .025 second delay fuses) were salvoed over land, 12 having hung up over the target and eight due to bombardier's error. No bombs were returned to base. 12 B.26's returned to base at 12.49 hours, three B.26's returned at 15.37 hours, after escorting a/c damaged by flak and circling after its crew baled out. Two B.26's lost in addition to the above.

Aircraft Battle No.86 was hit by enemy aircraft attack on the breakaway from the target. It dropped out of the formation, wheels were seen to go down, it nosed up sharply and then spun to the ground, crashing at A-6909 at 11.34 hours. No fire, explosion, or chutes were seen. Aircraft Battle No.84 was hit by enemy aircraft fire on the bomb run, continued in formation with three aircraft for escort. Crew baled out at 43° 18' North/09° 10' East at 13.15 hours. The crew is reported safe. No B.26's are missing. Four B.26's were slightly damaged by enemy aircraft: and two B.26's seriously damaged by enemy aircraft.

RESULTS: A good pattern of bombs covered the target, scoring probable hits. Some bombs landed over to the North.

ENEMY FIGHTER OPPOSITION: 12/15 enemy aircraft, consisting of eight Me109's, two Mc.202's and two FW190's attacked from 22 minutes, until formation returned to Desenzano, F-3059, after bombing. The initial attack by all E/A was made from 12 o'clock high, E/A going through formation. Subsequent attacks were made by groups of two, three, and four from the rear, level, at five, six, and seven o'clock. The attacks were aggressive and well executed. Attacks were pressed to 150 yards, some as close as 250 feet, some A/C hung directly behind the formation, at 1,000 yards, lobbing 20 mm cannon shells, with most of the shells falling short. After attacks, A/C broke off by diving to the right or left. Damaged A/C falling out of formation were concentrated on. Markings were black crosses on the wings and white crosses with black outlines on the fuselages. Some A/C had white spinners.

FLAK: Ten bursts of flak encountered from Genoa, C-9546, by escorting a/c. Flak was far out of range.

ROUTE: Base to Moneglia, F-4028, to Fidenza, P-9593, to Desenzano, F-3059, to IP. Ala, F-6891; to target on an axis of 06 deg. true; breakaway left to Desenzano, F-3059; reciprocal course to base.

The report of the action fits very neatly into the story by the fighter opposition of this sortie by the 320th Group. At 11.00 hours Allied aircraft had been reported in the Lake Garda area and 23 ANR (Aeronautica Nazionale Repubblicano) Me109s were scrambled from the Italian II° Groupo Caccia from Villafranca.

After the combat, five Italian pilots were each unofficially given credit for a bomber shot down for the three actually lost – two in combat and one which went into the sea later. The first was a 441st Squadron machine (01) flown by 2nd Lieutenant Truman C Cole and it seems this Marauder was shot down by Sergente Maggiore Pacini of the 3° Squadron. Marauder '86', piloted by 1st Lieutenant James R Longsdon, was shared between Capitano Mario Bellagambi and Sergente Maggiore Cavagliano, their report mirroring the 'dropping a leg, pulling up its nose and spinning into the mountain, east of Lake Garda' description.

Charles Kamanski and Leland Ford's B.26 appears to have been the machine attacked by Sergente Maggiore Loris Baldi and Tenente Antonio Camaioni. While it was credited to them, their last sight of it was leaving the target area trailing smoke.

Return fire from the B.26 gunners forced Sergente Maggiore Ancillotti to crash-land his 109 near Pescantina Veronese, and wounded Tenente Camaioni, compelling him to a one-wheel landing at Villafranca, followed by the 109G of Sottotenente Rosas of the 2° Squadron in a similar predicament.

More Americans
November 13 saw Sergeants E W Clarke and G H C Willing (R6547) flying 38 miles out from Fano with an escort of four Mustangs to rescue Lieutenant Robert R Blank of the 308th Fighter Squadron, 31st Fighter Group. Blank had been missing in his dinghy for two days, after having engine trouble which caused him to lose two con-rods on the 11th while on a mission. He had turned for home but the weather was murky. His plan had been to get to Ancona but he finally had to take to his parachute, hoping he was above it. The weather had caused him to misjudge the locality and in consequence he came down in the sea. Blank later became a captain with the 309th Squadron, and gained two combat victories in the final months of the European war.

On the 22nd, Sergeants D Newsome and E S Bilton were sent off at 14.55 in R6547 on a rescue mission. Twenty minutes later they over-flew Bellaria from where they set a course of 006 degrees, which they held for 55 miles. Nearing the spot, they could see in the distance two Spitfires circling, and as they arrived at 15.55 saw two dinghies below.

They quickly landed and taxied up to a 12th Air Force B.17 Fortress crew from the 429th Bombardment Squadron, 2nd Bomb Group. By 16.10 all ten men of Captain Joyce's crew were aboard, and Newsome started taxying towards Italy. A message had already gone out for extra help and this brought Walker and Burnett (L2170) who landed and took off four of the Americans, and Walker was able to take off and bring them back. Meantime, with daylight running out, Newsome, with his six Yanks, decided to anchor for the night and await daybreak.

He began taxying again at 06.20 and at 08.00 a HSL arrived and took off the B.17 survivors and towed the Walrus into Pesaro Harbour, where Newsome ran it onto the beach at 09.30.

While the HSL boys had managed to save Walrus R6547, an Australian fighter pilot with 450 Squadron RAAF wrote off one of her sister aircraft on 29 November. Warrant Officer J Boyd taking off in a Kittyhawk (FX591) swung as he became airborne and hit Walrus R6549 at its dispersal spot 140 yards from the runway. The smashed Walrus was towed to its last resting place in the nearby aircraft graveyard – 'with full military honours'. As it turned out, R6547 only had a couple more weeks of life to go herself.

Beagle Number Four

The team of Walker and Burnett used R6547 on 9 December 1944, to rescue yet another downed fighter pilot from the 2nd (Beagle) Squadron, 52nd Fighter Group. The Americans had been flying escort to B.17s attacking Brno, Czechoslovakia, but the American squadrons found themselves in heavy cloud. One Mustang pilot got into trouble. This was Lieutenant Greg Burdick, who sent his story to me on 9 December 1989:

> Today is really an appropriate day to write – the day I lost one of Uncle Sam's lovely birds and joined the Caterpillar Club and the Goldfish Club all at the same time.
>
> I believe I still have total recall of all the events of that memorable afternoon. The answer to the question, what happened, well, I lost my plane in the weather. As a pilot it is a hard thing to admit, that I goofed. I found many people to blame initially, and then to share the blame and then finally could say it was my own fault!
>
> When I was sitting in my dinghy, I passed the time thinking of the satisfaction I would get when I would discuss with my element leader how his breaking formation nearly killed me. After some time, I had some thoughts that if I had been paying attention more and not screwing up, I wouldn't have been in so close to him and suffered all the consequences.
>
> I had 'caged' my artificial horizon because it was processing too fast. If the artificial horizon had been operable I wouldn't be sending you this letter today.

The day before this mission, a new engine had been installed in my plane, and afterwards I had only spent about two hours flying it, but under reduced power. During the time I was 'slow timing' I never uncaged my gyro (artificial horizon). It was not until I was on the mission did I determine that the instrument had not been properly calibrated. Within about five minutes operating time in a position of level flight the gyro would show that I was in a ten-degree diving turn to the right. Since I was heading home and still had to make a let-down through about 30,000 feet of undercast, I made a conscious decision not to rely on the instrument and had so caged it or rendered it inoperable. I was counting on 'matching wings' with my flight leader, if I had to go on instruments.

The four flights of the sixteen planes that made up our Squadron were headed for home. We were at about 31,000 feet with a solid undercast beneath us. Somewhere below us were the northern Italian Alps and we were looking for a hole in the undercast that would let us fly visual to the deck. It is common to find such a break in the undercast at the coastline, so we searched. We found the expected 'hole' and since it was rather small, the four ships in my flight were probably diving at about a 40-degree angle to stay within its limits. Airspeed in such a dive would have been in excess of 350 mph. No.1 called to us to say they would not make it to the deck, so let us do a 360 degree turn and continue on down. I was on the outside of the turn, and maintained my position relying more on muscle than on trim to hold my position.

I didn't know that I already had two strikes against me with number three coming up. We levelled off at 2,000 feet and went into the overcast (scud) still carrying the high airspeed. Immediately we moved from a loose formation into a tight pack around our leader. I was still on muscle and not on trim. My element leader called No.1 to say that he was breaking formation. That meant I had to instantly duck – reduce power – and move away so that he could clear me – and I was not trimmed up. He disappeared into the soup and so did No.1. So there I was at 2,000 feet, with nothing but my rate instruments, doing 350 mph and really out of trim.

Chopping the throttle, the abrupt move to avoid my element leader's plane, had to induce vertigo. My immediate problem was to re-establish my power setting so that I could centre my needle and ball and begin to restore trim. With one eye I was looking for my airspeed and altimeter, with the other I was looking for the manifold pressure gauge so that I could re-establish the power setting, which would have the beneficial affect of helping to restore sanity to the cock-eyed needle and ball. I never did find the manifold pressure gauge; but I did zero in on my air speed and altimeter.

The aircraft was 190 and falling! Equally unsettling was the rate the altimeter was winding upwards. The rate of climb was glued straight up – bad news all the way. Standard stall recovery procedures call for the nose to be pushed over. A quick thought about the rapidity of the loss of air speed and the high rate of climb persuaded me that a push over would be too slow to avoid a stall and spin. At that point I shoved the throttle 'through the wall' and announced to the world that Burdick was baling out. I pulled the red handle, jettisoning the canopy, hit my seat belt release and jumped.

The damn seat belt release snapped shut as I pushed against it, so half in, half out of the aircraft, I managed to finally get loose, counted to five and pulled the release cord. Nothing happened! I tried again – nothing – what the hell . . . oh, my arm is broken, better use my left hand. Success.

I think that this was the point where all the things that could go wrong had already, and from here on things went right. However, looking down and seeing nothing but fog and the Adriatic I would not have guessed it. A buddy had heard my bale out call, and he saw my plane hit the water, then he saw me float out of the overcast on the end of my parachute. He called back and three flight mates and he sweated me until I was in the dinghy. No.1 climbed back to altitude to call air sea rescue.

Jerry Cook of the 2nd Squadron, flying with Dave Emerson, had heard Greg Burdick's call and turned back to look for him. He saw the Mustang go into the water and then the descending parachute. Both pilots circled above but being fairly low, could not raise the ASR boys on the radio, so Emerson climbed to where he could. Greg Burdick continues:

I went down shortly after 1 pm. I would guess that the Catalina flew over me along about 3.30. It continued to pick up the crew of a ditched B.24, and my three P.51 buddies headed for home as the Cat turned up. They had been airborne for over seven hours by this time. My buddy stayed with me when he saw the Cat fly by, and he stayed until the Walrus arrived. When he landed at Ancona he ran out of gas while still on the runway!

The Walrus had blown a cylinder on the way out to get me. With the lack of power and the rough water they couldn't take off. The Catalina returned from picking up the bomber crew and Lieutenant Walker said we were OK and for them to keep on going. Night fell quickly. Lieutenant Walker tried to taxi but the water was too rough so he shut down. E-boats were out looking for us, but as rough as the water was no way could they locate us.

In the small hours of the morning after taking a hell of a pounding all night long from the waves, Walker cautioned me that we might have to take to the dinghy. It didn't happen. Shortly after first light a Baltimore showed up to circle us. Later in the morning three Spitfires arrived to give us cover. Around noon the destroyer HMS *Bicester* arrived. They put out a longboat to retrieve us from the Walrus. After putting us in their lee, the destroyer recovered the longboat with all of us still in it. The waves were rough, but we arrived back at Ancona during the night, and in the morning I was turned over to the medics, and that is just about all there was to it. The muscles in my right arm were chewed up by the broken bone ends. The healing process was pretty long and I never did get back to operational flying.

I never did get to thank the ASR people who retrieved me. Burnett, poor guy, spent the night pumping out the bilge and throwing up. He was so seasick.

Lieutenant R G Burdick, 2nd FS, 52nd FG

It really had been an impossible night aboard the Walrus. It drifted all night long amidst six to seven foot waves. As dawn arrived it became even worse and at 07.00 Walker started up the engine. With four cylinders now gone, taxying was impossible with the sea breaking over the nose and lower wings. He cut the engine after fifteen minutes.

Two Spitfires arrived and later a Catalina, but it could not land. The bouncing around continued till 13.30, at which time the destroyer came to their rescue. The Walrus was badly strained, and with a hole in the port wing above the float, and water up to the cat-walk in the hull, the crew had no choice but to abandon it. The destroyer took them into Ancona at 16.15 and they returned to base by car. A later search for the Walrus found only an empty sea.

Other Happenings

Trevor Humphrey recalls an amusing incident which occurred shortly before Christmas 1944, concerning one of 293 Squadron's Warwick aircraft.

It happened at Biferno airstrip. We'd had a Walrus airborne the previous day and it had a bit of engine trouble, so the pilot put down on the airstrip, which was right on the seashore. He managed to get a message to me that he would like a fitter and some bits and pieces for a repair job, so I flew them over.

Whilst waiting for them to complete the work, I was sitting on the roof of the cockpit, gazing lazily out to sea, when I saw a Warwick come into view. It was a nice but misty day and I recognised the Warwick as coming from 293 and some minutes later it flew over at low level and promptly dropped a dinghy amongst a flock of ducks I could see on the water! I thought that was funny, they can't retrieve that, so I would have to do it. So later, I flew out to the dinghy, punctured it – it was a big 'un – took aboard its four containers, then took off and flew back to base at Foggia.

I presented my compliments to the CO and said, 'I've got a dinghy and stuff belonging to you.' I explained that I had seen someone drop it to a load of ducks off shore. 'Christ!' he exclaimed, 'don't tell anyone about this!'

As it turned out, I flew two other sorties on this day. The first was a scramble following a Baltimore crash after it had stalled when aborting a landing attempt. When I got to the scene all I could see was three dead bodies and a fourth man who was swimming ashore.

Later I had a call from the Baltimore squadron asking if I'd take another look round, did so, but found no further sign of life. However, I had to land and pick up an Italian ground crewman who had swum out and become exhausted.

Another incident worth recording concerned the American Brigadier-General Craigie, who raised a stink about losing a B.26 Marauder with six USO girls on board. They'd been flown out on a 'jolly' but the aircraft lost an engine, and had crashed, everyone being killed.

Flying Officer T H Humphrey, 293 Squadron

Chapter 8

NEARING THE END

294 Squadron Soldier On

While 293 Squadron were now taking the brunt of rescue operations beneath the 'armpits' of the Italian mainland, east and west, 294 Squadron were still covering the areas at the eastern end of the Mediterranean, even though the war had moved away by this time. Nevertheless, their expert help was needed on more than one occasion.

Walrus crews were not always able to make actual rescues but assisted numerous times to save downed airmen of either side. On 13 May 1944 for example, Flight Sergeant L Scarlett and his crew of Flight Sergeant Corkey and Warrant Officer Curnow, helped with the rescue of German airmen in position 34.25N/21.56E, a launch being their final saviour. A newspaper article read:

> YOUR LUCKY DAY: Message to Huns – May 13 Is Your Lucky Day.
> High Speed Launch and Walrus on the way was the message dropped by
> a Middle East Air Sea Rescue Wellington to four German airmen drifting
> in four dinghies lashed together 90 miles from the Cyrenaican coast. The
> Germans had fired a cartridge flare to an operational Wellington which
> radioed their position and circled the dinghies for three hours. Two
> Germans were found dead in the dinghies.

A sortie on 27/28 May 1944 wasn't a good night for 76 Operational Training Unit. Two Wellington Xs out on navigational exercises failed to get back. One (LP129) had crashed at Wadi Shari, 11 miles from Gaza at 03.30 hours, injuring one of the air gunners. This news that they were overdue came in just after base had become aware that another of its Wellingtons had gone missing on a similar training flight over the Arabian Desert. This was another Wellington X – LN956 – piloted by Flight Sergeant Ronald Jefferson.

A Wellington XI (HZ315) of 294 was flown out to search for it, with Flight Sergeant W J Parsons at the controls, joined later by a second Wellington, a type XIII (ME930), flown by Lieutenant J H Knoblauch SAAF. They located survivors in position 29.21N/31.57E (somewhere south of Alexandria) and called up the Walrus, which was flown by Flight Lieutenant D S Stothard, with Warrant Officer W A C Pratt and Flying Officer R J Stafford RAAF (Z1778).

When the call came, there was only one Walrus on the Squadron, and this was being serviced but the ground crew quickly got it fixed and within 1½ hours of the signal, it was airborne (11.40 am) and on its way. By this time a doctor had been flown from Halwen, the nearest airfield, to the spot in a Tiger Moth but the terrain was such that the pilot could see no way of landing without damaging either the biplane or its occupants.

Stothard arrived and also looked in anguish at the rock-strewn ground, but finally he chanced a landing on what appeared to be the best area – about a quarter of a mile from the crash. Dropping smoke bombs to establish the wind direction, he got down safely. Making their way to the crash, the Walrus crew began rendering first aid. One report suggests that of the seven crew, two were dead inside the burnt out wreck, the front gunner and navigator were seriously injured, while the pilot and flight engineer, while injured, could walk. Only the rear gunner was unhurt.

However, RAF records show that one of the two navigators was injured, the flight engineer and one air gunner were seriously injured and the other gunner slightly injured. The pilot, navigator/bomb aimer and the WOP/AG were alright.

It was obvious they would have to stretcher at least two of the men to the Walrus, so a stretcher was fashioned from pieces of parachute and bits from the Wellington's engine cowlings. With some effort they managed to get the injured to the Walrus (Sergeant Albert Harris the gunner and probably the engineer), Sergeant Richard Hallums jammed everyone in and even more successfully, took off without too many problems.

The Walrus brought them back to Heliopolis, although the front gunner died on the morning of the 29th. Upon later inspection of the Walrus's tyres, they were found to be completely unusable following the landing in such rough country.

It transpired that the training crew had become lost and didn't even know for certain if they were over land. The pilot had descended slowly, put his wheels down in case he was over land, but then came out of cloud too low to react and had crunched into the desert floor at 02.53.

Later the AOC wrote to 294 Squadron, praising the pilot by saying:

> Not only did he execute a successful landing in difficult circumstances and took off with a heavy load, but his rendering of first aid has, no doubt, greatly improved the chances of the injured survivors. I consider this rescue was in keeping with the high standards of the Air Sea Rescue Service.

The Squadron made another rescue on 30 June, this time a more conventional one. It was made from the detachment at Berka, commanded by Flight Lieutenant H G Litchfield. 335 Greek Squadron had sent out ten aircraft on a convoy patrol in the late afternoon, but Flying Officer G Pleonis in Spitfire Vb ER524 had suffered engine failure and had baled out in position 32.47N/20.29E. Being circled by his No.2, Flight Sergeant D Varverio, who called a Mayday, he hit the sea 20 miles out from the coast. Within two hours Pleonis had been rescued by a Walrus flown by Flight Sergeant L Scarlett, in company with Flight Sergeant A M Corkey, and Warrant Officer F O Curnow (W3107), and been

landed back at 335's airstrip at Bersis Landing Ground, on the Libyan coast. Les
Scarlett wrote in his log book:

> Scramble to 3247N 2029E for Spitfire of 335 Hellenic Sqdn. Picked up
> pilot and took him to his base at Bersis. What a night!!

Scarlett later told the following story about the aftermath of the rescue:

> Obtained permission after picking the Greek out of the water to go direct
> to his base, presumably not too far away. You can picture the excitement
> of the fighter boys on seeing the prompt return of their comrade. A party
> started and went on and on, and eventually the Walrus pilot had to stay
> overnight with his crew!

Later a letter came from Flying Officer George Pleonis, thanking him for saving
his life but went on to apologise that photographs taken of Les and his crew,
could not be forwarded as the pilot who was having them developed had gone
missing over Crete a few days later, presumably with the film on him.

Earlier in June (the 2nd) Les Scarlett and his crew had located a crashed 38
Squadron Wellington on the beach near Benghazi. He directed a launch to them
which picked up three survivors and collected three dead bodies. Scarlett
became a Warrant Officer and shortly before his tour ended in early 1945, he was
commanding a detachment at Mersa Matruh. When he left in March he was
assessed 'Above the Average'.

* * *

It was September before the next of 294's rescues occurred, a German airman,
on the 5th. The previous night a Ju88 D-1 of 2/(F)123 (coded 4U+KK), flown
by Hauptmann Helmut Weixelbaum and his crew, had been on a night
reconnaissance over Alexandria and had failed to return. Obviously there was
evidence that the 88 had gone in somewhere off the coast, hence 294 being
sent out.

Flying Officer T A Williams RCAF, with Flying Officer M A Brown RCAF
and Warrant Officer C E Pannell RAAF, took off in Z1757 at 11.05 am and
located a dinghy 37 minutes later. Having pulled one sole German airman
aboard, the difficulty of trying to get off soon became apparent. The three
attempts, including some spectacular porpoising, ended after hitting a large
wave, which damaged the Walrus and injured one of the crewmen.

A call had to be sent for assistance, resulting in the arrival of a HSL, which
towed them into Aboukir Harbour.

A Long Evening
Eight days later (the 13th) Flying Officer J S Turner, with Warrant Officers G R
Lowe and J D Ormesher, in Z1776, operating out of Gambut airfield, had a long
rescue, which lasted for over four hours.

Eight Beaufighters from 603 Squadron, operating out of Gambut, were out

on a sweep of the central Aegean Sea. At 14.15 pm the leader turned back with
an oil leak, so the sortie was taken over by Flight Lieutenant J R Keohaney, and
his navigator, Flight Sergeant A Fielding (NE593). However, this Beau too
developed an oil leak so aborted at 15.07. In view of the fact that only one of the
remaining crews was experienced, the formation was instructed to return to base
five minutes later.

Pilot Officer A B Woodier with Sergeant H Lee down at the back (NE367)
had returned with the leader, and this Beau too started to have problems and had
become separated. He called the others on VHF, was given a course to fly, but at
15.24, Woodier announced he was about to ditch, going in at position
33.33N/24.20E. Flight Lieutenant Keohaney turned back to help, making a
square search but had no luck finding the downed crew. Almost an hour later, in
position 34.07N/23.52E – some distance away from the first position given – he
finally spotted a V-shaped trail of oil on the sea, then some fluorescene, and then
two dinghies close together, downwards from the oil, with one man in each.

Keohaney circled at 3,000 feet as the men in the water fired off some flares.
He switched his IFF to 'distress', alternating with 'stud 1' at five minute
intervals, and showing 'stud 3' when it was thought relief aircraft were homing
in. Not wishing to lose sight of the dinghy, Keohaney continued to circle but by
18.49 he had reached PLE (Prudent Limit of Endurance) and had to set off for
base. The dinghies had now drifted three miles from the crash site.

Information from 235 Wing alerted an ASR Wellington of a downed aircraft
well north of the Libyan coast, at just after 16.00 hours, but the crew failed to
make any sighting. Meantime the Walrus went out at 16.48, initially for the pick-
up, and then to help search.

They too failed to find anyone or anything at the given position but they
continued to search until fuel began to run low, so decided, just before 7pm, to
head for Derna. Within ten minutes they sighted an oil patch, and then a red Very
flare arched up, and flying on they came upon the dinghies, now in position
33.58N/23.42E. The Walrus crew could see that the surface was far from
tranquil, with a heavy sea running, estimating the swell at between eight to ten
feet. As darkness was fast approaching, and with no other aircraft in the vicinity,
Turner decided to make a landing, despite the obvious dangers.

Turner got down safely, taxied up to the dinghies and took on the men, then
made an attempt to get off again. This proved very difficult due to the swell, and
also the port float was smashed and the underside of the same wing was
damaged. Despite the damage, Turner made another try and this time made it,
setting course for Derna, now desperately short of fuel.

At five minutes to eight pm, it was completely dark and they were unable to
get any QDMs from Derna. Either their radio was not working properly, or
Derna could not hear them. At 20.25 they crossed the coast but still could not
raise Derna control, while the petrol gauge was reading zero.

Twenty minutes later, obviously flying on fumes(!), Turner sighted Derna town
and sent out an SOS by flashing his navigation lights. Someone was obviously
alert for within minutes, the airfield flare path came on off to port. Turner put the
Walrus down at 20.55, with just one gallon of petrol left in the tank.

* * *

There is only one other recorded rescue by 294 Squadron, which occurred on 5 February 1945. Again it was a Beaufighter crew, this one on a training flight with 79 OTU at Lakatamia. Flying Officer T R Murdock, Warrant Officer R I Mowat and Sergeant E E L Crane were the Walrus crew (L2331) and they carried out a successful pick-up from position 33.10N/33.10E (an amazing numerical longitude/latitude coincidence) that afternoon, mid-way between Cyprus and Egypt.

A Not So Happy Christmas
War rarely stops for things such as Christmas, 1914 being perhaps the famous exception, and Christmas 1944 off Italy was a far cry from football between British and German troops in 'No-Man's-Land' on the Western Front.

Pilots of 450 Squadron were flying operations on the morning of 26 December, 11 Kittyhawks led by Flight Lieutenant D L Millar, attacking ammo dumps. Climbing to 7,500 feet along the Italian coast, then heading inland north-west to the south of Padova, the target was easily picked out and seven aircraft dive-bombed south-east to north-west, opening up with their guns too as they headed in. The bombing was reported to be concentrated at the south-west corner of the dump, but one pilot was in trouble.

Warrant Officer L G Robinson (FX710) called up to say his engine temperature was going off the clock and that he was going to have to leave. He was seen to bale out and later spotted by the colour of his Mae West, but he was not in his dinghy. This was both ominous and worrying, being late December. Three aircraft remained over him till some Spitfires arrived to take over.

Walrus L2170 of 293 was flown out by Sergeant R J Bickle, with Flight Sergeant Faulkner at 11.00, to position 44.34N/12.25E, off the coast at Porto Garibaldi. Looking down it seemed to the crew that the man in the water seemed lifeless but they landed at 11.30 and found he was indeed dead. They assumed he had been killed due to a low bale-out and he was face-down, suggesting that he had been unable to inflate his Mae West.

Sadly they were not able to recover the body due to the rough sea and being unable to take off commenced to taxi towards the shore at noon. At 14.15 the engine cut out and 50 minutes after this, the starboard lower wing broke inboard of the float. The Walrus was now in danger of foundering, so Bickle and Faulkner abandoned it and rowed ashore in their dinghy, which they reached at 15.30.

Later the Walrus was washed up nearby, in location 44.23N/12.19E, not far from Ravenna beach, at 17.00. Next morning some engineers cleared a path through a minefield and brought back the crew with the aid of two Italians, after walking to Ravenna. When Bickle returned to base he carried large blisters on both feet and swore never again to attempt a walk across country in flying boots!

1945
By the end of the year, 293 Squadron had detachments all over the place. The one at Ramatuelle in southern France had ended, but aircraft were at Bellaria just north of Rimini, Pomigliano, near Naples, and Foggia and Falconara, near Ancona.

The first rescue of the New Year came on 25 January. A 3 Squadron RAAF Mustang pilot, Pilot Officer D B Davies (KH821) was part of a 12-plane formation dive-bombing a bridge near Chuisaforte, that afternoon. Davies was hit in the engine, and with a dead motor ditched into shallow water off the River Po estuary. In fact he was only 200 yards off shore, close to Goro. The Mustang sank in eight to ten feet of water but he got out OK, and climbed onto the tail, which remained sticking out of the sea. Inflating his dinghy he paddled further out in order to increase his chances of avoiding capture. Four other Mustangs circled overhead until a Walrus arrived and pulled him from his dinghy just half an hour after ditching.

Davies was promoted to acting Flight Lieutenant at the end of the month, a rank confirmed later. However, on 1 April – All Fools Day – as well as the 27th anniversary of the birth of the Royal Air Force – he was hit again during a ground attack mission over northern Yugoslavia. He baled out and landed safely, and after living with local partisans as the war concluded, returned to his squadron on 1 June.

Unfortunately I was unable to locate any reference to which Walrus crew effected this rescue, but going through the diary of 293 Fighter Wing of the Desert Air Force to find some or any reference about it, as 3 RAAF Squadron operated in this Wing, I did find an amusing story which occurred during January, that I record here for some light relief. It was printed in the Wing Review and concerned one of the other units in the Wing, 260 Squadron.

> No combats with enemy aircraft occurred but on one occasion a pilot of 260 Squadron, intending to rejoin his squadron above cloud after bombing, started to join up with three Me109s. Having recognised them as hostile he was about to open fire when, remembering his Tee Emm[1], he looked behind and saw a fourth Me on his tail so he hastily took cover in cloud. His leader, who was below cloud heard frantic cries of "Help, help, I'm surrounded by Messerschmitts!" To which his leader dourly replied, "What is your call-sign, clot?", and was told it was Blue Two.
>
> After about five minutes of silence, leader called up, "Hello Blue Two, have you been shot down yet?" Blue Two replied, "No, I'm in cloud." The adventure ended happily.

* * *

293 Squadron had something of a lull in rescues in the early weeks of the New Year and it was not until 4 March that the next rescue was recorded. Sergeant F A Caie and Warrant Officer Taylor (L2207) were off at 10.15 am to pick up Lieutenant James O Spraley, from New Weston, Ohio, of the 87th Fighter Squadron, 79th Fighter Group. They were helped by a P.47 pilot who directed them to the exact spot. The American Group flew one hundred and nine sorties on the 4th, mainly against rail and road traffic, bridges and gun emplacements. Apart from Spraley, another pilot baled out over land and was taken prisoner.

---

[1] Tee Emm – Training Manual.

Mine-Spotting
Apart from picking up downed airmen from the sea, or rescuing soldiers and sailors from watery graves, the Walrus amphibian aircraft was given another task as the war entered its final phases, as Alex Stevens recalls:

> Back on the west coast I took part in several searches during which we sighted empty dinghies or oil patches, or a launch in the area made the pick-up while we guided them to the 'customer', but generally the ASR function for us became very quiet. Fortunately somebody discovered that in the Mediterranean, a mine can be seen down to a depth of about 30 feet whilst flying at about 200 feet so we were engaged from time to time surveying areas of sea and occasionally co-operating with minesweepers. Thanks to this we managed to get in some flying. Eventually 624 Squadron was formed early in 1945 for this specific function and I was posted to the new unit.
>
> Pilot Officer A G Stevens, 293 & 624 Squadrons

624 Squadron had originally been formed in September 1943, tasked with dropping agents and supplies to underground forces and partisans in Europe. For this it used four-engined Halifax aircraft and following a year of intense operations it was disbanded exactly one year later.

It was reformed in late 1944 at Gottaglie for mine-spotting, becoming operational in February 1945 from Foggia, and carrying out its work over the Adriatic. It was to continue in this role for the rest of the year, flying from Greece, Italy, Malta and North Africa. That last year saw Squadron Leader G M Gallagher as commanding officer, who had previously been with 284 Squadron.

Minefield Rescue
On the 11th, Flight Sergeant Bickle, with Flight Sergeants A S Goldstein and Burnett, again using L2207, were off shortly before 1 pm. The previous evening a Warwick had been out trying to locate the crew of a Mosquito XIII (MM527) of 256 Squadron lost on a Ranger Patrol. This crew had been north-east of Venice where they spotted a barge. Going down to attack it, the nose of the Mossie exploded as the cannons were fired. Heading for the coast, light flak came up from the mouth of the River Piave, causing them to evade and lose precious height.

Fragments of metal had already blown back into the radiator of the starboard engine from the exploding nose, and with the engine overheating, it had to be feathered. The Mosquito began to lose height, so the pilot, Warrant Officer R E Chamberlain, re-started the engine but soon had to feather it once more. Height was lost fairly rapidly now and finally Chamberlain was forced to ditch at 19.05. The navigator, Flight Sergeant N Goodyear, did not survive.

The Warwick that went out in order to locate the men and drop a Lindholme boat to them was assisted by a Baltimore and a Boston who were to drop flares as the night came on. They had no luck, and with an enemy night-fighter aircraft reported in the area, they finally had to call off the search till the next morning.

The first search was by a Walrus crew soon after dawn, but low cloud hampered their efforts. Later a Warwick found a dinghy and called up the Walrus. At 13.25, as the Walrus arrived, the Warwick dropped smoke floats to guide them to the customer. The main problem was that the man in the dinghy was right by a minefield.

Bickle landed and moved as close as he dared to the mines, then his two crewmen launched a dinghy and attempted to row to the survivor, through the minefield, but the current proved too strong and progress towards him was negligible. At 14.20 the Warwick (BV415, Flight Lieutenant A Rawling RAAF) dropped a lifeboat to the Walrus men, which proved to be very accurate, splashing down 50 feet up wind from them. Goldstein and Burnett paddled to it, climbed aboard, started the engine – at the sixth attempt – then proceeded into the minefield.

They reached Chamberlain, who was suffering from burns, exposure and a broken ankle. He told them his Mosquito had blown up shortly before he ditched, and his navigator had been killed. With their man safely aboard the lifeboat, they motored back to the Walrus, got aboard, and took off at 15.45. Escorting Spitfires then sunk the lifeboat and the dinghies.

Walker and Burnett were back on the score-sheet on 18 March (L2217), picking up Captain James C Hare, from the 57th Fighter Group Headquarters, after him being forced to ditch his Thunderbolt. They found him in his dinghy one and a half miles off Cérvia.

Under Shell Fire

Two days later, Warrant Officer C S Tod RNZAF with Sergeant Bilton – L2217 – had an early afternoon rescue. Spitfires of 601 Squadron were bombing barges at Guarda Veneta, led by Flying Officer T E Johnson. Diving down from 10,000 feet to 2,000 feet, his No.2 – Sergeant A R Charles (Spitfire IXE PT641) was hit by ground fire and after making the coast, had to bale out over the sea, landing some three miles east of Porto Garibaldi.

After spending almost two hours in his dinghy, and coming under shore fire as the Walrus arrived and landed, he was picked up unhurt and returned to his unit. To help keep the enemy gunner's heads down, Spitfires made strafing runs over them. As the Walrus moved across the water, one shell landed directly behind it, slightly damaging the rudder, but Tod got away after a very good effort all round.

A Busy Easter Sunday

After four successful rescues in March, April began with a double, the first by the redoubtable duo of Lieutenant K B Walker and Warrant Officer W Burnett, the second by Bickle and Goldstein.

Captain R Jacobs SAAF led an 08.50 escort mission of 92 Squadron Spitfires for a US Catalina, flying out to rescue Flying Officer C 'Hank' Beasly who had baled out two hours earlier. The Catalina landed and safely picked up its 'customer' but then Sergeant S Widdowson (Spitfire VIII MT667) developed engine trouble and had to bale out on the way back. Warrant Officer A Mitchell RAAF orbited round him until the Walrus hove into view and picked up Widdowson just before 10.30, off Porto Garibaldi.

Flight Sergeant W B Forster of 145 Squadron was the second rescuee. He had been No.3 to a four-plane element led by Squadron Leader S W F Daniel DFC, tasked with dive-bombing the railway line, which ran between Montebelluna and Castelfranco, taking off at 09.30. They met intense anti-aircraft fire and Forster was hit in the engine and radiator, which forced a bale out over the sea. Bickle and Goldstein were sent off at 11.05 and collected their man out from the Po estuary.

His wingman, Flight Sergeant A J Stacey may also have been hit, for he was last seen three miles out to sea, heading for home but then disappeared. However, two men had been saved, and later that afternoon, Group Captain Hugh Dundas DSO DFC, OC 244 Fighter Wing, telephoned the Squadron and thanked them for saving his two pilots.

Rescued Three Times
The final rescues of note also in their way became the most famous, for during the month of April 1945, one fighter pilot was rescued no less than three times, which has to be some sort of record.

Lieutenant R H Veitch was a South African pilot flying with 260 Squadron. On 2 April, flying Mustang KH592, he was one of ten pilots of the Squadron flying an armed reconnaissance mission to the Moribor-Graz area. Flight Lieutenant R S Brown led them out at 06.55. Trains were attacked with rockets and machine-gun fire, and then some motor transport became targets. Ray Veitch was hit by ground fire and he quickly turned for home, escorted by Lieutenant K Foster, but he was forced to bale out into a minefield. As it was soon to prove, nothing was going to be simple for this man.

A Warwick from 293 was already out on another rescue, piloted by Flying Officer F G Weaver (HF948), so he was called up by a Walrus when they – Flight Sergeant Newsome and Sergeant E S Bilton – found their man but were unable to land due to mines, clearly visible. Weaver arrived in due time and dropped him a lifeboat. Climbing in, Veitch sailed out of the danger area and in safer water, a US Catalina arrived, was able to land, and took him aboard.

Three days later, having hardly dried out, Veitch was back in a Mustang (FB315), on another early armed-recce along with five other aircraft. The area covered on this mission was Sesana-Ljubljana-Villach-Spittal-Drauberg. A locomotive was strafed but small arms fire from the ground struck Veitch's fighter which began to stream glycol. Again he headed for base and again he was forced to bale out before he got far over the sea. Escorted down by fellow-South African, Lieutenant Nelson, he gave a Mayday call, then watched as Veitch safely splashed down and clambered into his dinghy.

Nelson then saw a motor torpedo boat coming out from the nearby port of Trieste. To deter the hostile intent, Nelson dived down and fired rockets at the boat, which nearly capsized it. The message was clear, and the boat turned and limped back into port.

All this time, gunfire had been coming from the boat and from Trieste itself, but neither Nelson nor Veitch were hit, which was just as well, for Veitch had again put himself right in the middle of another minefield! 260 Squadron now flew a succession of sorties to cover their man and protect him from the hostile shore. On one, the CO, Squadron Leader P S Blomfield, saw a small boat with four blue-uniformed men in it, heading for Veitch's dinghy. Blomfield fired a warning burst towards them but they continued on undeterred, and even fired up at the Mustang. Having failed to take the hint, Blomfield curved down towards them, let go some rockets, which left the boat awash and with only two men in sight. Aircraft of 112 Squadron relieved 260 Squadron.

A Warwick of 293 Squadron flew out (BV449) skippered by Pilot Officer W W Huggins, entering the Gulf of Trieste with a Mustang escort. This escort was provided by Squadron Leader Blomfield, who had re-armed and refuelled, with three other Mustangs escorting the lifeboat-carrying aircraft. They located the dinghy and dropped the lifeboat despite intense AA fire from the coast. They could also see some heavy calibre shells falling around the South African in his dinghy; nine salvoes of three over the next half an hour – the nearest falling only 200 yards away.

Once again Veitch found himself moving from dinghy to lifeboat, started the motor and chugged away from both the minefield and the gunfire. He was still happily sailing along as night fell, but early the next morning, 260, led by Captain V B Ruiter, were out looking for him, finding him still motoring, and still looking happy.

A Catalina now arrived and still wary of mines, the Cat pilot dropped a message, telling Veitch to make for a smoke float they had dropped, six or seven miles away, in an area they knew was free of mines. Despite bad visibility, the Catalina and covering Mustangs kept the boat in view. Having reached the designated spot, the PBY landed, and taxied to the boat. Then one of the PBY's crew dived into the sea, swam to the boat, and helped Veitch swim to the aircraft and safety. Shortly afterwards, Raymond Howard Veitch was awarded the DFC.

That should have been enough for anyone, but on the 30th, Flight Lieutenant A Rawlings, in Warwick BV449, was scrambled at 18.00 hours to fly to a position 45.35N/13.12E. There he found a dinghy, with P.51s circling overhead. In the dinghy was Mr Veitch!

Veitch's squadron had been off on an armed recce at 08.25 and had not come back, reported to be down off the Italian coast. Once again they were over the Udine area. Road transport had again been attacked, and Veitch had rocketed a section of road, leaving it cratered. Pulling up from his last run, he was told he was streaming coolant and to head for home. He could see for himself a hole through his port wing. He eventually went over the side when he was down to 5,000 feet over the sea. His No.2, Warrant Officer L B Fricher, called control and circled high over Veitch to get a fix.

On 260 Squadron's second mission of the day, which had started just before 4 pm, the Mustangs attacked ground targets east of Udine. After the attack, the pilots flew down to take a look at two big fires, and saw a line of thatched buildings, two of which were burning, so they went in to shoot-up the rest. Letting go the last of their rockets, they scored three direct hits, then followed a road to strafe some motor transport they found. Four trucks were destroyed along with three trailers, and one scout car was set on fire.

Reforming, the aircraft set course for home, except for Squadron Leader Blomfield and his wingman, Pilot Officer Curtes, who flew out over the spot where Veitch had been reported to be blithely sitting in a dinghy. They stayed to orbit him pending the arrival of rescue aircraft. This time he was five miles out from Lignano.

The weather was far from good, and Rawlings in his Warwick had to coast-crawl north. By 19.30 the Warwick crew were encountering violent electrical storms and numerous water spouts, then heavy flak greeted them as they arrived in the Lignano area. What with storms and flak, and being unable to spot the dinghy, Rawlings had eventually to turn back for base.

At first light the next day, Rawlings was out again, but this time engine trouble forced a return, so 293 was denied a hand in Veitch's third rescue. In the event a lifeboat was dropped by an American B.17 and after making his way out to sea for the third time, he was located and picked up by yet another American ASR Catalina. Both the B.17 and the PBY came from the 1st Emergency Rescue Service.

In the summary of 260 Squadron's activities for the month, Squadron Leader Blomfield wrote:

> Of all the new records which were being established day by day, an all time one was established by Lieutenant R H Veitch, who baled out into the drink – the North Adriatic – three times during the month. His last effort on the 30th, resulted in his being in an open boat for 27 hours, and his subsequent appointment by the AOC Desert Air Force, as Commodore of the RAF Yacht Club – when formed!

Funn-eee!

There can be added to these gallant stories of the Walrus squadrons in the Mediterranean and around the coasts of Sicily and Italy, an amusing tale as this final chapter ends. On 19 April 1945, Flight Sergeant F Birch and Flight Sergeant J P Elkin of 293 Squadron – in W2729 – were hastily despatched in their amphibian to collect the Air Officer Commanding, Balkan Air Force, Air Vice-Marshal G H Mills DFC, from a high-speed launch, which had broken down in Rab Harbour on the Yugoslavian coast. They safely collected him, together with a group captain and a naval captain.

The group captain objected to the fact that the Walrus had landed, and then taken off again across a minefield, and that the two NCO airmen should have known better! The two NCOs were a little hurt by this and were about to mumble something about looking a "gift Walrus in the mouth", when the naval captain suddenly took their part. For no apparent reason, he chimed in to say that he thought it had been a very good show anyway!

The two airmen attributed the 'groupie's' bad mood to either sea sickness or to the fact that they had adopted the principle of Mr Keith and Mr Prowse – "We have the best seats, you want 'em?" – and sat the group captain on a pile of Mae Wests somewhere in the bowels of the Walrus. Anyway, the AOC seemed very happy and when they arrived at their destination, he departed gaily in a shower of salutes!

* * *

I have no particular reason for picking out Trevor Humphrey for special mention, except that he is one man I have met, and know that for his service to his country and to his fellow flyers, he, like so many others, had no reward. Apart from, that is, the personal satisfaction of having been able to save lives.

His record is probably as typical as any other Walrus pilot. He served in England with 278 and 277 Squadrons, then in the Mediterranean with 283, 284 and 293 Squadrons. In all he flew 118 rescue sorties and amassed some 350 flying hours on the Walrus. He rescued, or helped to rescue, 44 airmen, 21 in personal pick-ups, and a further 23 by directing surface craft to them. In addition to this, as an instructor on the various squadrons he was with, he converted 23 new pilots to fly the Walrus. He left the RAF in December 1945, with the rank of flight lieutenant.

Appendix A

AWARD CITATIONS FOR AIR SEA RESCUE WALRUS PERSONNEL IN THE MEDITERRANEAN THEATRE OF OPERATIONS

Distinguished Service Order

Squadron Leader Walter Sterne
283 Squadron. *London Gazette*, 28 September 1943

In Air Sea Rescue operations this officer has rendered most valuable service. During one period of six weeks the Squadron he commands was responsible for the rescue of many members of aircraft aircrew from the sea around Pantelleria and Sicily. These efforts were made under the supervision and direction of Squadron Leader Sterne who himself effected several of them involving abnormal hazard, near enemy territory. In June 1943, he undertook a search for a pilot reported adrift in a dinghy. After many hours flying, Squadron Leader Sterne located the dinghy very close to the Sicilian coast. The sea was extremely rough but, in circumstances which called for the utmost skill, Squadron Leader Sterne effected a successful rescue. This officer has displayed outstanding leadership and great courage.

Distinguished Flying Cross

Warrant Officer Gordon Frederick Brown RCAF
293 Squadron. *London Gazette*, 21 July 1944
(Joint citation with Flt Sgt C S Taylor, awarded DFM).

As pilot and wireless operator/air gunner respectively, Warrant Officer Brown and Flight Sergeant Taylor have completed many air sea rescue sorties. Their steadfastness and courage in the face of numerous difficult and dangerous situations has won the greatest praise.

Warrant Officer Kenneth George Hall RAFVR
284 Squadron. *London Gazette*, 1 October 1943.

Warrant Officer Hall displayed commendable courage, skill and devotion to duty, when on a recent occasion he rescued two pilots from their dinghies. His example is worthy of the highest praise.

162

Acting Flight Lieutenant Douglas John Garcia Harcourt RAFVR
294 Squadron. *London Gazette*, 26 November 1943.

Flight Lieutenant Harcourt has undertaken a large number of air sea rescue operations during which he has been responsible for some 43 personnel being rescued from the sea. Many of them he has saved himself by taking them aboard his aircraft, and others he has located and then remained with them whilst sending messages of guidance to surface craft which has taken them aboard. Flight Lieutenant Harcourt has displayed great courage and devotion to duty, setting an inspiring example.

––––––––––––

Flight Lieutenant Reginald Francis Hayes RAFVR
284 Squadron. *London Gazette*, 1 October 1943.

Flight Lieutenant Hayes has displayed great skill and devotion to duty in air sea rescue operations and his example is worthy of the highest praise.

––––––––––––

Flying Officer Anthony Bruno Morabito RCAF
283 Squadron. *London Gazette*, 30 November 1943.

(No citation gazetted)

––––––––––––

Warrant Officer Colin Ian Anthony Paterson RAFVR
284 Squadron. *London Gazette*, 25 August 1944.

(No citation gazetted)

––––––––––––

Warrant Officer Norman Pickles RAF
284 Squadron. *London Gazette*, 3 March 1944

Warrant Officer Pickles has taken part in a large number of air sea rescue operations during which he has assisted in rescuing ten members of aircraft crew. On one occasion whilst assisting a comrade from the sea, Warrant Officer Pickles was hit by machine-gun fire. Although in great pain and suffering from shock, he persisted in his efforts until the rescue was successfully effected. This warrant officer has invariably displayed praiseworthy courage, determination and devotion to duty.

––––––––––––

Flying Officer Harold Frederick Burditt RAF
293 Squadron. *London Gazette*, 29 May 1945.

(No citation gazetted) (noted as Lt Royal Regiment of Artillery)

––––––––––––

Flying Officer Alexander George Stevens RAFVR
293 Squadron. *London Gazette*, 29 May 1945.

Pilot Officer Stevens is a pilot of outstanding courage and determination who has always displayed exceptional keenness and great devotion to duty. In October 1944, he was detailed to search the sea off the north-west coast of Italy, for survivors of a minesweeper. Twelve survivors were sighted in an area heavily mined. Despite adverse weather and a high sea, this officer brought his aircraft down on the sea and managed to get nine of the men aboard. Three others were rescued by an Air Sea Rescue Launch which also entered the minefield. An attempt was made to transfer the survivors from the aircraft to the launch but owing to the adverse weather and a shortage of petrol, the aircraft was towed back to Leghorn by the launch. The gallantry and resolution displayed on this occasion was worthy of the highest praise.

Bar to Distinguished Flying Cross

Flight Lieutenant Reginald Frederick Hayes DFC RAFVR
284 Squadron. *London Gazette*, 25 August 1944.

(No citation gazetted)

Distinguished Flying Medal

Flight Sergeant John Rupert Berry RNZAF
284 Squadron. *London Gazette*, 7 January 1944.

On 17th August 1943, Flight Sergeant Berry was the wireless operator/air gunner in a Walrus from Cassibile which picked up two fighter pilots five miles north-east of Cape Spartivento on the toe of Italy in the face of heavy anti-aircraft fire and proximity of enemy aircraft, one pilot being but 150 yards from the enemy coastline. On 2nd September 1943, this airman was in a Walrus which rescued Wing Commander Duncan Smith DSO DFC and Bar. In this instance, the Walrus was attacked by two Me.109s and badly damaged by cannon shells below the water line. Flight Sergeant Berry covered the holes with his hands and prevented the aircraft from sinking so that a take-off from the sea could be effected. At all times, this airman has shown great keenness and tenacity of purpose and in the space of six weeks has helped to rescue eight members of aircrew, all from positions close to the enemy coastline.

Flight Sergeant Arnold Divers RNZAF
283 Squadron. *London Gazette*, 25 January 1944.

During the past four months, Flight Sergeant Divers has been responsible for 11 successful rescues of British or American aircrews. For example, on 3rd November 1943, although he had only been discharged from hospital on that day and said to be unfit for any duty until 18th November, he heard that a Mayday had been received from a position west of the Italian coast about 90 miles from base. The remainder of the squadron were

away on other sectors and were not available. Having no senior to refer to, this pilot, in spite of his weakened state of health, flew to the position given, located the dinghy and took five aircrew safely aboard. The dinghy was leaking badly and, coupled with stormy weather, these rescued aircrew could not have survived another two hours. The sea was so rough that the fabric of the Walrus was badly torn and take-off was impossible. Taxying too after a short while became impossible due to the extremely heavy seas. After managing to keep afloat for over ten hours, the crew of the Walrus and the five rescued airmen were at dawn on 4th November, taken aboard the USA Hospital Ship Seminole. The ship's log records: "Sea rough. Sky overcast. Rain squalls. It required considerable persuasion by the Chief Officer to induce the pilot to leave the damaged aircraft. In our estimation, the 'plane could not survive."
Other examples of the outstanding devotion to duty displayed by this airman are rescues effected on 3rd July 1943, when he rescued a pilot 15 miles off the Sardinian coast at a time when the island was still in enemy hands and again on 18th July when he rescued a pilot 20 miles off the Sicilian coast despite considerable enemy activity from the shore. Again, on 12th August 1943, a British fighter pilot was rescued about eight miles off Valcano and, on this occasion, heavy flak was experienced from enemy anti-aircraft batteries but, despite this, he successfully completed his task. The work of this pilot with 283 Squadron has always been of an exceptionally high order and his example has proved to be a keen incentive to the remainder of the squadron.

Flight Sergeant Edwin John Holmes
284 Squadron. *London Gazette*, 25 January 1944.

Flight Sergeant Holmes is a pilot of a Walrus aircraft of 284 Air Sea Rescue Squadron and has been actively engaged on operations since October 1942. Since August 1943, he has taken part in rescue work in both the Sicilian and Italian campaigns. Whilst operating from bases in Sicily and flying Walrus aircraft, he has carried out numerous searches well north of the enemy lines. On one occasion he rescued a pilot in the Messina Strait while the enemy was still in Sicily, south of Catania. In the space of one month, he rescued eight pilots alive, all in close proximity to the enemy coastline and several times under fire from shore batteries. At all times this airman has shown courage, determination and devotion to duty and as an Air Sea Rescue pilot, his flying has been outstanding and he has set a fine example to the rest of the squadron.

Flight Sergeant Colin Horne
283 Squadron. *London Gazette*, 30 November 1943.

This pilot of 283 Air Sea Rescue Squadron has successfully made 16 rescues off Pantelleria, Sicily, Sardinia and Italy, between 5th May and 31st August 1943. This is the highest individual score in his squadron. Even when fighter escorts were not available, he made sorties close to the enemy coast. During the operations against Pantelleria, he made four rescues in rough weather within sight of the shore in spite of constant enemy activity. On one occasion, the sea was too rough to allow for take-off and, in order to return to base, he taxied back 55 miles. His last rescue, on 25th August 1943, was made a few miles off the Italian coast.

Flight Sergeant Eric Frank Keeble
284 Squadron. *London Gazette*, 25 August 1944.

On 15th May, 1944, Flight Sergeant Keeble was the wireless operator/air gunner on a Walrus aircraft piloted by Warrant Officer Paterson of 284 Air Sea Rescue Squadron which effected the rescue from the sea of three members of a Mitchell crew of 466 Squadron USAAF. The aircraft had to land in a minefield only 100 yards from the shore of Elba in easy reach of the shore batteries and in constant danger from floating mines. Flight Sergeant Keeble, however, assisted three men into the aircraft unflurried and undeterred by the dangers with which they were surrounded. This is but one example of the excellent Air Sea Rescue record held by this NCO and he has assisted in the rescue of 18 other airmen during the period he has flown with Air Sea Rescue squadrons in this theatre, many of their lives being saved under the most dangerous circumstances and difficult conditions. His keenness to take part in rescue operations and the loyalty, courage and cheerfulness which he has shown at all times have been an inspiration to the other aircrew members.

Sergeant William Surtees Lambert
283 Squadron. *London Gazette*, 28 September 1943.

On 5th June, 1943, this pilot was ordered to pick up a Mitchell crew of four in a dinghy. The sea was extremely rough and difficult as well as hazardous to land on. This pilot located the dinghy and landed without damaging the aircraft and without regard to his own personal safety. He knew full well that he would be unable to take off again that evening. After transferring the four aircrew to his Walrus, he taxied to Sousse Harbour, the first 50 miles on his own power, the rest of the way he was towed by a Royal Naval launch. Three of the aircrew were badly wounded by enemy action and their recovery later in hospital must in a large measure be attributed to this gallant action. The rescue was effected 15 miles from Pantelleria when this island was still in enemy hands.

Sergeant Dennis John Lunn
284 Squadron. *London Gazette*, 1 October 1943.

Sergeant Lunn, on 27th July 1943, was ordered off from Cassibile within 30 minutes of arrival from Malta and without refuelling, to rescue a pilot five miles south-west of the toe of Italy which he did successfully while the enemy was still south of Catania. On 4th August 1943, Sergeant Lunn rescued three pilots on the same day, all within very close proximity of Catania and enemy guns and aircraft, one pilot being but 300 yards from the shore. Sergeant Lunn has always shown a great keenness and tenacity of purpose under the most difficult conditions and has proved himself as possessing courage and devotion to duty in the very highest traditions of the Service.

Flight Sergeant Kenneth Royden Pugh
283 Squadron. *London Gazette*, 1 October 1943.

This airman has on several occasions attended to wounded members of the crew under extremely difficult conditions. On one sortie, he gave attention to three severely wounded airmen and worked vigorously at the pumps in the intervals. Later he took part in the rescue of a pilot from the sea and when the dinghy became entangled with his aircraft's undercarriage, tied himself to a rope and cut the dinghy free. Although, meanwhile, he was partly submerged by the waves, he managed to haul the pilot aboard the aircraft. Sergeant Pugh has invariably displayed the greatest courage and devotion to duty.

———————————

Flight Sergeant Cyril Sidney Taylor
293 Squadron. *London Gazette*, 21 July 1944.

Flight Sergeant Taylor commenced his tour on night intruder work over France and Belgium. In February 1943, he started Air Sea Rescue work and since then has taken part in 72 rescue operations. He has, while flying with Warrant Officer Brown and other pilots, played a great part in the rescue of 24 persons and directing the rescue of 18 others. On one occasion a dinghy was sighted off the enemy coast and his aircraft landed to pick up a distressed pilot. Fire was opened on them from flak ships but, while Warrant Officer Brown manoeuvred the aircraft, Flight Sergeant Taylor, quite undaunted, played his part in catching the dinghy and helping the pilot aboard.
On another occasion, again with Warrant Officer Brown, a dinghy was found off the Italian coast before that country was invaded. This time, shore batteries fired on the Walrus but again Flight Sergeant Taylor helped a distressed airman aboard and a successful rescue was made. On 6th June, 1944, Warrant Officer Brown and Flight Sergeant Taylor carried out an extensive search off Civitavecchia. The dinghy was found half a mile from the enemy shore. The aircraft landed and in spite of being within sight and range of the enemy, another pilot was rescued and brought back to safety.
At all times when a rescue has been made beyond enemy lines, under fire from the shore and in rough and difficult sea conditions, Flight Sergeant Taylor has shown a very steady nerve in the face of danger. He has done splendid work in taking distressed and injured pilots and other aircrew from dinghies. By his magnificent teamwork with Warrant Officer Brown, his pilot, he shares the success of the rescues achieved.

American Distinguished Flying Cross

Squadron Leader Walter Sterne DSO
283 Squadron. *London Gazette*, 28 July 1944.

Flight Sergeant Colin Horne DFM
293 Squadron. *London Gazette*, 25 August 1944.

Flight Lieutenant Reginald Frederick Hayes DFC
284 Squadron. *London Gazette*, 28 July 1944.

Appendix B

WALRUS AIRCRAFT

K8549	Ex FAA 1940-41. 293 Sqn May 1944, from N Africa. Cat E after crash on take-off at Rimini, 9 Oct 1944.
L2170	Ex FAA 1939-44. 293 Sqn, coded 'Z'. Lost 26 Dec 1944.
L2207	275 Sqn UK. 293 1945.
L2223	Ex FAA 1939-43. 277 Sqn. 293 Sqn, coded 'U'. SOC 5 Aug 1944, strafed by Spitfires on beach.
L2266	Ex FAA 1940-44. 293 Sqn; sunk by MTBs 26 Oct 1944.
L2331	Ex FAA1939-43. 294 Sqn coded 'B1' 1945. SOC 6 Sep 1945.
P5667	Ex FAA 1940-44. 293 Sqn coded 'V', 1944-45. FAA 1945-46.
P5669	Ex FAA 1940-43. ASR Flt ME; damaged in Derna Harbour 25 July 1943.
P5718	Ex FAA 1940-43. 284 Sqn, coded 'P'. Trans to 283 1 March 1944. To 293 Sqn – wrecked by P.40 on ground, 22 May 1944 and SOC.
R6547	Ex FAA 1940-1944. 284 Sqn 1944; 293 Sqn, lost 9 Dec 1944.
R6549	Ex FAA 1940-44. 284 Sqn, coded 'B'. 293 Sqn. Badly damaged by P.40 on ground 29 Nov 1944 – Cat E.
R6588	Ex FAA 1941-43. 284 Sqn Aug-Nov 1943.
W2706	Ex FAA 1941-43; 700 Sqn rescued crew of Wellington 28 June 1942, and then beached. 294 Sqn coded 'E', Mar-Dec 1944.
W2708	Ex FAA 1941-43; 294 Sqn 'A' 1943-45.
W2709	Ex FAA 1941-43 (helped capture enemy submarine and sank another, also sank two surface vessels). ASR Flt/294 Sqn, coded 'H' 1943-45.
W2710	Ex FAA 1941-43; 294 Sqn Aug-Nov 1944.
W2719	Ex FAA 1941-44. 293 Sqn Sept 1944, coded 'Q'. SOC July 1945.
W2729	Ex FAA 1941-44. 293 Sqn Dec 1944, coded 'T'.
W2734	Ex FAA 1941-43. 283 Sqn. Lost at sea with crew 27 May 1943.
W2746	275 Sqn UK 1942-1944; 293 Sqn 1944-45. To 624 Sqn.
W2747	Ex FAA 1941-43. 283 Sqn 1944.
W2750	Ex FAA 1941-44. 293 Sqn 1945; damaged in crash, SOC Aug 1945.
W2757	Ex FAA 1941-43. 284 Sqn 1943. 293 Sqn coded 'P' Aug 1944.
W2772	Ex FAA 1941-44. 293 Sqn 1944-45, coded 'W', then 'N'.
W2787	Ex FAA 1941-1943. 283 Sqn Apr 1943; damaged Palermo in gale Oct 1943.
W2788	Ex FAA 1941-43. 283 Sqn 1943-44.
W2789	Ex FAA 1941-43. 294 Sqn Dec 1943; Cat E flying accident 17 Mar 1944.
W2796	Ex FAA 1941-44. 293 Sqn 1944-45.
W3010	Ex FAA 1942-44. 294 Sqn Oct 1944-Jan 1945.
W3012	Ex FAA 1941-43 (some rescues made SR Flt Malta 1943). 284 Sqn Jul 1943-Jan 1944.

W3013	Ex FAA 1941-44. 294 Sqn coded 'K', Feb-Oct 1944.
W3016	Ex FAA 1941-43. ASR Flt/294 Sqn 1943. 284 Sqn 1944.
W3017	Ex FAA 1941-43. 294 Sqn coded 'F' and 'O' Feb 1944-Apr 1946.
W3039	Ex FAA 1942-43. 294 Sqn – damaged Cat II; P.40 collided on take-off.
W3042	Ex FAA 1941-44. 293 Sqn Feb 1945.
W3044	Ex FAA 1942-43. ASR Flt ME Aug 1943 – Cat B damage 17 Sept 1943.
W3048	Ex FAA 1942-44. 293 Sqn, coded 'H' 1944 – Cat E damage 8 April 1945.
W3050	Ex FAA 1942-43. ASR Flt ME Aug 1943/294 Sqn, coded 'G' till 1945.
W3062	Ex FAA 1942-44. 294 Sqn, coded 'L' May 1945.
W3074	Ex FAA 1942-43. 283 Sqn Algiers, damaged in wheels-up landing 13 May 1943; repaired and with 283 till February 1944.
W3079	Ex FAA 1942; damaged in crash. 283 Sqn.
W3084	Ex FAA 1942. 276, 282, 278 Sqns UK – 1944. 293 Sqn 1945.
X9466	Ex FAA 1942-44. 294 Sqn Nov 1944, coded 'B' and 'M'.
X9471	Ex FAA 1942-43. 283 Sqn Algiers, Apr 1943. 284 Sqn 1943, then 283 Sqn 1944.
X9474	Ex FAA 1942-44. 293 Sqn, coded 'S', 1944.
X9479	Ex FAA 1942-43. ASR Flt 1943. Damaged in desert rescue 29 Aug 1943.
X9482	Ex FAA 1942-45. 293 Sqn, coded 'X' 1945.
X9498	Ex FAA 1942-43. 284 Sqn Aug/Sept 1943.
X9503	Ex FAA 1942-44. 284 Sqn, coded 'B'. Lost in sea landing 9 July 1945.
X9506	Ex FAA 1942-43. 284 Sqn, coded 'S'. Trans to 283 1 March 1944. To 293 Sqn, coded 'C'.
X9528	Ex FAA 1942-44. 284 Sqn 1944.
X9529	Ex FAA 1942-44. 293 Sqn, coded 'T' 1944. Hit by MTB gunfire and Cat E, 11 Sep 1944 off Rimini.
X9530	Ex FAA 1942-43. 283 Sqn Algiers Apr 1943. Lost 4 July 1943.
X9565	Ex FAA 1942-44; 284 Sqn Aug 1944; 293 Sqn Sept 1944. Crashed 19 Nov 1944 Elba, two RAF and two army men killed (non ASR).
X9579	Ex FAA 1942-43. 283 Sqn 1943. Abandoned 3 November 1943.
X9582	294 ???
X9584	ASR Flt/294 Sqn 1942, coded 'C' and 'D'. Lost in transit flight 14 Sep 1944.
X9590	Ex RN; RAF 1943; ASR & Comms Flt Malta; 294 Sqn 1944; SOC June 1944.
X9593	284 Sqn 1942 and again in 1943.
Z1756	Ex FAA 1942-43. 283 Sqn 1943; damaged in gale, Palermo, 2 Oct 1943, 284 Sqn 1943. 624 Sqn post war.
Z1757	Ex FAA 1942-43. 294 Sqn, coded 'F' and 'Z'. Damaged in sea crash 3 Oct 1943.
Z1769	293 Sqn Apr 1944, coded 'L'. (later 624 Sqn – coded 'A')
Z1776	ASR Flt ME coded 'E', Aug 1943/294 Sqn, coded 'P'. Cat Ac after rescue sortie, 13 Sept 1944.
Z1777	Gibraltar to 283 Sqn May 1943. To 293 Sqn, coded 'S'. Cat E, 31 May 1944.
Z1778	294 Sqn.
Z1779	284 Sqn Jan 1944, coded 'Z'. Trans to 283, 1 March 1944. 293 Sqn 1944. Crashed 9 June 1944.
Z1780	Ex FAA 1942. Gibraltar to 283 Sqn, coded 'W', Apr 1943. Damaged in gale at Palermo. Cat B, 2 Oct 1943.
Z1782	294 Sqn Feb-Apr 1944.
Z1783	283 Sqn from Gibraltar May 1943. Crashed on landing, La Sebala, 5 Aug 1943.
Z1784	283 and 284 Sqns to Apr 1944.
Z1805	283 Sqn from Gibraltar May 1943. Damaged in air raid 7 June 1943. Ditched off Palermo in bad weather, 23 Aug 1943, Cat E.

Z1809   Ex FAA Gibraltar 1942-43. 283 Sqn Apr 1943. Foundered off Palermo 3 July
     1943, Cat E.

Z1813   Ex FAA 1942-43. ASR Malta 1943. 284 Sqn July 1943. Trans to 283 1 March
     1944. To 293 Sqn Mar 1944-Aug 1944.

HK832   Fairchild 91 used by ASR Flight ME; lost in take-off accident 17 May 1943.

Appendix C

MAIN AIR SEA RESCUES BY WALRUS AIRCRAFT

283 Squadron

1943

Date	Crew	Aircraft	Rescue
5 May	F/Sgt C Horne Sgt S Prouse	Walrus	Body of a German pilot.
9 May	F/O R W V Jessett Sgt J V Botting	Walrus W3074	Three German soldiers, pm.
19 May	F/O K H Mears W/O N W Peat RCAF Sgt R B Hodges RCAF	Walrus	German airman. 21.20-23.50 hrs.
21 May	F/L W Sterne W/O N W Peat RCAF	Walrus Z1809	Petrol to downed Walrus W2734 allowing it to take off from the sea.
24 May	P/O A Hopkinson Sgt A B Morabito RCAF	Walrus	German crewman from a Ju88, 10.15-16.30 hrs.
27 May	W/O N W Peat RCAF Sgt F Bettridge	Walrus W2734	Lt F W Sanders, 48th FS, 14th FG, evening. All three men lost that night.
30 May	Sgt C Horne Sgt S Prouse	Walrus	Crew of US B.25, off Pantelleria, 340th BG. 10.50-12.05 hrs.
30 May	P/O A Hopkinson F/Sgt A B Morabito RCAF	Walrus X9471	Lt C M Lindstrom, US pilot. 17.30-19.30 hrs.
31 May	P/O A Hopkinson F/Sgt A B Morabito RCAF Sgt L H Newman Sgt K R Pugh	Walrus Walrus W2787	Seven men from a B.17 Fortress, 17.30-19.50 hrs. Four taken by Hopkinson, three by Newman. Off Cap Sidi Ali.
3 June	Sgt W S Lambert Sgt K R Pugh	Walrus Z1780	Guided minesweeper to three stranded US airmen on Zembra Island, am.
5 June	Sgt W S Lambert Sgt K R Pugh	Walrus W2787	Lt Schlitzkus and three crewmen, 310th BG, SE of Pantelleria, 16.50- 20.15 hrs. Walrus damaged and towed back by a minesweeper.
6 June	S/L W Sterne F/Sgt J V Botting	Walrus	Rescued four US airmen but Walrus damaged and all six men were taken onto a HSL and the Walrus towed in by a Naval motor launch. 04.45 -
6 June	Sgt C Horne Sgt S Prouse	Walrus	Two German airmen E of Kelibia. 07.35-09.10 hrs.
10 June	F/O K H Mears	Walrus	Lt P G McArthur, 31st FS, 79th FG,

	F/Sgt J V Botting		19.55-21.35 hrs. Towed to Kelibia by corvette.
11 June	Sgt C Horne Lt M Mosby USAAF Cpl Jaggers	Walrus	Lt G H Rich, 308th FS, 31st FG, off Pantelleria, shot down by Me109. 16.00-18.50 hrs.
13 June	F/O K H Mears F/Sgt J V Botting	Walrus	German pilot off Pantelleria, Ltn F Perz, II/SLG2, 16.10-18.10 hrs.
21 June	S/L W Sterne Sgt W S Lambert Sgt K R Pugh	Walrus Z1809	Capt R E Dekker, 14th FG, off Sicily, 05.30-08.45 hrs not found. Rescue made on sortie 10.50-14.20.
21 June	Sgt C Horne F/Sgt J V Botting	Walrus	Five crew of 142 Sqn Wellington; Sgts H L Pleydell, J Slater, H W Gee, J Lynch and A E Evans, 08.20-09.50 hrs.
30 June	F/O K H Mears F/Sgt J V Botting	Walrus	Crew of B.26 from 437th BS, 319th BG, Lts Davis, Matthews, Sgts Matunio, Disciscio and Chard.
2 July	S/L W Sterne F/O R G Eccles Sgt K R Pugh	Walrus Z1809	Crew of 47 Sqn Beaufighter X, JM324, F/Sgt J E Carroll and Sgt T Frewen, 14.15- ? hrs. Walrus sank 3 July.
3 July	Sgt W S Lambert Sgt A Divers RNZAF Sgt Cromie	Walrus Z1780	Crew of 47 Sqn Beaufighter X, F/O C A Ogilvie and Sgt A G Williams, a/c towed to Bone, 15.35-17.00 hrs.
4 July	F/Sgt L H Newman Sgt P M H Graham	Walrus X9530	Lt Marks, US pilot NE Cap Bon, but Walrus lost in heavy seas. Crew OK. 11.15-12.10 hrs.
5 July	Sgt C Horne Sgt P M H Graham	Walrus	Capt Carpenter, 316th FS, 324th FG. 09.00-10.00 hrs.
13 July	Sgt W S Lambert Sgt K R Pugh	Walrus W2787	Uffz F Schmidt, German Me109 pilot. 16.10-17.50 hrs.
18 July	Sgt A Divers RNZAF F/Sgt A Morabito RCAF	Walrus	Lt Townsend, 310 BS, 86th BG. In dinghy for 20 hours.
5 Aug	F/Sgt L H Newman F/Sgt P M H Graham	Walrus L1784	Three German soldiers, 1600 hrs - FTR. Later taxied to Ustica Island OK.
7 Aug	S/L W Sterne Sgt K R Pugh	Walrus	Spitfire pilot NE of Palermo, lost previous day. Lt H S Montgomery, 4th FS, 52nd FG. 11.15-13.10 hrs.
10 Aug	Sgt A Divers RNZAF F/Sgt A B Morabito RCAF	Walrus X9471??	Ltn J Zantropp, German pilot from III/KG100, 12.20-15.20 hrs.
12 Aug	Sgt A Divers RNZAF F/Sgt A B Morabito RCAF	Walrus X9471	S/L A C G Wenman, 154 Sqn, S of Vulcano Island. 14.40-17.40 hrs.
19 Aug	Sgt A Divers RNZAF F/Sgt A B Morabito RCAF	Walrus Z1784	Lt C E Simpson, 71st FS, 1st FG, NE of Ustica, 14.00-17.40 hrs. In dinghy for two days.
19 Aug	Sgt A Divers RNZAF F/Sgt A Morabito RCAF	Walrus Z1777	Wounded US soldier on beach near Termini, late pm.
22 Aug	P/O A Hopkinson F/Sgt J V Botting	Walrus	Four crewmen from 444th BS, 320th BG, evening.
25 Aug	F/Sgt C Horne F/Sgt K R Pugh	Walrus	Ltn R Bohn, German Ju88 pilot, 45 miles out from Termini.
19 Sep	F/O K H Mears Sgt E Smith	Walrus	Two German airmen, 80 miles off La Sebala. Crew of He111 shot down night of 18th.

19 Sep	F/Sgt W S Lambert Sgt E F Keeble	Walrus X9471	Two German airmen, He111, see above.
22 Sep	?	Walrus	11.45 hrs. 30 miles N of Stromboli.
22 Sep	?	Walrus	17.40 hrs. 5 miles N of Stromboli.
3 Nov	F/Sgt A Divers Sgt E F Keeble	Walrus X9579	Five US airmen, 82nd BS, 12th BG. Lts P Devlin, W E McGonigle, J L Steinberg, T/Sgt L A Stephens, Sgt J W Keyes. Walrus foundered, all rescued by hospital ship.

1944

3 Mar	W/O V L Prosser RAAF W/O J V Botting	Walrus Z1784	Lt J A Adams, 2nd FS, 52nd FG. 11.35-13.55 hrs.
7 Mar	Sgt J A Reid W/O J W Bradley	Walrus Z1779	Lt R F Harmeyer, 309th FS, 31st FG. am.
7 Mar	W/O V L Prosser RAAF W/O J V Botting	Walrus W2788	Lt H S Montgomery, 4th FS, 52nd FG. 16.45-18.50 hrs.
8 Mar	W/O A Divers RNZAF W/O P M H Graham	Walrus W2788	F/O J W Munro, 253 Sqn, 08.15-08.45. Walrus abandoned after damage from gunfire from Elba.
9 Mar	F/O K H Mears F/Sgt C I A Paterson F/Sgt E F Keeble	Walrus W3079	Adj J Doudies, GC 2/7. 16.30-22.00 hrs.
18 Mar	W/O A Divers F/Sgt E E Smith	Walrus W2747	Lt R C Curtis, 2nd FS, 52nd FG. 17.10-19.50 hrs.
2 Apr	P/O L H Newman F/Sgr S R Prouse	Walrus W2747	Lt J R Donahue, 65th FS, 57th FG. 10.50-13.20 hrs.
7 Apr	F/Sgt C I A Paterson F/Sgt E F Keeble	Walrus Z1784	F/Sgt Day, 253 Sqn, beach at Borgo. Grounded in shallow water, rescue completed by HSL 2600, 15.25-19.25.

284 Squadron

1943

27 Jul	Sgt D J Lunn Sgt G F Brown W/O N Pickles	Walrus X9506	Lt D E Harwood, 65th FS, 57 FG, 16.45-19.45 hrs.
31 Jul	F/L R F Hayes Sgt C S Taylor + USAAF pilot	Walrus W3012	Lt J C Kelly, 86th FS, 79th FG. 05.45-08.30 hrs, off Sicily.
1 Aug	F/Sgt E J Holmes Sgt R Brown Sgt C S Taylor	Walrus X9506	Lt H A Barker, 65th FS, 57th FG. NE of Catania, 19.15-21.15 hrs.
3 Aug	Sgt R Brown F/Sgt E J Holmes Sgt C S Taylor	Walrus X9506	Sgt J Howell-Price, 3 RAAF Sqn. 08.05-10.30 hrs, S of Riposto.
4 Aug	Sgt D J Lunn W/O N Pickles F/Sgt J Bradley	Walrus X9506	F/O G N Keith DFC RCAF, 72 Sqn, injured. (Died that evening). 10.20-12.30 hrs.
4 Aug	Sgt D J Lunn Sgt R Brown F/Sgt G W Paxton	Walrus X9593	Sgt A W Walker RAAF, 250 Sqn, off Catania, and P/O H J M Barnes, 112 Sqn, 12.40- beached S of Catania.

Date	Crew	Aircraft	Details
8 Aug	F/Sgt E J Holmes Sgt C S Taylor Sgt R Brown	Walrus R6588	Lt H Sherboudy, 65th FS, 57th FG. Trans pilot to HSL 2593.
13 Aug	F/L R F Hayes Sgt R Brown Sgt A J Heseltine	Walrus X9593	UntOff Arnold, from Do217. NW of Messina, 13.25- crash-landed five miles N of base, all OK.
17 Aug	W/O K G Hall F/Sgt J R Berry RNZAF	Walrus X9506	F/L N W Lee, 43 Sqn and P/O J L Griffiths, 1437 Flt, 14.05-17.35 hrs.
30 Aug	F/Sgt E J Holmes F/Sgt J R Berry RNZAF	Walrus X9498	1Lt M L Clark, 85th FS, 79th FG. 15.45/17.05-18.35 hrs, off Spartivento.
2 Sep	W/O K G Hall F/O R G Eccles F/Sgt J W Bradley	Walrus X9498	UntOffs W Young and J Bierer. 10.15-12.15 hrs.
2 Sep	Sgt R Brown F/O R G Eccles F/Sgt J R Berry RNZAF	Walrus X9498	15.30-19.00 hrs, W/Cdr W G G Duncan Smith DSO DFC, N of Vaticano. Shot- up by Me109 fighter.
21 Sep	W/O K G Hall Sgt A J Heseltine	Walrus W2757	Col J R Hawkins, 31st FG, 10.30-12.10.
21 Sep	F/Sgt J A Reid F/Sgt R C Glew	Walrus W2757	F/O C W Nelson, 309th FS, 31st FG. 17.40 hrs.
24 Sep	Sgt G F Brown RCAF F/Sgt J W Bradley	Walrus W3012	296 Sqn crew and passengers, F/O G L Wilson, F/O J G K Maxwell, F/Sgt R H Ward and Sgt H Lidgett. RSM Ryan and S/Maj Devine, 11.14- 14.00 hrs.
10 Oct	F/Sgt E J Holmes F/Sgt J R Berry RNZAF	Walrus W2757	F/Sgt L McKay RCAF, 92 Sqn. 11.25 – ?
10 Oct	F/Sgt E J Holmes F/Sgt J R Berry RNZAF	Walrus W2757	Three Croat airmen from Do17z. 13.50 – ?
20 Oct	F/O R G Eccles F/Sgt J R Berry RNZAF	Walrus X9506	Sgt H Ritchie, 14 Sqn, 12.45-15.00 hrs.
17 Nov	F/L R F Hayes F/Sgt R C Glew	Walrus R6588	Sgt Hilton USAAF, on Albanian coast, (321st BG). Attacked by Me109s – Walrus damaged. 06.45 -.
17 Nov	Sgt D J Lunn Sgt A J Heseltine	Walrus W3012	Rescued Sgt Hilton and Walrus crew – see above. 14.15-16.50 hrs.
16 Dec	Sgt D J Lunn W/O N Pickles F/Sgt G W Paxton	Walrus W3012	F/L J Beatson, 249 Sqn. Off Gulf of Drin. Pickles wounded.
22 Dec	F/Sgt E J Holmes F/Sgt J W Bradley	Walrus W3012	Lt K Hall SAAF, 4 SAAF Sqn. 15.05-16.50 hrs.
30 Dec	W/O K G Hall W/O M D Kelly	Walrus X9506	2/Lt Kelly, 523rd FS, 27th FG. 12.15-13.30 hrs.
1944			
30 Jan	F/Sgt E J Holmes F/Sgt J R Berry RNZAF	Walrus P5718	Lt L Sauer SAAF, 450 Sqn.
20 Mar	?	Walrus	Lt M Geeringh, 2 SAAF Sqn, 10 miles E of Trigno.
25 Mar	?	Walrus	Lt A W Homer, 1 SAAF Sqn.
11 Apr	P/O L H Newman	Walrus	Maj B Sanborn, 2nd FS, 52nd FG.

	F/Sgt E E Smith	Z1784	08.10-10.00 hrs (Newman on detachment from 283 Sqn).
15 Apr	P/O L H Newman	Walrus	Capt W P Benedict, 66th FS, 57th FG.
	F/Sgt E E Smith	Z1784	12.20 hrs. (Newman on detachment from 283 Sqn).
18 Apr	F/O T H Humphrey	Walrus	Lt K G Haydisx, 307th FS, 31st FG.
	Sgt A J Heseltine	W2747	E of Termoli.
24 Apr	F/O G M Gallagher	Walrus	Lt J A Eaglen, 65th FS, 57th FG.
	F/Sgt E E Smith	Z1784	14.35-15.20 hrs.
28 Apr	F/Sgt C I A Paterson	Walrus	Lt P W Magmuson and 2/Lt P F Rabne,
	F/Sgt E F Keeble	X9471	B.24 survivors from 320th Bomb Sqn. 16.15-01.30 hrs.
1 May	F/O T H Humphrey	Walrus	Survivors of B.17, 773rd BS, 463rd BG.
	Sgt A J Heseltine	W2747	Lts W A Hoffman & E T Betz, Sgts G Aletsee, O McCullers & L Fornia. 08.00 – beached at San Vito next day.
3 May	F/O G M Gallagher	Walrus	B.25 crew 447th BS, 321st BG, 08.45-
	F/Sgt E E Smith	Z1784	11.00 hrs. Lt H Beebe, 2/Lts W H Martin and N J Lunmark; Sgts I S Escher, R Sinclair and Korzeriowski.
3 May	F/Sgt C I A Paterson	Walrus	Four Italian workers escaping German
	F/Sgt E F Keeble	Z1784	labour camp on a raft off Pianosa Island.
12 May	W/O J A Reid	Walrus	Lt de Saboulin, 328 FF Sqn,
	F/O A B Morabito RCAF	Z1784	20.40-00.25 hrs.
15 May	F/O T H Humphrey	Walrus	B.25 crew off Elba, 466th BS:
	F/Sgt C I A Paterson	Z1784	Lt Sampson, 2/Lt F B White and
	Ff/Sgt E F Keeble		2/Lt W Warren. 10.05-12.10 hrs. Assisted HSL 2595.
21 May	F/Sgt C I A Paterson	Walrus	British soldier in dinghy off coast,
	F/Sgt E F Keeble	X9471	while HSL rescued four US soldiers who had tried to save him.
2 Jun	F/O G M Gallagher	Walrus	Lt Madon, 328 FF Squadron, 12.55-
	F/Sgt E E Smith	X9471	14.35 hrs.
2 Jun	?	Walrus	Lt J Gannon, P.39 pilot, 347th FS, 350th FG.
6 Jun	W/O C I A Paterson	Walrus	Lt P J S Louw SAAF, 242 Sqn. 15.40-
	F/Sgt E F Keeble	Z1784	take-off but Walrus lost; all three men rescued by HSL.
7 Jun	F/O T H Humphrey	Walrus	F/O G C W O'Neil MM RAAF, 451
	Sgt A J Heseltine	R6549	Squadron, 1150-1255 hrs.
14 Jun	F/O G M Gallagher	Walrus	F/O D C Dunn RAAF, 154 Sqn, 20.45-
	Sgt K R B Jones	X9503	23.30 hrs. Towed home by HSL.
	Sgt A J Heseltine		
15 Jun	F/O T H Humphrey	Walrus	2/Lt R L Johnson, 66th FS, 57th FG.
	W/O R G Hale	R6549	Took off 06.50 hrs.
20 Jun	S/L J S Barnett	Walrus	Lt Marril, 2/3 French Sqn, 13.20-15.45
	Sgt K R B Jones	X9471	hrs, towed into Bastia by HSL 2595.
	W/O R G Hale		
1 Jul	F/O T H Humphrey	Walrus	Lt T E Wright, 65th FS, 57th FG,
	Sgt W Burnett	X9471	11.10-11.40 hrs.
6 Jul	Lt K B Walker SAAF	Walrus	Lt H S Cleveland, 66th FS, 57th FG.

	W/O D P Devery RAAF	X9503	36 miles out, 07.50-09.20 hrs.
11/12 Jul	7 Warwick and three Walrus sorties	Walrus R6549	Aided rescue of Sgt Chef Courteville of 326 French Sqn, eventually picked up by HSL 2601 after 26 hours.
15 Jul	Lt K B Walker SAAF W/O D P Devery RAAF	Walrus R6549	Lt L J Pernicka, 66th FS, 57th FG, 17.05-18.10 hrs.
17 Jul	Lt K B Walker SAAF W/O D P Devery RAAF	Walrus X9565	W/O S L Kapner, 527th FS, 86th FG. 12.10-12.40 hrs.
19 Aug	W/O J A Reid W/O Rawding	Walrus X9503	Three survivors from US B.25, then transferred them to an HSL. 487th BS, 340th BG: Lts Farnnan, Evarts and Cpl Flynn.

293 Squadron

1944

3 Apr	F/Sgt E J Holmes W/O J R Berry RNZAF	Walrus Z1813	F/Sgt H E Eaves RAAF, 450 Sqn, 08.00-09.20 hrs.
4 Apr	W/O G F Brown F/Sgt C S Taylor	Walrus Z1813	Five crew of 40 Sqn – F/Sgt L J Redden RAAF, F/L L J Gillespie, F/Sgt W R Black, and Sgts L Carey and J P A Whitlock. 06.30 – taxied back – 11.10.
6 Apr	W/O G F Brown F/Sgt C S Taylor	Walrus Z1813	Six survivors from B.24 of 761 BS, 460th BG, in company with MTBs. 16.30-20.35 hrs. Those rescued were: 1/Lt F Smith, F/O H Mansdorf, 2/Lts B Budriunas, J Schwartz; Sgts H Wilson and H Breckenridge.
7 Apr	F/Sgt E J Holmes W/O J R Berry RNZAF	Walrus Z1813	Ten men from B.17, 774th BS, 463rd BG, 14.30- and taxied into Ortona at 17.45 hrs. Lt S L Florsham and crew.
10 Apr	W/O J A Reid F/O A B Morabito RCAF	Walrus Z1777	F/Sgt A G Newman, 145 Sqn, took off 1850, Walrus foundered in severe weather and all three men rescued by HSL at 20.15 hrs.
13 Apr	F/O T H Humphrey Sgt A J Heseltine	Walrus Z1813	Capt R E Ashmead, 48th FS, 14th FG. 10.50-14.00 hrs.
20 Apr	W/O G F Brown F/Sgt C S Taylor	Walrus Z1813	F/Sgt H E Eaves RAAF, 450 Sqn, 12.10-15.00 hrs. SE of Ancona. Same pilot as on 3 April.
3 May	W/O G F Brown F/Sgt C S Taylor	Walrus P5718	Three survivors of B.24 from 824th BS, 484th BG, Lts Rutter and Manhart, S/Sgt Schneider. 11.05-14.30 hrs.
12 May	F/Sgt E J Holmes W/O J R Berry RNZAF	Walrus X9506	B.24 crew, 830th BS, 485th BG, 14.10-15.55 hrs. Lts Martin, Strandord and Connolly Jr; F/O W S Lee, Sgts Knight, Mungier and Maxton; Cpls Longo and Hughes.
19 May	F/Sgt E J Holmes W/O J R Berry RNZAF	Walrus X9506	2/Lt S Molner, 315th FS, 324th FG. Off Gaeta Point, one mile off shore. RTB 10.50 hrs.
19 May	F/Sgt E J Holmes	Walrus	Six crewmen from a B.24 11.15-

	W/O E J Berry RNZAF	X9506	16.25, off mouth of River Volturno. Later transferred men to HSL 133.
24 May	P/O D J Lunn W/O M D Kelly	Walrus Z1779	Lt D T Gilson SAAF, 1 SAAF Sqn. 09.30-10.50 hrs.
26 May	W/O K G Hall W/O M D Kelly	Walrus Z1779	Lt R G Bosch SAAF, 4 SAAF Sqn. 07.20-08.55 hrs.
6 Jun	W/O G F Brown F/Sgt C S Taylor	Walrus X9506	Lt G A Bell 84th FS, 79th FG, 13.35-15.15 hrs.
10 Jun	P/O D J Lunn W/O N Pickles	Walrus L2170	Wellington crew, F/Sgts Slade and Briscoe; Sgts Barber, Taylor and Best. 05.40-06.55.
10 Jun	P/O D J Lunn W/O N Pickles	Walrus 'W'	Seven survivors from B.24, 726th BS, 451st BG: Lts H Guiness, Bird and McDowell; Sgts Langlois, Whitlow, McPeak and Walthen. 11.25-14.10 hrs.
25 Jun	W/O K G Hall W/O M D Kelly	Walrus K8549	F/O J Johnstone, 241 Sqn (JF701). 17.30-20.45 hrs.
8 Jul	Sgt P F Lydford W/O J A Slater	Walrus L2223	Ten men from US bomber; 13.35-15.50 hrs.
	Lt J V Peters SAAF F/O I Morgan	Walrus L2170	ditto.
20 Jul	Lt J V Peters SAAF F/O I Morgan	Walrus L2170	F/O H G Proudman, 601 Sqn (MK481). 07.10-09.15 hrs.
21 Jul	Lt J V Peters SAAF F/O I Morgan	Walrus L2170	2/Lt Eastman, 537th FBS, 07.25-09.15 hrs.
22 Jul	Lt A G Riley SAAF F/O A A O'Dell	Walrus W2757	Lt Taylor, 526th FBS, 86th FG, 12.30-15.30 hrs.
5 Aug	Sgt P F Lydford W/O J A Slater	Walrus L2223	Sgt K Etchels, 241 Sqn, early am. Beached due to rough sea and although an HSL picked up Etchels, the Walrus crew were taken prisoner.
22 Aug	Lt J V Peters SAAF F/O I Morgan	Walrus L2170	F/O G L Garnham, 241 Sqn (JF339) 08.25- ?
24 Aug	Lt J V Peters SAAF F/O J W Bradley	Walrus L2170	F/L D M Leitch, 241 Sqn, 05.45-08.10.
24 Aug	Sgt R J Bickle F/O J W Bradley Sgt D Newsome W/O M D Kelly	Walrus L2170 Walrus 'Y'	Five survivors from B.24 465th BG: Lts Mills, Fritts & Dionne; Cpls Marchese and Nichols. 12.30-21.20 hrs.
30 Aug	Sgt W J Bishop F/O A A O'Dell	Walrus X9474	Sgt J A Bridger, air gunner, 114 Sqn Boston IV (BZ506). Two other crew killed, a fourth found later. 06.00-07.10.
11 Sep	Sgt D Newsome W/O M D Kelly	Walrus X9529	Capt M D Lawton SAAF, 92 Sqn (JF704), 19.30-. Walrus abandoned after hit by RN MTB gunfire.
13 Oct	F/Sgt A G Stevens F/Sgt R Barnes	Walrus W2719	Nine crewmen from minesweeper N of Isola di Gorgona. Three more rescued by HSL.
16 Oct	F/O H F Burditt F/O I Morgan	Walrus L2266	Lt J L Slatton, 85th FS, 79th FG. 16.30-17.35 hrs.
21 Oct	F/O H F Burditt	Walrus	Sgt P Estep, B.24 survivor, 758th BS

	F/O I Morgan	L2266	459th BG: Capt A W Meikle, 7 SAAF Sqn and Sgt A W Jones, 112 Sqn (HB925). 08.00- transferred to Catalina after the engine stopped. Walrus crew were later taken prisoners.
5 Nov	F/L G M Gallagher W/O V Udberg	Walrus W3048	Lts L Ford & C Kamanski, 444th BS, 320th BG. Others rescued by HSL.
13 Nov	Sgt E W Clarke Sgt G H C Willing	Walrus R6547	Lt R R Blank, 308th FS, 31st FG, 12.25- ?
22 Nov	Sgt D Newsome Sgt E S Bilton Lt K B Walker SAAF F/Sgt W Burnett	Walrus R6547 Walrus L2170	Ten men, Capt Joyce and crew of B.17 429th BS, 2nd BG, 14.55- beached. 15.40-17.30 hrs.
9 Dec	Lt K B Walker SAAF F/Sgt W Burnett	Walrus R6547	Lt R G Burdick, 2nd FS, 52nd FG. Walrus abandoned and men picked up by a destroyer next day.
19 Dec	F/O T H Humphrey LAC Bisset AC Stemp	Walrus L2217	After abortive search, landed and picked up exhausted Italian airman who had swum out to help.

1945

25 Jan	?	Walrus	P/O D B Davies, 3 RAAF Sqn (KH821), mouth of River Po.
4 Mar	Sgt F A Caie W/O C S Taylor	Walrus L2207	Lt J O Spraley, 87th FS, 79th FG. 10.15-12.20 hrs.
11 Mar	F/Sgt R J Bickle F/Sgt A S Goldstein F/Sgt W Burnett	Walrus L2207	W/O R E Chamberlain, 256 Sqn, customer in minefield, so Walrus crew sailed lifeboat from a Warwick to pick him up and take him back to the Walrus.
18 Mar	Lt K B Walker SAAF F/Sgt W Burnett	Walrus L2217	Capt J C Hare, 57th Ftr HQ. 16.10-17.00 hrs.
20 Mar	W/O C S Tod RNZAF Sgt E S Bilton	Walrus L2217	Sgt A R Charles, 601 Sqn (PT641), 12.55-14.40 hrs.
1 Apr	Lt K B Walker SAAF W/O W Burnett	Walrus W2772	Sgt S Widdowson, 92 Sqn (MT667), 09.35-11.00 hrs.
1 Apr	F/Sgt R J Bickle F/Sgt A S Goldstein	Walrus X9482	F/Sgt W B Forster, 145 Sqn (JG247), 11.05-12.55 hrs.

ASR Flight, Middle East

1942

12 Feb	? (det of 700 Sqn FAA)	Walrus	SubLt L Polwin FAA, Fulmar Defence Flight. (X8685)
23 May	?	Fairchild HK832	Crew of Ju88, NE Mersah Matruh.
2 Jun	?	Walrus	Six men from 221 Sqn in dinghy for three days, 40 miles from Bardia.
	?	Fairchild HK832	Each aircraft took three men each. F/Sgt H Nixon and crew.
28 Jun	?	Walrus	Crew of Wellington (W5732) 20 miles

		W2706	N of El Amaid. Beached later.
10 Jul	?	Walrus	Picked up captain of Wellington from desert, rest brought in overland.
6 Aug	?	Walrus	Six men from 10/207 Sqn (Halifax), picked up three and later directed a HSL to remaining three.

1943

19 Apr	Lt Borland ?	Walrus	F/Sgt J Goodfellow and Sgt L G Maynard of 603 Sqn (V8372).
25 Apr	Sgt H G C King ?	Walrus 'C'	F/L I H R Shand, 145 Sqn (ER982), 11.55-13.55 hrs.
25 Apr	SubLt Oldknow ?	Walrus 'A'	F/O R H Probert, 92 Sqn (EN458), E of Korba. Took off 13.15 hrs.
27 Apr	Sgt H G C King ?	Walrus	Lt C A Halliday SAAF, 1 SAAF Sqn, S of Hammamet, late pm.
16 May	Sgt H G C King ?	Walrus	Ltn B Losen, German pilot of 2/(F)122, (Me410), pm.
7 Aug	?	Walrus	P.40 pilot. Taxied into Tripoli. 16.55 -.
18 Aug	Lt A Whitworth Sgt R W J Forbes LAC Taylor	Walrus X9584	American P.40 pilot. 06.15-09.20 hrs.

Flight became 294 Squadron effective 24 September 1943.

26 Sep	F/L D J G Harcourt Sgt A J Christian P/O C R Berry	Walrus W2709	P/O P T P Temple-Murray, 213 Sqn. 10.00-12.30 hrs.
17 Oct	W/O F E Tutton W/O C W Batten F/Sgt R D Drake	Walrus W2709	Sgt J R Reid and Sgt H C Seymour, 227 Sqn off Cape Pamos, 10.10-11.55 hrs.

1944

30 Mar	F/Sgt H G C King F/Sgt J M Frater F/Sgt J Welsh	Walrus Z1782	Capt K Muir and Lt Strydom, both SAAF from 16 SAAF Sqn, S of Berka, 12.05-13.00 hrs.
29 Apr	P/O J S Turner W/O J D Ormesher F/Sgt G R Lowe	Walrus W3013	Oblt H Jonas and his Ju88 crew from 2/(F)123. 07.45-09.45 hrs.
28 May	F/L D S Stothard W/O W A C Pratt F/O R J Stafford RAAF	Walrus Z1778	Desert rescue of crew of 76 OTU Wellington LN956. 11.40-13.30/17.30-18.22. F/Sgt R Jefferson, Sgt K Beecher (N), Sgt J Purnie (N/BA), Sgt R Hallums (FE), Sgt A Brown (WOP/AG), Sgt D Cook (AG) and Sgt A Harris (AG) who died of his injuries.
30 Jun	F/Sgt L Scarlett F/Sgt P M Corkey W/O F O Curnow	Walrus W3107	F/O G Pleonis, 335 Greek Sqn, (ER524), off Libyan coast late pm. 18.50-19.55 hrs.
5 Sep	F/O T A Williams RCAF F/O M A Brown RCAF W/O C E Pannell RAAF	Walrus Z1757	German airman, survivor of Ju88 of 2/(F)123, 11.05 – towed back by HSL.

13 Sep	F/O J S Turner	Walrus	P/O A B Woodier and Sgt H Lee, 603
	W/O G R Lowe	Z1776	Sqn (NE367). Landed back after dark.
	W/O J D Ormesher		16.48-20.55 hrs.

1945

5 Feb	F/O T R Murdock	Walrus	Survivors from 79 OTU Beaufighter,
	W/O R I Mowat	L2331	12.45-16.00 hrs.
	Sgt E E L Crane		

Appendix D

THE WALRUS SQUADRONS

283 Squadron   **Motto:** *Attende et Vigila*   **Squadron code – FD**

Formed in Algiers, February 1943, equipped with Walrus amphibian aircraft. In April 1944, Walrus crews went to 293 Squadron, 283 becoming a Warwick aircraft unit. Known rescues over 90.

Bases:		
	Hussein Bay, Algiers	Feb 1943 – May 1943
	Maison Blanche	May 1943 – May 1943
	Tingley	May 1943 – May 1943
	La Sebala, detachments Pantelleria and Palermo, Sicily	May 1943 – Aug 1943
	Palermo, detachment at Monte Corvino	Aug 1943 – Dec 1943
	Ajaccio, Corsica	Dec 1943 – Dec 1943
	Borgo, detachment at Alghero	Dec 1943 – Dec 1943
	Hal Far, Malta	Apr 1944 – Mar 1946
	Disbanded 31 March 1946	

CO:		
	S/Ldr W Sterne DSO	Feb 1943 – Apr 1944
	S/Ldr R B Crampton	Apr 1944 –

Main equipment: W3734; W2747; W2788; W3074; X3079; X9471; X9488 'B'; X9506; Z1777 'S'; Z1813; Z1780 'W'; Z1784.

---

284 Squadron   **Motto:** *From the Deep*   **Squadron Code: ?**

Formed at Gravesend, Kent, 7 May 1943, with Walrus aircraft for overseas duty with the planned invasion of Sicily. Known rescues were in the region of 70+.

Bases:		
	Gravesend	May 1943 – May 1943
	Martlesham Heath	May 1943 – May 1943
	en-route to Middle East	Jun 1943 – Jul 1943
	Hal Far, Malta, detachment Algiers	Jul 1943 – Jul 1943
	Cassibile, Sicily	Jul 1943 – Aug 1943
	Lentini East, detachment at Milazzo	Aug 1943 – Sep 1943
	Scarzano, Italy	Sep 1943 – Oct 1943
	Gióia del Colle, detachment at Triola	Oct 1943 – Nov 1943
	Brindisi, detachments at Capodichino and Cutella	Nov 1943 – Mar 1944

Alghero, detachments at Ramateulle, Borgo and Elmas (Sardinia)	Mar 1944 – Aug 1944
Borgo, detachment at Calvi	Aug 1944 – Aug 1944
Bone, detachments at Elmas, Istres and Pomigliano	Sep 1944 – Apr 1945
Pomigliano, Italy	Apr 1945 – Sep 1945
Disbanded 21 September 1945	

COs:	F/Lt R F Hayes	May 1943 – Jul 1943
	S/Ldr J H Ashton DFC	Jul 1943 – Apr 1944
	S/Ldr J S Barnett	Apr 1944 – Sep 1944
	S/Ldr A I James	Sep 1944 – Mar 1945
	S/L S H Troughton-Smith	Mar 1945 – Jul 1945

Main equipment: L1784; P5718; R6549; W2705; W2747; W2757; W3012 'W'; X9471; X9498; X9503; X9506; X9565; X9593.

---

293 Squadron   **Motto:** *Ex Aere Salus*   **Squadron Code: ZE**

Formed at RAF Bircham Newton on 28 June 1943, for training with Warwicks for rescue work in the Middle East. Unit's Walrus detachment in the Middle East, in April 1944, finally became 293 Squadron in August 1944, merging with crews from 283 Squadron. Rescues by Walrus aircraft were well over 100.

Bases:	Bircham Newton	Jun 1943 – Oct 1943
	Blida, Algeria	Nov 1943 – Dec 1943
	Bone, detachment at Pomigliano, Italy	Dec 1943 – Mar 1944
	Pomigliano, detachments at Foggia, San Vito, Capodichino, Cutella, Nettuno, Sinello, Fermo, Tarquinia, Ramatuelle, Bellaria, Falconara and Calvi	Mar 1944 – Mar 1945
	Foggia and Tortoreto	Mar 1945 – Jun 1945
	Pomigliano, Italy	Jun 1945 – Apr 1946
	Disbanded 5 April 1946	

COs:	S/Ldr R H McIntosh DFC AFC	Jun 1943 – Sep 1943
	S/Ldr R W Pye	Oct 1943 – Oct 1944
	S/Ldr W R Gellatly RNZAF	Oct 1944 – Aug 1945
	S/Ldr R J Cruttenden	Aug 1945 – Apr 1946

Main equipment: K8549; L1769 'L'; L2170 'Z'; L2217 'P'; L2266; P5718; R6547; W3048 'H'; W2729 'T'; W2772 'W'; X9474 'S'; X9506 'C'; X9529; Z1777 'S'; Z1779; Z1813.

---

294 Squadron   **Motto:** *Vita Ex Undis Abrepta*   **Squadron Code: FD**

Formed in the Middle East in July 1941, initially as the Middle East Air Sea Rescue Flight, based at Kabrit, under 201 Group control. Equipped with Wellingtons and in November a Walrus was attached at Mersa Matruh. In 1942 it formed a Walrus Flight with FAA personnel, operating from Benghazi. Continued operations with Wellingtons, Blenheims and Walrus, plus a Fairchild 91 amphibian. Became 294 Squadron on 24 September 1943 at Berka, Libya. Unit operated mainly at the eastern end of the Mediterranean and over the desert. In all over 50 lives were directly saved by Walrus aircraft.

Bases:	Kabrit	Aug 1941 – Sep 1941
	Burg-el-Arab, Benghazi	Sep 1941 – 1943
	Walrus detachment at Misurata (Libya) and Sidi-Bou-Cobrine	Apr 1943 – Apr 1943
	Amriya South, detachments on Cyprus and in Palestine; Walrus detachment at Hergla	May 1943 – Jun 1943
	Idku, detachments Cyprus and Greece	Aug 1943 – May 1945
	Walrus detachments at Gambut (LG07) El Arish, Mulatten and Nicosia.	
	Basra, detachments on Persian Gulf and Arabian Sea.	Jun 1945 – Apr 1946
	Disbanded Basra, Iraq, 8 April 1946	
COs:	F/Lt P W Dawson	Aug 1941 – Feb 1942
	S/Ldr S W R Hughes OBE	Feb 1942 – Nov 1942
	F/Lt G Wright DFC	Nov 1942 – Sep 1943
	F/Lt S A M Morrison	Sep 1943 – Dec 1943
	W/C R G M Walker DFC	Jan 1944 – Feb 1945
	W/C D B Bennett DFC	Feb 1945 – Jun 1945

Walrus equipment:

W2708; W2709; W2710; W2789;
W3013; W3017; W3018; W3039;
W3050 'G'; X9466; X9479; X9584 'C';
X9590; Z1757; Z1776; Z1778; Z1782.

SITES OF MAIN RESCUES

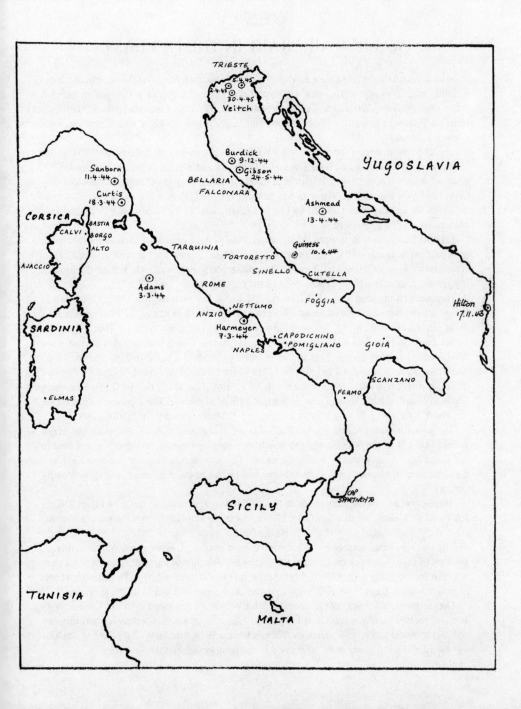

Appendix F

WALRUS AIRCRAFT IN THE FAR EAST

In order to round off the air sea rescue Walrus story it is necessary to cover the somewhat limited activities of 292 Squadron. This unit was formed at Jessore on 1 February 1944 and in March it was operating from Ratmalana, Ceylon. Commanded by Wing Commander E A Starling it operated Warwicks as well as Walrus amphibians. Later it had Sea Otter amphibians and four-engined Liberators.

However, the first recorded rescue with a Walrus was not made until 5 December 1944. Flight Lieutenant B T Holmes, with Flight Sergeant A G Barlow and Warrant Officer R King, in JM767, went out to search for a missing P.40 pilot in the Barisol area. Sighting the man in the water, they landed and took him aboard. The man was carrying important despatches and was in a hurry to deliver them, so rather than transferring him to a nearby launch, the Walrus crew flew him to his destination, safe, wet, but well.

Like the European Walrus units, the squadron's flights were spread out to cover the maximum area, and on 1 January 1945, E Flight moved to Cox's Bazaar on the Arakan coast, under command of Flying Officer D J Barnett. The rescue Flight here was right behind the forward operational area, although, of course, most of the fighting was on land.

However, on the afternoon of 9 January, 292 lost a Supermarine Sea Otter, shot down in flames off the Japanese base at Akyab, Warrant Officer W J Horan being killed. Horan, a New Zealander, had been with 277 Squadron in England before going out to the Far East.

Six Japanese Nakajima Ki43s (Army 01 *Oscars*) from the 64th Sentai, escorted aircraft of the 50th Sentai, and were approaching Akyab in order to bomb and strafe it. Five Spitfires of 67 Squadron had been scrambled and in the air fight which followed, 67 Squadron claimed five shot down, two by the leader, Squadron Leader R W R 'Bob' Day DFC, two by Flight Lieutenant Clyde M Simpson RNZAF, and one by Warrant Officer McQuarie. The Japanese estimated the number of Spitfires as 30 with another 20 joining in!! They claimed three Spitfires shot down.

The pilot who attacked and claimed the Sea Otter, in company with his wingman, was Major Toyoki Eto, CO of the 64th Sentai. Eto was a long serving veteran, having flown in China in 1938, and later over Burma in WW2. He gained 12 victories. On this date his own Ki43 was damaged after he claimed one of the Spitfires and he had to make a forced landing in friendly territory.

Three days later, on the 12th, the Squadron suffered another casualty, this time Flying Officer J A Hickson, a navigator in a Sea Otter. He was hit in the stomach by small arms fire over the coast, and transferred to a hospital ship. He died of his wounds on the 20th.

The other recorded rescues by 292 Squadron both involved Liberator and Warwick aircraft. The first of these was back on 12 August 1944, by the detachment based at China Bay, Ceylon. A search for a missing American B.29 bomber found two dinghies and a Lindholme lifeboat was parachuted down. Later HMS *Redoubt* was homed to the spot and picked up the survivors.

During the 23/24 April 1945, Liberator VI EW240 'J', captained by Pilot Officer W G Tomkins located survivors from a 354 Squadron Liberator. A Lindholme lifeboat was dropped and later a coaster picked up a survivor – Warrant Officer W M Ashton. William Gordon Tomkins was awarded the DFC later in the year, for this and another successful rescue mission.

INDEX OF PERSONNEL